Intensive Longitudinal Methods

Methodology in the Social Sciences

David A. Kenny, Founding Editor
Todd D. Little, Series Editor
www.guilford.com/MSS

This series provides applied researchers and students with analysis and research design books that emphasize the use of methods to answer research questions. Rather than emphasizing statistical theory, each volume in the series illustrates when a technique should (and should not) be used and how the output from available software programs should (and should not) be interpreted. Common pitfalls as well as areas of further development are clearly articulated.

RECENT VOLUMES

ADVANCES IN CONFIGURAL FREQUENCY ANALYSIS
Alexander A. von Eye, Patrick Mair, and Eun-Young Mun

APPLIED MISSING DATA ANALYSIS
Craig K. Enders

PRINCIPLES AND PRACTICE OF STRUCTURAL EQUATION MODELING,
THIRD EDITION
Rex B. Kline

APPLIED META-ANALYSIS FOR SOCIAL SCIENCE RESEARCH
Noel A. Card

DATA ANALYSIS WITH Mplus
Christian Geiser

INTENSIVE LONGITUDINAL METHODS: AN INTRODUCTION
TO DIARY AND EXPERIENCE SAMPLING RESEARCH
Niall Bolger and Jean-Philippe Laurenceau

DOING STATISTICAL MEDIATION AND MODERATION
Paul E. Jose

LONGITUDINAL STRUCTURAL EQUATION MODELING
Todd D. Little

INTRODUCTION TO MEDIATION, MODERATION, AND CONDITIONAL
PROCESS ANALYSIS: A REGRESSION-BASED APPROACH
Andrew F. Hayes

Intensive Longitudinal Methods

An Introduction to Diary and
Experience Sampling Research

Niall Bolger
Jean-Philippe Laurenceau

Founding Editor's Note by David A. Kenny

THE GUILFORD PRESS
New York   London

Library of Congress Cataloging-in-Publication Data

Bolger, Niall.
  Intensive longitudinal methods : an introduction to diary and experience
  sampling research / Niall Bolger and Jean-Philippe Laurenceau.
        p. cm. — (Methodology in the social sciences)
    Includes bibliographical references and index.
    ISBN 978-1-4625-0678-1 (hbk. : alk. paper)
    1. Social sciences—Methodology. 2. Social sciences—Longitudinal
  methods. I. Laurenceau, Jean-Philippe. II. Title.
  H61.B62165 2013
  001.4′33—dc23
                                                            2012032402

For Brian and Pauline, Con and Gertie
N. B.

For Linda, Kelley, Papá Philippe, Abuelita,
Grammie, and Grampie
J.-P. L.

Founding Editor's Note

One of the most exciting developments in social and behavioral methodology is the development of diary methods, or as they have come to be known, "intensive longitudinal methods." I remember in the late 1980s hearing Harry Reis discuss a whole host of interesting findings using the Rochester Inventory Record, which was an early instrument used in diary studies. As was the case for many methodological advances, substantive researchers like Reis were asking questions from the data for which methodologists had not developed the proper statistical tools—or if there were the proper tools, they were buried in the statistical literature. Additionally, practitioners did not have access to computer software to obtain the proper answer to these questions. After Reis's talk, Deborah Kashy and I began work on a diary study with the goal that she and I would advance quantitative methods in this area. Very early on we realized that we were in way over our heads in this area, and we sought out someone who could assist us in this project. That person was Niall Bolger.

I first met Niall at a cocktail reception in Buffalo at the meeting of the Society of Experimental Social Psychology. Niall at the time was a postdoctoral fellow at the University of Michigan. To steal a line from *Casablanca*, this was "the beginning of a beautiful friendship." Niall appreciated the importance of diary methods in our field, and he had an understanding of the difficult statistical and computational issues in this area. After Niall moved to New York City, I even convinced him to visit the village of Storrs to continue our collaboration, and he convinced me to visit Gotham several times.

I have not known Jean-Philippe Laurenceau, or J.-P., for as long or as well, but I do know that he has been integral to the successful development of this book. Like Niall, J.-P. has both the statistical and substantive interests, his area of interest being clinical psychology. Like Niall, J.-P. is a dedicated scholar. I remember a meeting a few years back at a University of Massachusetts conference on dyadic data analysis, and both Niall and J.-P. were up until 3 in the morning making the final changes to their presentation.

The book does an excellent job of explaining the usefulness of intensive longitudinal methods, and provides both an intelligent and intelligible discussion of a topic of compelling interest. It discusses why and when you would want to use these methods; how you would collect such data; the analysis of such data; and the meaning of these analyses. For each, substantive examples and computer setups are given. I feel very privileged to have played a role in bringing this book to fruition. Enjoy.

DAVID A. KENNY
Storrs, Connecticut

Preface

We begin with a bald definition: An intensive longitudinal study is one with enough repeated measurements to model a distinct change process for each individual. By this definition, intensive longitudinal data can be laboratory-based measures of physiology or brain activation as well as field-based, ambulatory measures of affect, physiology, or behavior. Our focus in this book, however, is on using these methods to understand people's thoughts, feelings, and behaviors *in situ*. Used in this way, intensive longitudinal methods represent a core research strategy that both contrasts with and complements traditional laboratory experiments. Although laboratory experiments excel in testing causal hypotheses, intensive longitudinal field methods are essential for determining whether particular causal processes actually occur in real-world settings. We believe that an adequate understanding of human behavior requires both approaches.

Our desire to promote the use of these methods has been tempered, however, by the many hurdles we have experienced over the years in working with intensive longitudinal data. In fact, this is the book we would have liked to have had when we began this work, in the mid-1980s to 1990s. At that time, there was a lot of uncertainty about fundamentals such as design, measurement, data analysis, and power. In the intervening years, there have been so many important developments that it has now been possible to produce a comprehensive *Handbook of Research Methods for Studying Daily Life* (Mehl & Conner, 2012).

Our book is intended to complement this handbook. Whereas the handbook is wide-ranging and reviews findings in specific fields (e.g., health psychology, organizational psychology), our book provides in-depth coverage of two central issues: research design and data analysis. We intend it to be a practical how-to book written by researchers for researchers. Such methods books can sometimes gloss over important technical or statistical issues, but one must weigh this concern against the danger that an overly formal and abstract treatment will be useless to practicing researchers. Our hope is that we have succeeded in combining rigor with accessibility, but whether we have or not is, of course, for others to judge.

We assume that our readers are researchers who have collected or are planning to collect intensive longitudinal data, including researchers in training such as graduate students and postdoctoral fellows. Although many of the data examples we use are from social and clinical psychology, our hope is that the book will be useful to researchers across the behavioral and social sciences, including those in communication, health, business, and policy domains.

In our experience, the best way to learn a statistical method is to work with an example dataset, and most of the chapters are constructed around specific datasets and analyses. For three of the data chapters (Chapters 4, 5, and 8) we also include example write-ups of results, as one might prepare them for a manuscript to be published as a journal article. We encourage readers to download these datasets and syntax files from the website for our book (*www.intensivelongitudinal.com*) and try the analyses themselves.

There is a variety of software that can be used to analyze intensive longitudinal data. In the book we present syntax and output files for SPSS, SAS, and Mplus. These can also be found on our website, including equivalent syntax and output files for R, HLM, and Stata. Also on the website are links to facilitate any comments or corrections readers would like to bring to our attention. We would very much welcome the feedback.

Acknowledgments

There are many people to thank for making this book possible. We both would like to thank Dave Kenny, whose career as a theorist and methodologist has been our fundamental inspiration in writing the book; at The Guilford Press, Editor-in-Chief Seymour Weingarten, for his amazing patience with and encouragement of a book project that took almost two decades to complete, and Publisher extraordinaire C. Deborah Laughton for her unmatched skill and enthusiasm; and the reviewers, Larry Cohen, Howard Tennen, Tamlin Conner, Matthias Mehl, Honor Nicholl, and Joel Hektner. We are also grateful to Aline Sayer at the UMass–Amherst Center for Research on the Family as well as Linda Collins and Stephanie Lanza at the Penn State Methodology Center for supporting the summer workshops we have given over the past several years. Through these workshops, particularly those at UMass, we refined much of the material in the book.

Niall Bolger would like to thank John Eckenrode for introducing him to the wonders of intensive longitudinal methods in the first place; Ron Kessler, Camille Wortman, Anita DeLongis, and Jim Coyne for postdoctoral support and guidance; and especially Pat Shrout for his intellectual and emotional support at all stages of the project.

Jean-Philippe Laurenceau is grateful to his former doctoral advisor, Lisa Feldman Barrett, for first exposing him to experience sampling and diary methods. He is also especially thankful to Chuck Carver, S. T. Calvin, Larry Cohen, Adele Hayes, Michael Kozak, and Blaine Fowers for inspiration, motivation, and support at varying stages in the life of the book. Finally, J.-P. particularly appreciates his coauthor, Niall Bolger, for having invited him to take a journey of learning, growth, and camaraderie that has changed him in a fundamental way.

There are many other people who contributed ideas, motivation, direct help, and inspiration to the project. Here is a partial list: colleagues Walter Mischel, Rena Repetti, John Nesselroade, Jerry Suls, John Lydon, Glenn Affleck, Art Stone, Joe Schwartz, Alex Zautra, Rich Gonzalez, Karen Rook, Mary Anne Stephens, Melissa Franks, Nilam Ram, Andrew Fuligni, Art Aron, Harry Reis, Peggy Clark, Bram Buunk, Ben Karney, Shelly Gable, Eva Pomerantz, Chip Reichardt, Rob Roberts, Susan Harter, Harry Gollob, Shelly Chaiken, Diane Ruble, Yaacov Trope, Ted Huston, Dan Ames, Sheena Iyengar, Tory Higgins, Andrew Gelman, Steve West, Dave Krantz, Dave Almeida, Michael Sobel, Martin Lindquist, Tor Wager, Valerie Purdie-Vaughns, Kevin Ochsner, Patrick Wilson, Chris Rini, Jen Bartz, Nina Knoll, Urte Scholz, Mike Rovine, Peter Molenaar, Ellen Hamaker, Steve Boker, Joanne Davila, Maria Llabre, Scott Siegel, Mike McCullough, and Paul (B. W.) Quinn; graduate students Beth Schilling, Roger Giner-Sorolla, Roeline Kuijer, Angie Davis, Janet Kennedy, Jeannette Alvarez, Anne Thompson, Gisela Michel, Adam Zuckerman, Marci Gleason, Ozlem Ayduk, Chris Burke, Lexi Suppes, Masumi Iida, Maryhope Howland, Sean Lane, Jamil Zaki, Lauren Atlas, Becca Franks, Lauren Aguilar, Canny Zou, Mona Xu, Melissa Boone, Jeff Craw, Kenzie Snyder, Joy Xu, Grace Jackson, Christine Paprocki, Michelle Herrera, Matthew Riccio, Yael Avivi, Adam Troy, Brighid Kleinman, Amber Belcher, Elana Graber, Elizabeth Pasipanodya, Amy Otto, Kimberly Dasch-Yee, Brendt Parrish, Stefanie LoSavio, and Lauren Courtright; and postdocs Joy McClure, Eshkol Rafaeli, and Turu Stadler.

Finally, we thank our families. Niall Bolger wishes to thank his mother, Pauline; father, Brian; brother, Dermott; father-in-law, Con Downey; and most of all his wife, Geraldine Downey. J.-P. Laurenceau wishes to thank his father, Philippe; mother, Marietta; brother, Jean-Pierre; and his wife and daughter, Linda and Kelley.

Contents

Datasets and output in SPSS, SAS, Mplus, HLM, MLwiN, and R for
the examples are available on the companion website
www.intensivelongitudinal.com.

1

Introduction to Intensive Longitudinal Methods

Like its companion, the *Handbook of Research Methods for Studying Daily Life* (Mehl & Conner, 2012), this volume highlights the value of studying people in their natural settings. Although laboratory experiments can be powerful tools for testing theories about social and psychological processes, for practical or ethical reasons many of these processes do not lend themselves to experimentation. Even in cases where experiments can be conducted, phenomena demonstrated in the laboratory may not actually occur in the real world. For these reasons, we see great value in studying social and psychological processes as they unfold naturally and believe the best way to do so is to use intensive longitudinal methods.

Intensive longitudinal methods involve sequences of repeated measurements sufficiently frequent to allow one to characterize a separate change process for each subject (which can be a person or other sampling unit such as a dyad or group). By characterize we mean not only the functional form of the change but also its causes and consequences. The purpose of this book is to provide guidance on how to do so.

When conducting nonexperimental studies, researchers in the behavioral and social sciences have traditionally relied on questionnaire surveys, longitudinal studies, and behavioral obser-vations. There is no doubt that these methods have provided many important insights. Nevertheless, what these methods have lacked is a focus on what Gordon Allport (1942) called the "particulars of life" and what Wheeler and Reis (1991) call the "little experiences of everyday life that fill most of our working time and occupy the vast majority of our conscious attention" (p. 340). Intensive longitudinal designs permit this kind of focus and allow us to realize Allport's vision that "Psychology needs to concern itself with life as it is lived, with significant total-processes of the sort revealed in consecutive and complete life documents" (p. 56).

A second justification for these methods comes from the work of Peter Molenaar (2004; Molenaar & Campbell, 2009). According to Molenaar, almost all biological and social processes are nonergodic, which means that regularities found by comparing subjects (or other sampling units) with one another are unlikely to mirror regularities in how subjects change over time. In other words, if one wishes to understand within-subject changes, one must either directly produce those changes through experimentation or obtain measurements on them as they evolve naturally. Research designs based on observing between-subjects differences will not suffice. Hamaker (2012) pre-sents a compelling discussion and several examples of nonergodicity within the context of intensive longitudinal data.

Now for a more specific definition: an intensive longitudinal design involves sequential measurements on five or more occasions during which a change process is expected to unfold within each subject (e.g., person or other sampling unit). Although specifying a minimum number of measurements is somewhat arbitrary, we chose five because with five observations it is possible to estimate within each subject a linear model with an intercept, a slope for time, a slope for a prior value of the outcome, and a slope for one putative causal antecedent. Such a model would indeed be minimal, having just one degree of freedom to assess the goodness of fit. Nonetheless five observations could be descriptively and graphically informative about change for a given subject over a particular time interval, and if the observations were combined with data from many persons in a suitable multilevel model, it could be very informative about the typical subject.

1.1 WHAT ARE INTENSIVE LONGITUDINAL METHODS?

New researchers embarking on research in natural settings face a frustrating impediment: the variety of names used to describe relevant methods. Experience sampling, daily diaries, interaction records, ecological momentary assessment, ambulatory assessment, and real-time data capture—these all share fundamental similarities that are obscured by terminology. Although the term *intensive* has been used in the past to describe the dense measurement in these designs (Almeida & Kessler, 1998; Bolger, 1990; Bolger, DeLongis, Kessler, & Schilling, 1989; Stone & Shiffman, 1992), it is Walls and Shafer (2006), in their edited volume, who are responsible for coining *intensive longitudinal* as an umbrella term. One of us was a contributor to the volume (Boker & Laurenceau, 2006) and to the meetings at Penn State University that preceded it. As a result of that experience and of our perception that the lack of an overarching term is impeding cumulative work and training efforts, we have chosen to adopt theirs.

To date there are a number of general reviews of research using intensive longitudinal methods (Bolger, Davis, & Rafaeli, 2003; Laurenceau & Bolger, 2005; Reis & Gable, 2000; Shiffman, Stone, & Hufford, 2008; Wheeler & Reis, 1991). Authored and edited volumes summarizing intensive longitudinal research in particular domains (e.g., psychopathology by Delespaul [1995] and deVries [1992]; behavioral medicine by Stone, Shiffman, Atienza, and Nebeling [2007]) have also appeared. A volume devoted specifically to experience sampling methods was published in 2006 (Hektner, Schmidt, & Csikszentmihalyi, 2007). Also, Stone and Shiffman (2002) provided useful guidelines for reporting intensive longitudinal studies. Most recently, the *Handbook of Research Methods for Studying Daily Life* (Mehl & Conner, 2012) has provided a comprehensive overview of various forms of intensive longitudinal methods.

1.2 APPLICATIONS OF INTENSIVE LONGITUDINAL METHODS

The two earliest published accounts of intensive longitudinal research that we located are *How Working Men Spend Their Time* (Bevans, 1913) and *Round about a Pound a Week* (Pember-Reeves, 1913), both of which focused on how individuals use their time. An early and influential intensive longitudinal study was by sociologists Sorokin and Berger (1939), who asked a sample of individuals to record the starting and stopping times of daily activities, whether others were present, and the motivation for the activity. Some of the earliest work in personality and social psychology was by Csikszentmihalyi and colleagues (Csikszentmihalyi & Larson, 1984; Csikszentmihalyi, Larson, & Prescott, 1977), who studied emotional processes in the daily lives of adolescents; Wheeler, Reis, and Nezlek, who invented the Rochester Interaction Record for use in research on daily social interactions (Reis, Nezlek, & Wheeler, 1980; Reis & Wheeler, 1991; Wheeler & Nezlek, 1977); and Diener and colleagues (Diener & Emmons, 1985; Diener & Larsen, 1984), who studied patterns of mood across situations in daily experience. Other notable pioneering work was conducted by Hurlburt and Sipprelle (1978), Hormuth (1986), and Pawlik and Buse (1982).

The intervening years have seen the expansion of these methods to a wide range of topics including personality processes (e.g., Bolger & Zuckerman, 1995; Fabes & Eisenberg, 1997); affective processes and dynamics (e.g., Barrett, 2004; Kuppens, Oravecz, & Tuerlinckx, 2010), physical health (e.g., Stone & Shiffman, 1994); racism and sexism in daily life (e.g., Swim et al., 2001, 2003), developmental psychopathology (e.g., Schneiders et al., 2007), mental health (e.g., Alloy et al., 1997), and drug and alcohol problems (e.g., Litt, Cooney, & Morse, 1998).

An area of notable growth in the use of intensive longitudinal methods is the study of interpersonal processes in dyads and families (see Laurenceau & Bolger, 2005, for a review). One of the first applications of intensive longitudinal methods to close relationships was by Wills, Weiss, and Patterson (1974), who examined the link between daily pleasant and unpleasant behaviors (over 14 days) and global ratings of marital satisfaction in seven nondistressed married couples. Since then, a growing number of studies have taken advantage of intensive longitudinal procedures to investigate marital and family phenomena, including work on intimacy in marriage (e.g., Laurenceau, Barrett, & Rovine, 2005), work–home spillover (e.g., Repetti & Wood 1997), family emotional transmission (e.g., Larson

& Almeida, 1999), the effect of marital conflict on child outcomes (e.g., Cummings, Goeke-Morey, Papp, & Dukewich, 2002), and family regulation of emotion (e.g., Perrez, Schoebi, & Wilhelm, 2000). Because intensive longitudinal studies of dyads and family members present unique methodological and data-analytic challenges, we devote Chapter 8 in this book to the collection and analysis of dyadic intensive longitudinal data.

1.3   WHY USE INTENSIVE LONGITUDINAL METHODS?

One of the fundamental benefits of intensive longitudinal methods is that they can be used to examine thoughts, feelings, physiology, and behavior in their natural, spontaneous contexts. The data that result can show the unfolding of a temporal process, both descriptively and in terms of causal analysis. Thus, for example, it is possible to examine how an outcome Y changes over time and how this change is contingent on changes in a putative causal variable X.

Although traditional longitudinal designs can also examine temporal unfolding, they are often limited by few repeated measurements taken over long time intervals. If a researcher is interested in examining the degree to which intimacy fluctuates within a marriage, a longitudinal design consisting of four or five assessments over months or years would likely be inadequate. Because intimacy is theorized to vary over the course of daily interactions (Reis & Shaver, 1988), the density of assessments needs to reflect the underlying theory of change. Moreover, depending on when a variable X measured at one point in time has its maximal causal effect on Y at a later point in time, the precise temporal design of a longitudinal study can greatly influence the observed effects (Collins, 2006). Intensive longitudinal designs allow researchers to directly capture these day-to-day (or within-day) processes.

In our definition above, intensive longitudinal methods have sufficient repeated measurement to permit researchers to characterize a within-subject process. All too often, hypotheses about within-subject processes are tested using between-subjects data. Consider the following two approaches to studying the link between stressful events and negative affect. In the first, a researcher obtains stressor and emotion data at one point in time for a sample of individuals. In the second, stressors and emotion are measured on several occasions for a particular individual (or a sample of individuals). Will both approaches yield similar results? Most likely, no. The first approach can determine whether individuals who report more stressors also tend to report higher levels of negative affect. The second can determine whether occasions when an individual's stressors are higher are occasions when the individual's negative affect is higher.

A similar contrast can be drawn when assessing whether anxiety and depression are correlated. In a between-subjects approach, measures of anxiety and depression are obtained at one point in time from a sample of individuals. In a within-subjects approach, anxiety and depression are measured on a number of occasions for a particular individual (or sample of individuals). If we observe that those individuals who are higher than others in anxiety tend to also be higher than others in depression, this does not imply that on occasions when an individual is higher than usual in anxiety the individual will be higher than usual in depression. Although such an inference does not follow either logically or mathematically, in the social and behavioral sciences, we often make inferences about within-subject processes based on between-subjects associations (Borsboom, Mellenbergh, & van Heerden, 2003; Molenaar & Campbell, 2009). By contrast, intensive longitudinal methods permit us to answer questions within subjects, while also allowing us to determine whether these processes are mirrored in between-subjects associations.

Of course, these designs involve important trade-offs. These include increased cost to the investigator in terms of data management, complexity of data analysis, and (increasingly) management of technology for data collection (e.g., PDAs, online web surveys). There are also increased costs to participants in terms of level of intrusiveness. To get a sense of this, we invite readers to imagine themselves being in a study where they are asked to complete a brief diary after every social interaction lasting 10 minutes or more over the course of 7 consecutive days. Although there are many people who could take on this task in their stride, there are many who would find it unmanageable. In the next chapter, we consider these and other drawbacks in more depth.

In the not-too-distant future, intensive longitudinal methods will be used not just for the assessment of everyday experience but also for momentary intervention. For example, a certain constellation of negative affect scores could trigger prompts to address an impending behavioral problem relapse (e.g., cigarette smoking, alcohol drinking, binge eating). These applications are already being investigated by some research groups (e.g., Intille, 2012; Nusser, Intille, & Maitra, 2006) and such work is sure to increase with time.

1.4 GOALS FOR THIS BOOK AND INTENDED AUDIENCE

Despite the promise of intensive longitudinal methods, these methods raise a variety of important practical issues of design, measurement, analysis, and write-up. The purpose of this book is to provide basic guidance on these issues so that readers can plan, carry out, analyze, and publish their own intensive longitudinal studies. Thus, we attempt to provide a practical, self-contained guide for those interested in conducting intensive longitudinal studies to understand behavioral and social phenomena.

This book is geared toward faculty, postdoctoral fellows, and advanced graduate students in the biomedical and social sciences, whether or not they have previous experience with intensive longitudinal methods. For example, we believe the book will be of use to graduate students planning dissertation studies and faculty seeking grant support for their first intensive longitudinal study. For those who already have experience with intensive longitudinal methods, the book provides guidance on more advanced topics such as mediation, psychometrics, and power analysis.

1.5 ORGANIZATION OF THIS BOOK

The remainder of the book is organized into nine chapters. Chapter 2 covers types of designs and research questions including choosing a design appropriate to your research question. It also includes a brief review of the range of technologies available for collecting intensive longitudinal data. Chapter 3 discusses the conceptual and methodological issues that arise when one wishes to study a within-subject process using intensive longitudinal designs. Chapter 3 is necessary before we move onto the more detailed data analysis chapters that form the remainder of the book.

Chapter 4, the first and most straightforward analysis chapter, is devoted to modeling the temporal form of a within-subject change process for continuous outcomes. Chapter 5 tackles the much more difficult goal of modeling causes and consequences of the change process, again for continuous outcomes. A particular challenge that surfaces in this chapter and resurfaces in future chapters is the need to separate within-subjects from between-subjects variability in key longitudinal predictors of interest. Chapter 6 describes how analyses of causal processes can be conducted with categorical outcomes. Chapter 7 is devoted to the psychometrics of intensive longitudinal assessments of psychological states.

The final three chapters of the book cover advanced topics. Chapter 8 addresses intensive longitudinal studies of dyads, studies that are growing in popularity in social, personality, and clinical psychology. Here the special challenge arises from the additional interdependence that comes from collecting data from partners in the same relationship. Chapter 9 tackles another difficult issue—assessing within-subjects mediation using intensive longitudinal data. Within-subjects mediation involves complexities that are absent from traditional between-subjects mediation and requires either a complicated restructuring of the data or the use of specialized software. Chapter 10, the final chapter, is on estimating power for intensive longitudinal studies. Conducting a power analysis is usually an essential task for those seeking grant support for intensive longitudinal research, but it presents a challenge because of the multiple sources of random variability in models of intensive longitudinal data.

Throughout the book, we use example datasets, all of which are available on the website for this book. Within many chapters, we provide syntax code pertaining to three popular statistical software programs: SPSS (version 19), SAS (version 9.3), and Mplus (version 6). This code, as well as corresponding code for HLM, Stata, and R, can also be found on the book's website. We encourage readers to use the datasets and code to gain experience with data analysis prior to, or in parallel with, analyses of their own data.

1.6 RECOMMENDED READINGS

Bolger, N., Davis, A., & Rafaeli, E. (2003). Diary methods: Capturing life as it is lived. *Annual Review of Psychology, 54, 579–616.*

> This article provides a review of diary designs, the research questions to which they can be applied, and the statistical models that permit one to answer each type of research question.

Mehl, M. R., & Conner, T. S. (Eds.). (2012). *Handbook of research methods for studying daily life.* New York: Guilford Press.

> This first-of-its-kind handbook contains 36 chapters on research that is real-world, real-time, and within-subjects.

2

Types of Intensive Longitudinal Designs

The purpose of this chapter is to differentiate among intensive longitudinal designs and help you pick the right one for your research objectives. We begin by reviewing common strengths across all designs. We then address the types of research questions to be covered in the book. Next, we review the types of designs and give examples of work using each type. Finally, we address the main limitations of each design and give advice on choosing the right one.

2.1 STRENGTHS OF INTENSIVE LONGITUDINAL DESIGNS

The literature describing, reviewing, or reporting findings based on intensive longitudinal methods is large and growing rapidly. For example, a recent keyword search for the terms *diary method, experience sampling, daily diary, diary study, ecological momentary assessment, intensive longitudinal, ambulatory assessment,* or *real-time data capture* in the PsycINFO database came up with a total of 2,222 entries covering the period from 1980 to March 2012. Of the total number of entries, 1,117 (50%) came from just the past five years. An analogous search in the Medline database shows a similar rapid rate of increase. We believe that this trend will continue, given the resurgence of interest in studying behavior in psychology (e.g., Baumeister, Vohs, & Funder, 2007; American Psychological Association Decade of Behavior 2000–2010: *www.decadeofbehavior.org*), health and biomedical fields more generally (Nilsen, Haverkos, Nebeling, & Taylor, 2010; Stone et al., 2007), and even the U.S. Food and Drug Administration (2009).

Researchers have turned increasingly to methods involving intensive longitudinal measurement because they afford important advantages over cross-sectional and experimental methods. First, intensive longitudinal methods allow researchers to study the relationships within and between everyday behaviors, activities, and perceptions. Indeed, some of the most interesting behavioral and social science phenomena occur outside the confines of a controlled laboratory (Reis & Gosling, 2010). Second, intensive momentary measurements of variables can help to reduce the effects of recall biases that often affect global measurements (Tversky & Kahneman, 1982), particularly when assessing emotional experiences (Robinson & Clore, 2002).

Third, using an intensive longitudinal design can allow researchers to directly observe processes of change—processes that can at best be only indirectly inferred using cross-sectional designs. Fourth, intensive longitudinal designs allow researchers to study low-intensity behaviors or events that might not be detected in more traditional designs. Lastly, as has already been emphasized, data collected using an intensive longitudinal design enable researchers to identify relationships among variables within each subject.

2.2 TYPES OF RESEARCH QUESTIONS

Intensive longitudinal studies produce data that vary between subjects and within subjects, in mean levels and in variances. There is a wide variety of research questions to which they can be applied, as Bolger, Davis, and Rafaeli (2003) detailed in their article in *Annual Review of Psychology*. In this book, as has already been emphasized, our central focus is on the extent and causes of within-subjects changes.

This does not mean that we ignore between-subjects variability altogether, but we consider it only as it relates to within-subjects changes. In examining the course of within-subjects changes over time (see Chapter 4), for example, we consider the extent to which there are between-subjects differences in those changes.

Table 2.1 presents an overview of the research questions to be covered. In the leftmost column we list (1) the measurement reliability of within-subjects changes in a dependent variable Y, (2) the temporal course of those changes, (3) the causal antecedents to those changes (symbolized as $X \rightarrow Y$), and (4) the intervening variables in the causal process of change (i.e., mediation, symbolized as $X \rightarrow M \rightarrow Y$).

The second column shows which chapters deal with these questions for studies where the subjects are persons and the dependent variable Y is continuous as opposed to categorical (note that the independent variables, the X's, can be either continuous or categorical). In order to have the book progress from relatively easy to relatively difficult topics, it was not possible to have the order of the chapters follow the order of these research questions: Although assessing measurement adequacy is logically prior to modeling the

TABLE 2.1. Overview of Research Questions Covered in This Book

	Person (continuous Y)		Person (categorical Y)		Dyad (continuous Y)	
	Data analysis	Power analysis	Data analysis	Power analysis	Data analysis	Power analysis
Measurement (can within-person change be assessed reliably?)	Ch. 7					
Time course (is there a systematic trend over time?)	Ch. 4	Ch. 10	Ch. 6	Ch. 10	Ch. 8	Ch. 10
Causal process: $X \rightarrow Y$ (is there evidence that changes in X cause changes in Y?)	Ch. 5	Ch. 10	Ch. 6	Ch. 10	Ch. 8	Ch. 10
Causal process: $X \rightarrow M \rightarrow Y$ (is there evidence for causal mediation?)	Ch. 9	Ch. 10				

time course, the relatively complex issue of measurement is covered in Chapter 7, whereas the relatively simple issue of modeling the time course is covered in Chapter 4.

The third column addresses planning an intensive longitudinal study as opposed to analyzing data from a study that already has been conducted. Perhaps the most important issue in planning is determining the number of subjects and time points that will produce powerful tests of key hypotheses. In Chapter 10, we show how this can be accomplished for the majority of research questions considered in the book.

Columns 4 and 5 concern data analysis and power assessment, respectively, for the case of categorical dependent variables assessed repeatedly on persons. Columns 6 and 7 are the equivalent for continuous dependent variables assessed repeatedly on members of dyads. The reader will notice that certain cells of Table 2.1 are empty. There is no power analysis for measurement reliability, for example. Our intention is to fill in many of these empty cells in future editions of the book. Although not depicted in the table, we also provide write-ups of analyses in American Psychological Association manuscript style (American Psychological Association, 2009) for three of the data chapters (Chapters 4, 5, and 8).

In summary, the book's central questions are about measuring, tracing the trajectory of, and explaining the causes of within-subjects changes. These questions are covered for analyses of existing data as well as for planning future data collection. They are covered for studies of persons and of dyads, and for dependent variables that are continuous as well as those that are categorical.

2.3 TYPES OF DESIGNS AND PROTOTYPICAL EXAMPLES

Three general categories of intensive longitudinal methods are usually distinguished: interval-contingent designs, signal-contingent designs, and event-contingent designs (Eckenrode & Bolger, 1995; Wheeler & Reis, 1991). Bolger et al. (2003) make a conceptually simpler distinction between time-based designs (including interval- and signal-contingent designs) and event-based designs. In this section, we return to the traditional tripartite framework and extend it to include a fourth that has emerged from technological advances in computerized recording devices: device-contingent designs.

Interval-Contingent Designs

In interval-contingent recording, participants record experiences at regular and predetermined intervals of time selected by the researcher. The researcher may ask participants to report based on what has occurred since the last recording or on what the participant may be doing or feeling at that exact moment in time. An example of the use of interval-contingent recording is a study by Bolger and Schilling (1991) on the relationship between neuroticism and daily stress. In this article, the researchers sought to determine whether individuals high versus low in neuroticism differed in overall daily negative affect, in exposure to daily stressors, and in reactivity to daily stressors. Data consisted of daily reports of stressors and distress from a sample of married couples over a 6-week period. Results indicated that participants high in neuroticism reported being exposed to more daily stressors than those low in neuroticism. They also were more reactive to the stressors to which they were exposed, and this mechanism, in particular, was the most important in explaining overall differences in daily distress between the two groups.

Prototypical intensive longitudinal studies that fall under the heading of interval-contingent designs are what have been called daily process designs (Affleck, Zautra, Tennen, & Armeli, 1999) wherein "repeatedly measured dependent variables are thought to change in meaningful ways from day to day (or within a day) and are measured prospectively at daily (or within-day) intervals" (p. 747). Daily process designs have been used in various areas of psychology, including personality (Bolger & Zuckerman, 1995), health (Belcher et al., 2011; Tennen, Affleck, & Armeli, 2003), close relationships (Laurenceau et al., 2005), emotion (Feldman, 1995), and psychotherapy (Cohen et al., 2008).

Another prototypical approach under this heading is ambulatory assessment, defined as the "use of (mainly) electronic devices and computer-assisted methods of data collection suitable for use in the field to collect self-report data, behavior observation data, psychometric behavior measures, and physiological data in unre-strained daily life settings" (Fahrenberg, Myrtek, Pawlik, & Perrez, 2007, p. 207). Ambulatory assessment in the behavioral sciences has had a long tradition in Europe (particularly Germany and Switzer-land), where these methods have been used to study personality, daily experiences, stressors, coping, and physiological outcomes (Fahrenberg & Myrtek, 2001). The Society for Ambulatory Assess-ment hosts international and interdisciplinary conferences and maintains a website with a frequently updated bibliography of pub-lished papers making use of intensive longitudinal methods (at *www. ambulatory-assessment.org*).

We have some final comments on interval-contingent designs. Given that they often involve only one or two assessments per day, these designs tend to be less intrusive than the other designs. More-over, because they involve assessments taken at regular, fixed, equi-distant intervals, their data lend themselves to a variety of types of longitudinal and time-series modeling. However, because of the relatively infrequent assessments, interval-contingent designs often involve more retrospection than other designs (but not, of course, if the assessments are about momentary states at the time of assess-ment, such as mood and energy upon waking).

Signal-Contingent Designs

In contrast to interval-contingent designs, where participants report experiences at regular intervals, signal-contingent designs require participants to report when prompted to do so by a researcher's signal. The researcher determines whether the signals are fixed or random, and participants usually report on their experience at that point in time. To take an early example of this design, McAdams and Constantian (1983) investigated the relationship between inti-macy motivation and self-reported thoughts, emotions, and behav-iors. Participants were given an electronic beeper to carry for a 7-day period and during waking hours were signaled randomly to provide reports. The authors hypothesized that intimacy motiva-tion would be related to the number of reported thoughts concern-ing people and relationships as well as the number of conversa-tions and letter-writing episodes that were occurring at the time the participant was signaled. As expected, the motivation toward warm, close, and communicative relationships was positively related to having more thoughts about specific others or specific relationships. In addition, greater intimacy motivation significantly predicted self-reported behaviors such as letter writing and engaging in conversations.

Prototypical signal-contingent designs are the experience sampling method (ESM) developed by Mihalyi Csikszentmihalyi and colleagues (e.g., Larson & Csikszentmihalyi, 1983) and ecological momentary assessment (EMA) developed by Shiffman, Stone, and colleagues (e.g., Shiffman et al., 2008; Stone & Shiffman, 1994; Stone, Shiffman, & DeVries, 1999). As described in Hektner et al. (2007),

> ESM is a means for collecting information about both the context and content of the daily life of individuals. This purpose is shared by other methods, but the unique advantage of ESM is its ability to capture daily life as it is directly perceived from one moment to the next, affording an opportunity to examine fluctuations in the stream of consciousness and the links between external context and contents of the mind. (p. 6)

EMA is most often used in health psychology and is described by Shiffman et al. (2008) as a class of "methods using repeated collection of real-time data on subjects' behavior and experience in their natural environments" (p. 3).

Both ESM and EMA approaches typically focus on momentary, *in situ* subjective assessments of behavior and experience obtained in response to random signals each day over several days. These designs potentially provide a random sampling of real-time thoughts, feelings, and behavior in context. No retrospection is involved. However, depending on the sampling schedule and response burden, signal-ontingent designs can be perceived as somewhat to very intrusive by participants.

Event-Contingent Designs

In event-contingent designs, participants are asked to report every time a predefined event has taken place. An example of a study using this method is Tidwell, Reis, and Shaver's (1996) study of the degree to which attachment styles predicted behavior in everyday social interactions. They obtained the attachment styles for 125 participants and asked them to complete a Rochester Interaction Record (RIR; Reis & Wheeler, 1991) immediately after any social interaction that lasted more than 10 minutes. The RIR is a structured social interaction diary containing rating scales for various interaction variables. In this study, it was used to measure the degree of self-disclosure, other-disclosure, and intimacy participants experienced in the interaction, among other variables. Results provided evidence that in opposite-sex social interactions, individuals with avoidant attachment styles reported less disclosure and intimacy than both securely and ambivalently attached individuals.

Prototypical intensive longitudinal studies that fall under event-contingent designs are those using the above-mentioned RIR (Reis & Wheeler, 1991; Wheeler & Nezlek, 1977) or the Iowa Communication Record (Duck, 1991), both of which have been used to address questions concerning the quality and nature of social interactions. Event-contingent designs provide researchers with the potential to obtain detailed information on all events of a particular kind or class. With these designs, it is important to concretely define the event that participants are to report on so that they can do so reliably. Because event-contingent designs rely on the participant detecting an event and reporting on it soon afterwards, they can sometimes be disruptive to the participant. Also, unlike the previous designs, compliance usually cannot be evaluated. Nonetheless, with properly trained and motivated participants, they are the best way to obtain detailed reports on important events in daily life.

Device-Contingent Designs

Given the many advances in recording devices in recent years, we feel that the categories of interval-, signal-, and event-contingent intensive longitudinal designs should be extended to include a fourth: device-contingent designs. With the growing use of smart phones that run Windows Mobile OS, MacOS, and Android operating systems, researchers are now capable of collecting intensive longitudinal data in ways that were inconceivable two or three decades ago when these methods first became popular.

To introduce the expanded possibilities, imagine the following scenario. A sample of participants carry around smart phones that are wirelessly connected to a cell phone network and have Bluetooth capability to make wireless connections to other devices. The smart phones come with a camera, video and audio recorder, accelerometer, global positioning system (GPS), and touch-screen input. The researcher is interested in understanding the context of everyday distress. Participants are asked to wear a Bluetooth wireless heart rate sensor that is monitored by the smart phone. Imagine that periods of sustained heart rates of over 100 beats per minute are identified by an algorithm that triggers the device to signal the participant to enter her momentary mood and thoughts, identify the context by speaking a description into the device microphone, take a photo of her immediate surroundings, and have the built in GPS identify her exactly spatial location. The device time-locks these various data streams for later analysis.

As illustrated in the above example, device-contingent designs can (simultaneously) collect data from several different modalities: (1) self-reports of experience (e.g., affect, behavior, perceptions), (2) physiological indices (e.g., heart rate), (3) performance on tasks (e.g., cognitive tasks presented on the smart phone), (4) environmental indices (e.g., ambient sound, temperature, photograph of context), and (5) spatial data (e.g., GPS information). This list will expand as more mobile sensor technologies become cheaply available.

This approach was first exemplified by Intille and colleagues' context-aware experience sampling (CAES; Intille, Rondoni, Kukla, Anacona, & Bao, 2003). Sensors were used as input to a palm-top device that responded to a particular context (e.g., elevated heart rate) by triggering self-reports of experiences *in situ*, thus allowing for "just-in-time" intensive longitudinal sampling (Intille, 2005). Sampling occurred when particular situations or constellations of measurements were detected by the mobile sensors.

There are important advantages to a context-driven sampling approach. First, the participant is not required to use cognitive resources to detect a particular event of interest—the technology takes on this burden, allowing participants to respond to prompts about the contextualized momentary state. Second, the momentary assessments can be more focused by homing in on particular classes of experience-in-context information. Third, data about context (e.g., spatial position, temperature, physiological states) can be collected continuously and with little to no awareness on the part of the participant.

There is a small but growing number of examples of device-contingent intensive longitudinal designs. Mehl and colleagues (Mehl, Pennebaker, Crow, Dabbs, & Price, 2001) have developed a device they call the Electronically Activated Recorder (EAR), which continuously takes 30-second samples of ambient sound. In a clever use of this approach, Mehl and colleagues (Mehl, Vazire, Ramirez-Esparza, Slatcher, & Pennebaker, 2007) sought to answer the question of who talks more in everyday life: women or men? Using the EAR, they were able to estimate across several independent samples that both women and men use approximately 16,000 words per day. Although the EAR recording is not triggered by specific device-determined contexts, it does collect data about participants' contexts in an unobtrusive way. A more sophisticated example of device-contingent sampling comes from Froehlich, Chen, Smith, and Potter (2006), who created a sensor-based experience sampling tool called *My Experience*, developed for mobile phones. They used a GSM place-tracking algorithm to trigger *in situ* sampling of momentary assessments of liking of particular locations. A more recent effort by members of the MIT Media Lab has led to an extremely promising open source application, the extensible sensing and data-processing framework for mobile devices called Funf (Aharony, Pan, Ip, Khayal, & Pentland, 2011). Another example of a less sophisticated yet effective device-based intensive longitudinal design is the collection of medication compliance data by instrumented pill bottles (Byerly et al., 2005).

Device-contingent designs reflect the newest developments in intensive longitudinal research. In addition to having context-sensitive algorithms that can trigger assessments, these designs permit "just-in-time" experience sampling interventions of the kind mentioned in Chapter 1. Moreover, the potential of these devices to allow researchers to reach a wide and diverse participant pool is immense. For example, 83% of U.S. adults currently have a cell phone of some kind, and 42% of them own a smart phone with mobile online capabilities (Smith, 2011). The proportion of U.S. adults with smart phones is expected to exceed 50% sometime during 2012. The true potential of device-contingent data collection designs has yet to be fully exploited in behavioral and social science research. To do so, however, behavioral and social researchers will need to develop research teams with proficiency in programming, in device management, and in handling the large amount of data that these devices will soon be capable of gathering. We predict that the most effective lines of intensive longitudinal research in the future will pair leading-edge technological innovations with compelling and significant social and behavioral science research aims.

2.4 LIMITATIONS OF INTENSIVE LONGITUDINAL DESIGNS

Intensive longitudinal designs are not without disadvantages. First, they can be burdensome and time-consuming for participants. For example, an intensive longitudinal study can involve interruptions to participants at inappropriate times. Also, too much response burden on participants can increase their forgetfulness or noncompliance and can result in missing data and attrition from the study.

Second, participating in a study may itself be an intervention that influences ratings of experiences, an effect often called *reactivity*. For example, individuals who participate in an event-contingent sampling study in which they report on the frequency and severity of headaches may learn to attend to bodily sensations and cues more than usual (or alternatively habituate to certain bodily sensations). Interested readers can consult Iida, Shrout, Laurenceau, and Bolger (2012) and Barta, Tennen, and Litt (2012) for more detailed discussions on the topic of reactivity in intensive longitudinal methods.

Third, intensive longitudinal designs may require researchers to reevaluate their notions of measurement reliability (Duck, 1991). For example, the standard approach to assessing the reliability of measures of emotional expression is to rely on between-subjects differences in expression. However, in intensive longitudinal designs it often emerges that emotional expression is an intrinsically variable phenomenon that changes from assessment to assessment. Assessing reliability in intensive longitudinal data is considered in Chapter 7.

Fourth, intensive longitudinal designs are not useful for studying rare events such as the breakup of an intimate relationship. For this reason, it is not feasible to use such methods to understand psychological and interpersonal processes during or immediately following such an event.

Lastly, depending on the specific self-report method used, retrospective biases, although reduced, may still be present to some degree. For example, when using an interval-contingent sampling procedure, reports may be provided after a delay of many hours. This may be more problematic for some questions than for others. A report of one's mood at work provided at bedtime is less likely to be accurate than it would have been at the end of the workday. This problem may also be present when using an event- or signal-contingent sampling method, to the extent that participants delay providing responses.

2.5 WHICH INTENSIVE LONGITUDINAL DESIGN IS BEST FOR YOU?

Which intensive longitudinal design you choose should depend on a number of issues. One is whether the phenomenon you want to study is discrete (e.g., a conflict, a drink of alcohol, smoking a cigarette) or continuous (e.g., ongoing emotional experience, hunger, intimacy). Discrete events are more likely to be recalled than continuous events and some can be assessed hours later (e.g., at the end of the day) rather than at the moment they occur. A second is the response burdens and intrusiveness that participants can bear. Certain designs are more burdensome and intrusive than others. We would not recommend a random signal-continent design be used for participants in high stress occupations. Such a design, however, could be acceptable in assessing physical symptoms in patients with chronic illnesses.

Frequency of intensive longitudinal assessment is a third important issue, and ideally it should be guided by a theory of how the phenomenon of interest changes (Collins, 2006; Collins & Graham, 2002). In general, phenomena that are slow moving or have little variability can be assessed less frequently and less densely, whereas those that are faster moving or have high variability should be assessed more frequently and more densely. For example, a nonlinear, oscillating pattern will need more assessments than a smooth, monotonically increasing pattern (e.g., Boker & Laurenceau, 2006). Unfortunately, theories of social and behavioral phenomena rarely specify the temporal course of associations between predictors and outcomes or the shape of an outcome's trajectory over a specified period of time. One useful piece of advice on this problem comes from Collins (2006): When there is little theory or past work to go on, researchers should obtain frequent assessments over small units of time. If the process turns out to be more regular and less dynamic than anticipated, the data can be aggregated before analyses are conducted (e.g., daily measurements could be aggregated to the weekly level).

A further design consideration is how soon after a daily experience occurs should it be assessed? If your interest is in the experience of a relatively rare event, then an event-contingent design with information about the context of the event is warranted. If your interest is in experiences that are momentary and ephemeral, then frequent real-time assessments throughout the course of the day are called for. If the experiences of interest can be easily remembered (did you have an argument at work today?), then assessments once or twice a day may be sufficient. If the experiences of interest are tied to particular times of day, as in the case of quality of sleep and level of energy upon waking, then obviously measurements should coincide with those particular times.

Finally, your access to resources (e.g., funding, time, technology, participants) will undoubtedly affect your choice of design and the scope of the design you choose. It is important, however, to know when these resource constraints seriously compromise the scientific value of your study. One way in which studies can be compromised is when researchers cannot afford to collect a large enough sample of participants to ensure powerful tests of hypotheses. We treat this issue in depth in Chapter 10.

2.6 CHAPTER SUMMARY

In summary, when based in a sound theoretical model of change and its corresponding statistical model (Collins, 2006), an intensive longitudinal design can be a powerful tool for understanding within-subject change processes. The continued growth of technologies for *in situ* data collection, technologies we have considered only briefly, will ensure continued growth of intensive longitudinal methods as engines of knowledge generation.

2.7 RECOMMENDED READINGS

Conner, T. S., & Lehman, B. J. (2012). Getting started: Launching a study in daily life. In M. R. Mehl & T. S. Conner (Eds.), *Handbook of research methods for studying daily life* (pp. 89–107). New York: Guilford Press.

This chapter provides a practical guide to planning and implementing an intensive longitudinal study.

Iida, M., Shrout, P. E., Laurenceau, J.-P., & Bolger, N. (2012). Using diary methods in psychological research. In H. Cooper, P. M. Camic, D. L. Long, A. T. Panter, D. Rindskopf, & K. J. Sher (Eds.), *APA handbook of research methods in psychology: Vol. 1. Foundations, planning, measures and psychometrics* (pp. 277–305). Washington, DC: American Psychological Association.

The chapter also provides advice on selecting an appropriate intensive longitudinal design.

Reis, H. T., & Gosling, S. D. (2010). Social psychological methods outside the laboratory. In S. Fiske, D. Gilbert, & G. Lindzey (Eds.), *Handbook of social psychology* (5th ed., Vol. 1, pp. 82–114). New York: Wiley.

This chapter argues for the importance of collecting data outside of the laboratory and reviews various methodologies for doing so.

Shiffman, S., Stone, A. A., & Hufford, M. R. (2008). Ecological momentary assessment. *Annual Review of Clinical Psychology, 4,* 1–32.

This article reviews methodological issues specific to momentary assessment and experience sampling.

3

Fundamentals of Intensive Longitudinal Data

Intensive longitudinal data are complex, but we believe that if you adhere to five basic guidelines, you will be well on your way toward analyzing them effectively. The *first* guideline is to carefully distinguish the between-subjects and within-subjects levels of analysis in your statistical model. As will be seen, between- and within-subjects relationships can be different in size and in sign, and a failure to distinguish them can result in erroneous conclusions. The *second* guideline is to allow for random effects, that is, to allow subjects to differ from one another in within-subject processes. One of the central benefits of intensive longitudinal data is the possibility of estimating these between-subjects random effects. The *third* guideline is that even if temporal change, per se, is not of direct interest in your study, the influence of time should always be taken into account in your statistical model. That is, time should be an explicit factor, or predictor, in any model of interest. The *fourth* guideline concerns specifying the appropriate number of independent units in models of intensive longitudinal data. Although in special circumstances it is possible to treat the total number of observations (N subjects * T time points) as independently sampled, we advise treating only upper-level units (i.e., subjects) in this way. The *final* guideline is that you should be careful to choose interpretable zero points for within-subject independent variables. Whereas this issue can often be ignored in models of between-subjects data, it can almost never be ignored in models of intensive longitudinal data. More detail on each of these issues follows.

3.1   AN EXAMPLE DATASET

In the chapters that follow you will encounter concrete examples of datasets and how to analyze them effectively. Here, to introduce the guidelines, we use a highly simplified dataset with just five participants, five variables, and five observations per participant, as shown in Figure 3.1. The first thing to notice about the dataset is that each observation for each participant is given a separate data line, which results in 25 lines of data. This is an essential feature of the way repeated measurements are treated in later statistical modeling. The first variable is an ID code that uniquely identifies each participant (with values ID_1, ID_2, ID_3, ID_4, ID_5). Following the convention established in Chapter 1, the "participant" in an intensive longitudinal study can be an individual person, animal, or indeed any other sampling unit that is expected to undergo change over the course of the measurement period.

The variable T indexes the time point or occasion on which observations were obtained on the participants. It is common to use a code of "0" for the first observation T_0, and if the observations are equally spaced, to use integers 1, 2, 3, etc., for the subsequent values within a person. For the simplified dataset, we have five equally spaced observations (at T_0 to T_4) on an independent variable X and a dependent variable Y. We will encounter examples of Y's in later chapters that are daily diary ratings of relationship intimacy and negative mood. Examples of X's we will encounter include daily stressful events, such as whether an interpersonal conflict has occurred. The X's and Y's, although they are measured repeatedly and can be expected to vary within subjects, can also vary in their mean levels between subjects. Finally, W stands for a predictor variable that varies between subjects only. Examples will include treatment versus control status in a clinical trial, and relationship quality.

ID_j	T_i	X_{ij}	Y_{ij}	W_j
1	0	x_{11}	y_{11}	w_1
1	1	x_{21}	y_{21}	w_1
1	2	x_{31}	y_{31}	w_1
1	3	x_{41}	y_{41}	w_1
1	4	x_{51}	y_{51}	w_1
2	0	x_{12}	y_{12}	w_2
2	1	x_{22}	y_{22}	w_2
2	2	x_{32}	y_{32}	w_2
2	3	x_{42}	y_{42}	w_2
2	4	x_{52}	y_{52}	w_2
3	0	x_{13}	y_{13}	w_3
3	1	x_{23}	y_{23}	w_3
3	2	x_{33}	y_{33}	w_3
3	3	x_{43}	y_{43}	w_3
3	4	x_{53}	y_{53}	w_3
4	0	x_{14}	y_{14}	w_4
4	1	x_{24}	y_{24}	w_4
4	2	x_{34}	y_{34}	w_4
4	3	x_{44}	y_{44}	w_4
4	4	x_{54}	y_{54}	w_4
5	0	x_{15}	y_{15}	w_5
5	1	x_{25}	y_{25}	w_5
5	2	x_{35}	y_{35}	w_5
5	3	x_{45}	y_{45}	w_5
5	4	x_{55}	y_{55}	w_5

FIGURE 3.1. A hypothetical intensive longitudinal dataset with five participants and five time points.

3.2 BETWEEN-SUBJECTS AND WITHIN-SUBJECTS LEVELS OF ANALYSIS

When the Outcome Y Varies at Both Levels of Analysis

Given that each person in an intensive longitudinal study contributes his or her own set observations to the resulting dataset, it is important to allow for the possibility that there are between-subjects differences on the dependent variable. If, for example, Siobhán, a generally relaxed subject, provides five consecutive daily reports on her anxiety, it is not unreasonable that her five anxiety scores should be more similar to one another than they are to an equivalent five anxiety scores provided by Sinéad, who is frequently nervous. On the left-hand side of Figure 3.2, along the Y-axis, are five normal distributions. Each distribution is meant to summarize a large number of repeated measurements on each of five participants whose average scores on Y differ markedly. This simple idea can be captured numerically by what is called the intraclass correlation (ICC).

The ICC can be thought of as the percentage of the total variance in Y that is due to mean differences between subjects. When the ICC is 0, participants do not differ from one another in their average levels of Y. When the ICC is 1.0, then all of the variability in Y is between subjects. In intensive longitudinal studies involving self-reports (i.e., the typical diary study), it is usual to have ICCs in the .2–.4 range. This level of nonindependence, if ignored, causes tests of significance to be incorrect and biased in the direction of concluding that effects exist when they do not (Kenny, Kashy, & Bolger, 1998, p. 235).

Before multilevel models became generally available, it was common for researchers with nested data to estimate and test the significance of the ICC, and if it was nonsignificant, to treat the data as if they were independent. This was an imperfect approach because of the typically low power to detect appreciable ICCs (Kenny et al., 1998). These days, experienced researchers with nested data routinely use multilevel models, and this is the approach we take in this book. Multilevel models allow us to calculate ICCs, but more importantly, to estimate models that incorporate the nonindependence

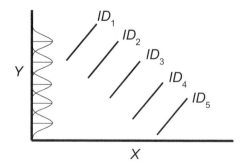

FIGURE 3.2. When the X-to-Y relationship exists between-subjects and within-subjects.

along with the influence of other factors. Detailed examples of this procedure are given in subsequent chapters.

When the X-to-Y Relationship Exists at Both Levels of Analysis

Just as emotional states such as anxiety can vary at both the between- and within-subject levels, so also can its causes, such as daily stressors. Some people, for example, report more stressors on average than others; and the average person reports more stressors on some days than on others. When X and Y vary at both levels, this opens the possibility that they will covary at both levels, and, in addition, that the level of covariance will differ between levels. The body of Figure 3.2 illustrates how, in general, the X-to-Y relationship can be very different—and even of opposite sign—when viewed at the between-subjects versus within-subjects level. We can see from the figure that X is positively related to Y within each subject but that subjects with higher mean levels of X have lower mean levels of Y. Although both types of variability can be informative, researchers testing causal hypotheses tend to focus on the within-subject level.

The reason for favoring the within-subject level is that omitted and confounding variables are less likely to be a problem when analyses focus on how and why people change over time than on how people differ from one another. Multilevel models appear to be an ideal framework for distinguishing the two levels of analysis because, as their name suggests, multilevel models can handle data that vary at two or more levels. When it comes to the outcome variable, Y, this is true. However, when it comes to predictor variables and their relationship to Y, it is not.

The problem originates in the statistical theory underlying mixed models, and it has been known in the field of econometrics for decades (e.g., Judge, Griffiths, Hill, & Lee, 1980, chap. 13). When X varies between and within subjects, and when it relates to Y at a between- and within-subject level, the coefficient for X in a mixed-model analysis is a weighted average of the between- and within-subject relationships (Allison, 2005, 2009).

To prevent this confounding of levels from occurring, it is necessary to separate X into its components at each level, usually called person-mean centering or group-mean centering (Kreft, de Leeuw, & Aiken, 1995; Raudenbush & Bryk, 2002; Snijders & Bosker, 2012). The simplest way to do this is to calculate each subject's mean on X and to subtract it from the subject's raw score on X. The multilevel analysis then is conducted with two X's: the between-subjects means and the within-subjects deviations. There is no necessary connection between the results for mean X and mean-deviated X, and for the purposes of intensive longitudinal analysis, the results for mean X can often be ignored.

3.3 ALLOWING FOR BETWEEN-SUBJECTS HETEROGENEITY: RANDOM EFFECTS

Although the terms *fixed* and *random* effects may be unfamiliar to many readers, they refer to core ideas in the sense that all statistical analyses can be thought of as modeling fixed and random effects. The mean and standard deviation of a variable are its fixed and random effects, respectively. The mean is often used as the single, fixed value that best represents the individual scores, and its counterpart represents how spread apart the scores are. In a simple regression model, the fixed effects are the intercept and slope that best represent the X-to-Y relationship, and the random effects are how spread apart the Y values are around the regression line.

These same ideas apply to models of intensive longitudinal data, except we now have random effects at two levels of analysis. Take a look at Figure 3.3. In it there are separate within-subject regression lines for each of five participants, ID_1 to ID_5. The thick regression line represents the fixed effects, namely, the regression intercept and slope for the average person. The random effects are represented by between-subjects variability around this average. For example, ID_1's intercept is smaller than the average intercept, but its slope is greater than the average slope.

Random effects are valuable in intensive longitudinal data analysis because they can document variability without requiring that the analyst know what its causes or sources are. A research program can begin by assessing variables X and Y in intensive longitudinal

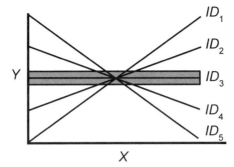

FIGURE 3.3. X-to-Y regression lines for five hypothetical subjects. The thick shaded line is the X-to-Y relationship for the average subject.

design, showing (1) that X and Y covary within subjects, but also showing (2) that the X-to-Y relationship differs across subjects. If the extent of these differences is large, then the variance of the random effect will be large, and the next step in the research program is to understand what explains the variability. This strategy of characterizing the typical person (fixed effect) and between-subjects differences (random effect), then explaining between-subjects differences, was laid out by Bolger et al. (2003) in the *Annual Review of Psychology*.

3.4 TAKING ACCOUNT OF TIME

Time as a Third Variable

Intensive longitudinal data not only differ across subjects, they are also strictly ordered in time, such that values of Y for Time 2 always follow those for Time 1 and precede those for Time 3. Because of this time ordering, it is possible that concurrent changes in X and Y are not due to any causal process but may be due to the passage of time (or to other variables correlated with the passage of time). For example, imagine that the data in Figure 3.4 are time series of five consecutive measurements of workload X (square data points) and concurrent measures of marital conflict (round data points) for a single participant. In this highly simplified example, both sets of

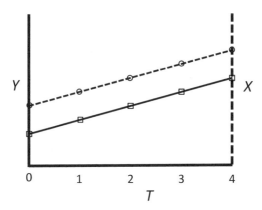

FIGURE 3.4. When the X-to-Y relationship is confounded with time (T).

data points lie on lines that have identical slopes. The data show a perfect positive relationship between X and Y. However, it is also apparent that X and Y have equally perfect relationships with time T. This situation means that we cannot rule out the possibility that the X-to-Y relationship is spurious, a consequence of time itself or of some third variable (or confounder) that changes linearly with time. Indeed, if T were included in a regression analysis of the X-to-Y relationship, there would be no independent relationship between the two. In this case, and more generally, if one wants to rule out time as a source of confounding of within-subject X-to-Y relationships, then time must be included as a predictor in the analysis.

Residual Nonindependence Due to Time Ordering (Autocorrelated Errors)

Even if time is included in the model as a predictor, it may still be the case that time can be a source of nonindependence in level-1 residuals. This type of nonindependence, called *autocorrelation*, was first discovered in analysis of economic time-series data (Wold, 1938; Yule, 1926). Autocorrelation in the errors in Y usually means that measures of Y taken close together in time are more similar to one another than measures taken further apart in time. If the values of Y behaved as if they were sampled independently, there would be no relation between values adjacent in time (nor would there be a relation for values nonadjacent in time). Figure 3.5 shows two situations: The situation in the upper panel is one in which over and above the linear effect of time as a predictor, the residuals in the model are scattered randomly around the regression line; the lower panel displays a situation in which the residuals are (positively) autocorrelated, in the sense that adjacent residuals tend to have the same sign.

Autocorrelation can come about, for example, when a person in a diary study of daily mood suffers from a cold. If, as is usually the case, the cold persists over several days and each day it has a depressing effect on mood, then this situation will result in autocorrelation in Y. Strictly speaking, is it not autocorrelation in Y that causes analytic problems but rather autocorrelation in the errors in Y. As we will see in the next chapter, adequate statistical models of intensive longitudinal data test for, and correct for if necessary, any autocorrelation in errors.

Like correlation due to nesting, autocorrelation tends to be positive: If an omitted variable such as having a cold depresses mood today, it is likely to also depress mood tomorrow, resulting in a positive correlation between the errors in Y from day to day. Autocorrelation effects, however, tend to fade rapidly over time, such that the correlation between errors 2 days apart is much lower than for those 1 day apart, and they are often negligible for those 3 days apart.

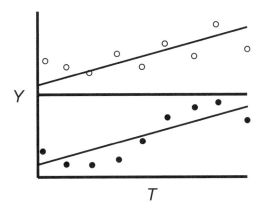

FIGURE 3.5. Depiction of nonautocorrelated residuals (upper panel) and positively autocorrelated residuals (lower panel).

3.5 HOW MANY INDEPENDENT UNITS ARE THERE IN INTENSIVE LONGITUDINAL DATASETS?

We now arrive at the thorny question of how many independent units there are in an intensive longitudinal design. The answer requires us to return to the issue of between-subjects and within-subjects variation in Y. But first, let us approach the question with an example. Imagine that you conducted a cross-sectional phone survey with $N = 100$ participants, all of whom were sampled randomly and phoned on one particular evening with questions about their emotional experiences that day. In this case the answer is easy: There are 100 independent units. If, for one of the emotions (let's say, anxiety), you used the data to calculate a sample estimate of the population mean, and you wanted to test a hypothesis about that mean (e.g., whether it is different from the midpoint of the scale), it would be standard practice to carry out a one-sample t-test with 99 degrees of freedom.

Why 99 degrees of freedom? The answer is 99 because to conduct the inferential test, you need to estimate the sampling variability of the sample mean—that is, its standard error (to see how easy it would be to get a sample mean that differs considerably from the population value by chance). To estimate the standard error, you have to first estimate the standard deviation, and because estimating the standard deviation requires you to have already estimated the mean, there are only $100 - 1 = 99$ independent pieces of information upon which to base that estimate.

Now imagine that the phone survey continued every subsequent evening for $T = 14$ days, and (to keep things simple) that there are no missing data (thus ensuring a balanced design). Imagine that you again calculated a mean, now based on 1,400 observations, and you wanted to test the same hypothesis. What are the degrees of freedom in this case? The answer is not *1,399*, unless you make highly unrealistic assumptions about the process that generated the data.

The more justifiable answer is *99*, and the reasoning is as follows. Variation in daily anxiety scores usually has at least two major components. The first is between-subjects differences in average levels; this influence would be indicated by a positive intraclass correlation between scores from the same person. The second component would be all the temporary influences on anxiety at each time point. If the first influence is appreciable—a case that is typical for anxiety and many other psychological and biomedical states—then it is appropriate to base the degrees of freedom on the number of participants rather than the total number of observations. A detailed discussion of this issue can be found in Kenny et al. (1998).

The example above concerns estimating a population mean, but the same reasoning applies to the estimation of a slope, such as the within-subject relationship between daily events and anxiety. If you have evidence that the slope varies across subjects—in the language introduced above, that there are *random effects*—then for hypothesis tests on the average slope, you should base the degrees of freedom on the number of subjects rather than on the total number of observations. Here, however, you must also consider the possibility that your design is underpowered to detect the random effect of slopes. Our advice is that even in the absence of significant random effects, it is still prudent to operate as if they exist and base degrees of freedom on the number of participants. For some data analysis software this would require that you carry out additional, but relatively minor, calculations.

There is another way of viewing this issue that avoids the problem of degrees of freedom altogether: If your sample size is sufficiently large, you can use a z-distribution in place of a t-distribution (and an χ^2 in place of an F). Some statisticians argue that multilevel models of the sort described in this book are suitable for large samples only (e.g., see Fitzmaurice, Laird, & Ware, 2011), and therefore when one conducts an analysis on such samples, one can rely on what are called *asymptotic tests* such as those based on a z-distribution. It is fair to say, though, that this is not a majority view. When is a sample large enough to use large-sample tests? One answer is to use the rule of thumb that when the degrees of freedom for one's hypothesis is 30 or larger, the t-distribution on which most tests are based approximates a z-distribution, and so one can justify reporting a z-test rather than a t-test.

3.6 CHOOSING AN APPROPRIATE ZERO POINT FOR X

Choosing a zero point, also called *centering*, is a type of rescaling of predictor variables, and its purpose is to make the results of a statistical analysis more interpretable (Aiken & West, 1991). The most common form of centering involves subtracting the sample mean of a predictor variable. Evaluating Y when X is at its typical value is often more useful than evaluating it when X is 0. Sometimes $X = 0$ is not even a legitimate value. Figure 3.6 is designed to illustrate how centering can affect the results of analyses of multilevel data, including intensive longitudinal data. We can see that if X is centered at X_0, there are no between-subjects differences in the Y intercept, whereas if it is centered at X_2, there are large intercept differences. Centering at X_1 results in intermediate differences.

If, instead of indicating subjects, the separate lines indicated levels of a between-subjects variable W (an example of which is shown in the data matrix at the beginning of this chapter), then at X_0, there would be no Y differences due to levels of W; at X_2 those differences would be large; and at X_1 the differences would be intermediate in size. The implication of these differences is that, in the presence of X-slope differences due to subjects (i.e., due to random effects) or due to a measured between-subjects variable W, centering of X needs to be considered carefully. Usually, though, centering on the mean is better than no centering at all. The one exception to this rule is time; *time* = 0 can be a very informative value at which to evaluate Y. Making *time* = 0 allows the intercept to represent the model-implied mean Y at the first time point of the study (Bollen & Curran, 2006).

Discussions of centering in multilevel modeling often contrast

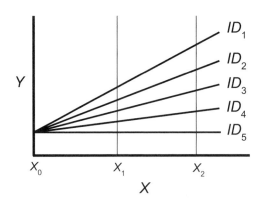

FIGURE 3.6. How centering X at different values can affect the mean and variance of the intercept in multilevel models.

grand-mean versus group- or person-mean centering (e.g., Rauden-bush & Bryk, 2002). In this book, we argue that it is frequently use-ful to do both. Grand-mean centering establishes an interpretable zero point for X, and person-mean centering splits this centered variable into between- and within-subjects components. A concrete and detailed example of this approach is provided in Chapter 5.

3.7 CHAPTER SUMMARY

We have reviewed five basic guidelines that are fundamental to working effectively with intensive longitudinal data: (1) distinguish between-subjects and within-subjects levels of analysis; (2) allow for between-subjects random effects; (3) include time in your model; (4) specify the appropriate number of independent units in your model; and (5) choose interpretable zero points for within-subjects variables. By following these guidelines you will circumvent major analysis pitfalls and draw more sound inferences from your data.

3.8 RECOMMENDED READINGS

Hox, J. J. (2010). Multilevel analysis: Techniques and applications (2nd ed.). New York: Routledge.

Chapter 5 of this book discusses specific analysis issues that arise when using a multilevel framework to analyze longitudinal data.

Snijders, T. A. B., & Bosker, R. J. (2012). *Multilevel analysis: An introduction to basic and advanced multilevel modeling* (2nd ed.). Thousand Oaks, CA: Sage.

Chapter 15 of this book covers basic issues on analyzing longitudinal data using a multilevel modeling framework.

Walls, T. A., & Schafer, J. L. (Eds.). (2006). *Models for intensive longitudinal data.* New York: Oxford University Press.

This edited volume popularized the term *intensive longitudinal data* and covers several advanced modeling approaches not covered in this book.

4

Modeling the Time Course of Continuous Outcomes

Having presented some fundamental guidelines for working with intensive longitudinal data—the need to take account of the between-subjects influences and heterogeneity, to take account of temporal influences, and to use interpretable measurement units—we are now in a position to implement these guidelines in our first data analysis example. According to Bolger et al. (2003), the most basic feature of an intensive longitudinal outcome is its time course. Questions regarding the time course are of two basic kinds: First, what is the time course for the typical subject? Second, how much do subjects differ from one another in their time course?

We address these questions using the example of a two-group intervention study with weekly diary assessments. Although our example dataset involves equal intervals between measurements and has no missing data, the analysis method we describe can be used for designs with unequal intervals (e.g., experience sampling designs) and for designs where missingness is unrelated to the change process (see Black, Harel, & Matthews, 2012). Finally, we provide an example write-up of the findings in a format suitable for publication.

4.1   THE TIME COURSE DATASET

The time course dataset contains simulated data on an outcome where, as the result of an intervention, there is reason to expect group differences in the time course and, over and above these, subject-level differences within each group. The dataset is intended to represent a study of wives from 50 heterosexual married couples, randomly assigned to a 16-week marital therapy treatment condition (*n* = 25) or a 16-week wait-list condition (*n* = 25). The reader should imagine that (1) in the treatment group each wife completed a web diary each week on the evening prior to the day of the therapy session, and (2) in the control group each wife completed a web diary on a fixed day each week.

Figure 4.1 shows the multilevel structure of the time course dataset. Like the multilevel structure of the example dataset in the previous chapter, the upper-level units or subjects are persons, and the lower-level units are time points. There are 16 lines of data for each subject, resulting in 16 * 50 = 800 rows in all. There are four variables in the dataset: *id*, which takes integer values from 1 to 50; *time*, which takes integer values from 0 to 15; *intimacy*, which ranges from 0 to 10; and *treatment*, which takes the value 0 for the control group and 1 for the intervention group.

4.2   AN APPLICATION OF LINEAR GROWTH CURVE ANALYSIS

Before beginning the statistical analysis of an intensive longitudinal dataset, it is essential to visualize the raw data. There are many ways to do this, but we recommend one that creates separate panels of a dependent variable for each subject (i.e., person, or other upper-level unit) and examine the time course by "joining the dots." Given that our example concerns the efficacy of a between-groups intervention, separating the panels by group also makes sense. Details about how these graphs can be created are provided in the appendix to this chapter.

For each group, the graphing procedure places the data in panels

id	time	intimacy	treatment
	(T_{ij})	(Y_{ij})	(W_j)
1	0	2.96	0
1	1	2.34	0
⋮	⋮	⋮	⋮
1	14	1.15	0
1	15	4.54	0
2	0	0.64	0
2	1	3.1	0
⋮	⋮	⋮	⋮
2	14	0.65	0
2	15	2.21	0
⋮	⋮	⋮	⋮
25	0	3.09	0
25	1	2.59	0
⋮	⋮	⋮	⋮
25	14	4.9	0
25	15	2.1	0
26	0	1.8	1
26	1	2.5	1
⋮	⋮	⋮	⋮
26	14	3.46	1
26	15	3.78	1
⋮	⋮	⋮	⋮
50	0	1.47	1
50	1	4.17	1
⋮	⋮	⋮	⋮
50	14	3.01	1
50	15	3.54	1

FIGURE 4.1. Structure of the time course dataset.

in a 5×5 grid ordered by ID number. Figure 4.2 shows the resulting paneled data. The first point to notice in this figure is that *intimacy* changes markedly from week to week in the majority of subjects. The second pattern is that some subjects show an overall increase in intimacy over the 16 weeks. The third pattern is that, consistent with the goal of a marital therapy intervention, there are more people showing increases in intimacy in the treatment than in the

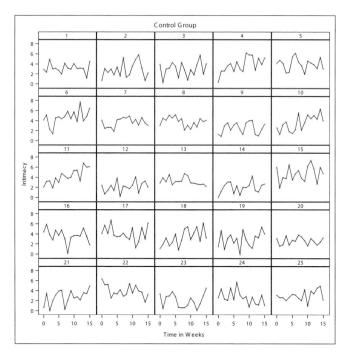

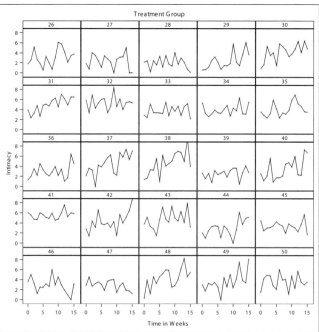

FIGURE 4.2. Panel plots of the 16-week time course of intimacy for each subject in the control and treatment groups.

control group. The group differences are not that striking, though, and no conclusions can be drawn until we can estimate a formal statistical model.

We first need appropriate notation for representing a multilevel model of individual and group differences in change over time. In this book we use notation drawn largely from Raudenbush and Bryk (2002). Figure 4.3 is a schematic of two groups that differ on change but which also shows between-subjects, within-group variation. To keep things as simple as possible, there are only two subjects in each group, and we have made the groups differ markedly in average intercepts and slopes. The dependent variable is Y_{ij}, representing the weekly intimacy score of subject j at time i. We know from the design (and from Figure 4.1) that there are $j = 1$ to 50 persons and $i = 16$ time points in the study. The single within-subject independent variable is T_{ij}, the times of measurement i for subject j (note that the j subscript could have been omitted because each subject was measured at the same time points). The single between-subjects independent variable is the intervention group (0 = control vs. 1 = treatment), represented by W_j. We do not show a subscript i for this variable because it is constant across time points for any given subject. These variables are called *intimacy*, *time*, and *treatment*, respectively, in Figure 4.1.

The multilevel statistical model to be estimated is most easily

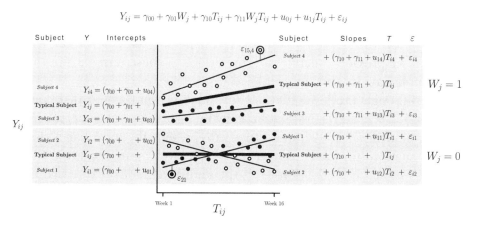

$$Y_{ij} = \gamma_{00} + \gamma_{01}W_j + \gamma_{10}T_{ij} + \gamma_{11}W_jT_{ij} + u_{0j} + u_{1j}T_{ij} + \varepsilon_{ij}$$

FIGURE 4.3. Simplified depiction of a longitudinal multilevel model with average (thick) and subject-specific (thin) regression lines.

understood as a set of algebraic equations specified by level of analysis. At level 1, the within-subject level, *intimacy* is specified to be a linear function of time:

$$Y_{ij} = \beta_{0j} + \beta_{1j}T_{ij} + \varepsilon_{ij} \tag{4.1}$$

Equation 4.1 is a within-subject equation that focuses on particular time points i for a particular subject j. One way to think about what this part of the model is doing is that it is specifying an intercept, β_0, and a slope, β_1, for each subject in the population, resulting in a distribution of j intercepts and j slopes. ε_{ij} is a within-subject residual term representing the difference, at a given time point between the predicted intimacy for a given subject and the actual value. At level 2, the distribution of individual intercepts and slopes is modeled in the following way:

$$\beta_{0j} = \gamma_{00} + \gamma_{01}W_j + u_{0j} \tag{4.2}$$

$$\beta_{1j} = \gamma_{10} + \gamma_{11}W_j + u_{1j} \tag{4.3}$$

Equations 4.2 and 4.3 are between-subjects equations specifying that (1) any subject's intercept is determined by a common (fixed) intercept for the population, γ_{00}, a common (fixed) effect of the level-2 variable W_j for the population, γ_{01}, and a subject-specific intercept deviation, u_{0j}; and (2) any subject's slope is determined by a (fixed) common slope effect, γ_{10}, a (fixed) common effect of the level-2 variable W_j on the slope, γ_{11}, and a subject-specific slope deviation, u_{1j}. (Soon we provide concrete interpretations of these terms using the example data for this chapter.)

Although the level-1/level-2 formulation represented in Equations 4.1, 4.2, and 4.3 are a didactically useful way of understanding a multilevel model, one can also represent the model as a single equation (through substitution of the level-2 equations into the level-1 equation). Equation 4.4 is the multilevel model expressed in a single-equation form, often called a *mixed model* form. When the focal explanatory variable at level-1 is *time*, as it is in this case, the model is also usually called a *linear growth model* (Raudenbush & Bryk, 2002; Singer & Willett, 2003):

$$Y_{ij} = \gamma_{00} + \gamma_{01}W_j + \gamma_{10}T_{ij} + \gamma_{11}W_jT_{ij} + u_{0j} + u_{1j}T_{ij} + \varepsilon_{ij} \qquad (4.4)$$

It is useful to think of this linear growth model as a regression model with terms for the intercept, group, time, and group-by-time interaction. These are called the *fixed effects*, and they are shown as the first four terms to the right of the equal sign in Equation 4.4. The heavy black regression lines in Figure 4.3 also show this aspect of the model. Yet another way of thinking of this aspect of the model is that it represents the typical person within the control and treatment groups, respectively. Bearing in mind the coding of the variables (see Figure 4.1), the first term, γ_{00}, is the intimacy level of the control group at Time 0; the coefficient for the second term, γ_{01}, is how much higher or lower the treatment group's intimacy level is at Time 0; the coefficient for the third term, γ_{10}, is the change in intimacy per week for the control group; and the coefficient for the fourth term, γ_{11}, is how much higher or lower the rate of change for the treatment group is compared to the control group. As one would expect for a therapeutic intervention, the treatment group members are expected to show increases in intimacy over time, whereas the control group members are expected to show either no increase or a smaller increase.

Although it is an important interpretation of the model, a traditional regression-with-interactions interpretation is also an inadequate one, because it ignores the possibility that within the control and treatment groups, people may not be exactly the same in their starting position and/or rate of change. The coefficients u_{0j} and u_{1j}, known as *random effects*, capture the (assumed-to-be) normally distributed random deviations of subjects above or below their group average in terms of intercepts and slopes, respectively. These two terms, together with the fixed effects terms, allow us to arrive at subject-specific regression lines. For example, Subject 1 in Figure 4.3 is a wife in the control group with a starting level of intimacy that is lower than her group average, but she has a rate of change that is more positive than that of her group average. As another example, Subject 4 is a woman in the treatment group whose starting value and rate of change in intimacy are higher than her group average.

Although as we will see, it is possible to obtain model-based predictions of the upper-level random effects (and therefore the specific regression lines) for each subject in a sample, a more central concern in modeling intensive longitudinal data is to estimate the population variances and covariances of these effects. These allow us to know how much subjects differ from one another within the treatment and control groups, and, in the case of the intercept–slope covariance, whether there is any tendency for subjects with larger or smaller intercepts (i.e., starting levels) to have larger or smaller slopes. Using the Raudenbush and Bryk (2002) notation, the variance of the intercepts is τ_{00}; the variance of the time slopes is τ_{11}; and the covariance of the intercepts and slopes is τ_{01} (or equivalently, τ_{10}). These three parameters (τ_{00}, τ_{11}, and τ_{10}) are the lower triangle elements of the covariance matrix of the random effects, called Tau.

The random effects for the intercept and slope are what are termed *upper-level* or *between-subjects random effects*; there are also lower-level or within-subjects random effects. These are the ε_{ij}'s, and they capture the extent to which a wife's intimacy on a given week deviates above or below the value predicted by her specific regression line. Two example residuals are highlighted in Figure 4.3: The intimacy for Subject 1 on the second week is lower than predicted by her regression line, whereas the intimacy level of Subject 4 on the 15th week is higher than predicted. As was the case for the upper-level random effects, we are especially interested in the variance of the residuals, σ^2.

We assume that the ε_{ij}'s are normally distributed with a mean of zero, but because our data are longitudinal, strictly ordered in time, we cannot take for granted, as we often do with cross-sectional data, that pairs or sequences of ε_{ij}'s are uncorrelated. As discussed in the previous chapter (Section 3.5), a likely reason why one might expect to find serial correlation in the residuals is that there are within-subject variables that temporarily influence Y_{ij} that are omitted from the model. If, for example, a wife was afflicted by a cold or flu over multiple weeks, this could result in lower intimacy scores during those weeks than would be expected by the wife's general time trend. The simplest form of serial correlation is where the current error, ε_{ij}, is a linear function of the previous error, $\varepsilon_{i-1,j}$, plus an additional error that is truly random, v_{ij}, as follows:

$$\varepsilon_{ij} = \rho\varepsilon_{i-1,j} + v_{ij} \tag{4.5}$$

Ignoring autocorrelation in errors typically leads to estimates of fixed effects (e.g., γ_{00}) that have standard errors that are too small and test statistics that are too large (Greene, 2008), leading to Type I errors. Consequently, one must take account of autocorrelation if one wants to make valid population inferences.

The model shown in Equation 4.4 (together with assumptions about random effects) can be estimated by general purpose software (e.g., IBM SPSS [IBM Inc., 2010], SAS [SAS Institute Inc., 2011], STATA [StataCorp LP, 2011], and R [R Development Core Team, 2011]) as well as by software specific to multilevel modeling (e.g., HLM [Raudenbush, Bryk, Cheong, Congdon, & du Toit, 2011], MLwiN [Rasbash, Charlton, Browne, Healy, & Cameron, 2011]), and software specific to structural equation modeling (e.g., Mplus [Muthén & Muthén, 1998–2010], LISREL [SSI Inc., 2010], and EQS [Multivariate Software Inc., 2011]). Below we show extracts of relevant SPSS and SAS code; at the end of the chapter we include more complete versions of SPSS, SAS, and also Mplus code; the companion website for the book has the equivalent code for HLM, MLwiN, STATA, and R. When presenting syntax, we use the convention that terms in uppercase refer to (mostly) unchanging program commands, whereas terms in lowercase refer to user-provided information, such as variable names and analysis options. In other words, when modifying the code to suit your own analysis needs, you will most likely modify the terms in lowercase.

SPSS Code

```
MIXED intimacy WITH time01 treatment
 /FIXED=time01 treatment time01*treatment | SSTYPE(3)
 /METHOD=reml
 /PRINT=g solution testcov
 /RANDOM=INTERCEPT time01 | SUBJECT(id) COVTYPE(un)
 /REPEATED=time | SUBJECT(id) COVTYPE(ar1).
```

SAS Code

```
PROC MIXED COVTEST DATA=intimacy METHOD=reml cl;
```

```
CLASS id time;

MODEL intimacy=time01 treatment
      time01*treatment/solution cl

      DDF=48,48,48,48 OUTP=intp OUTPM=intpm;

RANDOM intercept time01/SUBJECT=id TYPE=un s g gcorr;

REPEATED time/SUBJECT=id TYPE=ar(1);
```

In addition to estimating the model, we believe that a crucial accompanying step involves graphically inspecting the predictions of the model, both alone and in combination with the raw data. In fact, we recommend examining the predictions of the model visually before doing so numerically. There are two visualizations we recommend: First, create an analogous panel plot to Figure 4.2 but with both the raw data and the predictions of the multilevel model included; and second, create what is called a *spaghetti plot*, which presents the predicted regression lines for each person for each group in a compact way (Singer & Willett, 2003).

Figure 4.4 shows the output of this analysis, and it is in our view the single most important representation of the success of multilevel modeling in terms of support for a hypothesized intervention effect. From the two sets of panels in this figure we can see that the raw data are well described by the model-implied regression lines, and that there are no anomalous individuals or even data points. This is not always the case in analyses of intensive longitudinal data. Any problems of model fit will be evident from panel plots of the kind shown in Figure 4.4.

Although some indication of group differences can be seen from Figure 4.4, a much more effective way of visualizing these is through the use of the second visualization we recommend, a spaghetti plot, shown in Figure 4.5. Again, the code for producing these plots is detailed in the chapter appendix.

The thick black lines in Figure 4.5 show that the typical person in the treatment group had similar levels of *intimacy* to the typical person in the control group in week 0. Both groups show a rise in *intimacy* over time, but the slope for the average subject in the treatment group appears steeper. The thin black lines show the fitted lines for each subject in the study, and they indicate that there is considerable variability in intercepts and slopes within each group.

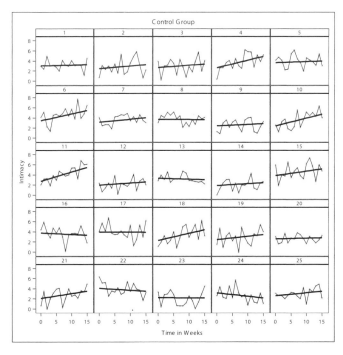

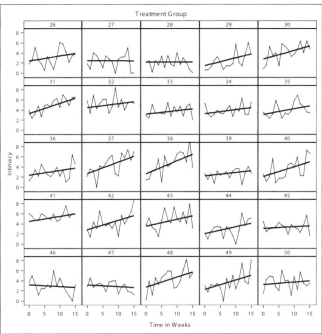

FIGURE 4.4. Panel plots of the actual and model-predicted time course of intimacy for each subject in the control and treatment groups.

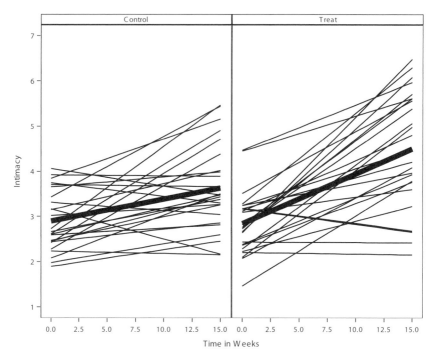

FIGURE 4.5. Model-predicted time course of intimacy: Spaghetti plot of average (thick) and subject-specific (thin) regression lines for the control (left) and treatment (right) groups. (This figure has been duplicated as Figure 1 of the example write-up.)

The variability is large enough that there are many in the control group who have trajectories as steep as the average for the treatment group, and vice versa. Therefore, these graphical patterns do not necessarily imply that the group differences in average slopes are statistically significant using standard criteria.

Before taking a detailed tour of the results of statistical program output, it is worth noting some similarities and differences among SPSS MIXED, SAS PROC MIXED, and Mplus. For the models in this and most chapters in the book, SPSS and SAS produce identical results (within rounding error). Mplus will produce results that are very close to those of SPSS and SAS, but may differ a bit due to two model specification differences. First, Mplus does not have a feasible way of incorporating autocorrelated residuals as part of a multilevel model, and, to the extent that autocorrelated residuals are present in the data, its results will diverge from those of SPSS and SAS. Second, the REML estimator (which is the default in SPSS MIXED and SAS PROC MIXED) does not exist in Mplus, and models in the program are run using ML. Although REML estimation is preferred when sample sizes are small, it is also well known that REML and ML estimation converge to the same estimates asymptotically (i.e., as sample sizes become large).

We now turn to the numerical output of IBM SPSS MIXED (as noted, SAS produces equivalent results). Tables 4.1 and 4.2 contain the fixed and random effects results, respectively. Please note that we are displaying excerpted parts of the output only. Readers are invited to view the complete output on the companion website, and if they wish, to replicate it using the Time Course dataset also on that website. We begin with a table of estimates and tests of fixed effects.

Recall that the fixed effects are displayed as thick dark lines in Figure 4.5. Consistent with the visual evidence from that figure,

TABLE 4.1. Fixed Effects Output for Time Course Data Example from SPSS (top) and SAS (bottom)

Estimates of Fixed Effects[a]

Parameter	Estimate	Std. Error	df	t	Sig.	95% Confidence Interval	
						Lower Bound	Upper Bound
Intercept ($\hat{\gamma}_{00}$)	2.898974	.207030	47.975	14.003	.000	2.482707	3.315242
time01 ($\hat{\gamma}_{10}$)	.735201	.347199	47.998	2.118	.039	.037111	1.433292
Treatment ($\hat{\gamma}_{01}$)	-.056442	.292785	47.975	-.193	.848	-.645134	.532249
time01*treatment ($\hat{\gamma}_{11}$)	.921436	.491013	47.998	1.877	.067	-.065813	1.908686

a. Dependent Variable: intimacy.

Solution for Fixed Effects								
Effect	Estimate	Standard Error	DF	t Value	Pr > |t|	Alpha	Lower	Upper
intercept ($\hat{\gamma}_{00}$)	2.8990	0.2070	48	14.00	<.0001	0.05	2.4827	3.3152
time01 ($\hat{\gamma}_{10}$)	0.7352	0.3472	48	2.12	0.0394	0.05	0.03710	1.4333
treatment ($\hat{\gamma}_{01}$)	-0.05644	0.2928	48	-0.19	0.8479	0.05	-0.6451	0.5323
time01*treatment ($\hat{\gamma}_{11}$)	0.9214	0.4910	48	1.88	0.0667	0.05	-0.06583	1.9087

Note: The Greek symbols in parentheses are Raudenbush and Bryk (2002) notation for each parameter.

TABLE 4.2. Random Effects Output for Time Course Data Example from SPSS (top) and SAS (bottom)

Estimates of Covariance Parameters[a]

Parameter		Estimate	Std. Error	Wald Z	Sig.	95% Confidence Interval	
						Lower Bound	Upper Bound
Repeated Measures	AR1 diagonal ($\hat{\sigma}^2$)	1.692482	.092127	18.371	.000	1.521216	1.883031
	AR1 rho ($\hat{\rho}$)	-.000034	.042175	-.001	.999	-.082507	.082439
Intercept + time01 [subject = id]	UN (1,1) ($\hat{\tau}_{00}$)	.685773	.221288	3.099	.002	.364344	1.290771
	UN (2,1) ($\hat{\tau}_{01}$)	-.516135	.306251	-1.685	.092	-1.116375	.084105
	UN (2,2) ($\hat{\tau}_{11}$)	1.893711	.623774	3.036	.002	.992966	3.611547

a. Dependent Variable: intimacy.

Covariance Parameter Estimates								
Cov Parm	Subject	Estimate	Standard Error	z Value	Pr z	Alpha	Lower	Upper
UN(1,1) ($\hat{\tau}_{00}$)	id	0.6858	0.2213	3.10	0.0010	0.05	0.3977	1.4559
UN(2,1) ($\hat{\tau}_{01}$)	id	-0.5162	0.3063	-1.69	0.0919	0.05	-1.1165	0.08409
UN(2,2) ($\hat{\tau}_{11}$)	id	1.8939	0.6238	3.04	0.0012	0.05	1.0875	4.0963
AR(1) ($\hat{\rho}$)	Id	-0.00005	0.04217	-0.00	0.9991	0.05	-0.08271	0.08261
Residual ($\hat{\sigma}^2$)		1.6925	0.09213	18.37	<.0001	0.05	1.5255	1.8886

Note: The Greek symbols in parentheses are Raudenbush and Bryk (2002) notation for each parameter.

there were no initial group differences in intimacy at the beginning of the study ($\hat{\gamma}_{01}$ = −0.1 units on a 0–10 scale; the 95% confidence interval, CI_{95}, ranges from −0.6 to 0.5). The time slope for the typical wife in the control group (the thick black line in the left panel of Figure 4.5), $\hat{\gamma}_{10}$, is 0.7 units, $t(48) = 2.12$, $p = .04$, $CI_{95} = 0.04$, 1.4. The time slope estimate for the treatment group is 0.9 units steeper than the control group, $t(48) = 1.88$, $p = .07$, $CI_{95} = -0.07$, 1.9. So, despite the visual evidence of a between-groups slope difference, we cannot rule out the possibility that the true difference in the population is zero (as the CI for this effect contains zero). Note, however, that we also cannot rule out the possibility that the population difference is as large as 1.9 units. We now turn to the SPSS MIXED output for the random effects.

As was shown in Figure 4.4, there are both between-subjects and within-subjects random effects. We begin with the between-subjects variety. In Figure 4.5 we can see that at the beginning of the study, there is considerable variation within the control and the treatment groups in intimacy. This variability, assumed to be the same for both groups, is $\hat{\tau}_{00}$ and has a value of 0.69 units, which corresponds to 0.84 in *SD* units, $z = 3.10$, $p = .001$. Note that we report the Wald z-test rather than the more appropriate and powerful likelihood ratio (LR) test because they agree in their conclusions (see Raudenbush & Bryk, 2002, and Singer & Willett, 2003, for a discussion of this issue). Combining the point estimates of fixed and random effects of the intercept, we can calculate the PI_{95}, the 95% prediction interval for the distribution of random intercepts to be $2.9 \pm 2 * 0.8 = 1.3$ to 4.5. Thus the model predicts that 95% of the population intercepts will lie within $\pm 2 * 0.8 = \pm 1.6$ units of their respective group-level intercepts.

The slope variance is 1.89, which corresponds to an *SD* of $\sqrt{1.89} = 1.4$ units. Analogous to the intercept variance, this indicates that 95% of the population slopes should vary between $\pm 2.8 = 5.6$ units of the typical slope for their group. This variability is very large and helps explain why, despite the fixed effect estimates shown in Figure 4.4, we cannot rule out the possibility that the typical slopes for control and treatment groups are the same.

There is a final upper-level covariance parameter estimate, $\hat{\tau}_{01}$. This shows the linear relationship between intercept differences and slope differences (i.e., do those people who have larger intercepts tend to be the same people who have larger slopes?). The estimate is -0.50 in covariance units, which is -0.43 in correlation units. The LR test is $\chi^2(1) = 2775.2 - 2770.9 = 4.3$, $p = .038$, whereas the z-test is -1.70, $p = .090$. This is an example of a marginal Wald test, where one should carry out the more involved LR test. Thus, it appears that those with more positive intercepts tend to have less positive slopes.

Turning to the within-subjects random effects, recall from Figure 4.4 that these are the deviations of the observed data points from the individual-specific fitted lines. On the assumption that these residuals are draws from a normal distribution with a common variance (an assumption that seems reasonable, given the visual evidence of Figure 4.4), the estimate of that variance, $\hat{\sigma}^2$, is 1.7 units, $CI_{95} = 1.5, 1.9$. Note also that there is essentially no first-order autocorrelation; that is, there is no tendency of adjacent residuals to be correlated: $\hat{\rho} = 0.00$, $CI_{95} = -0.1, 0.1$.

Although the focus of our growth curve example in this chapter has been on linear change, it is important to consider nonlinear time-based trajectories when analyzing longitudinal data. Inspection of individual panel plots, like those shown in Figure 4.2, will be useful when determining what functional forms should be considered. Interested readers can consult Grimm and Ram (2009) for examples of how to fit various nonlinear functions to longitudinal data.

4.3   EXAMPLE WRITE-UP OF TIME COURSE DATA

Presenting the Results as in a Journal Article

We assume that you, the readers of this book, are substantive researchers who are using, or wish to use, intensive longitudinal methods to study some social or behavioral phenomenon. Having done so, you will surely want to communicate relevant results in the form of a journal article to be read by your peers. Although norms have been developing slowly, it is still fair to say that journal articles show great variability in their reporting of results of intensive longitudinal studies. What follows is our attempt to provide guidance on this issue. Given how much detail we have provided on data analysis in this chapter, you may be surprised at the brevity of the results we recommend presenting in a journal article: one table, two graphs, and (in general) no use of multilevel-model equations. We consider the last of these first.

In the late 1980s and through the 1990s, when multilevel models were unfamiliar, many authors provided formal details on these models that would have been judged unnecessary for more standard procedures such as regression and analysis of variance (ANOVA). In particular, thanks to the popularity of stand-alone multilevel software such as HLM and MLwiN, multilevel models were often presented formally as equations for each of the multiple levels. For intensive longitudinal designs, at least, and when the goal of the journal article is to communicate substantive results, we now feel that this approach is often counterproductive.

In fact, we recommend that reporting results should begin, where possible, with a graph and not a table. Perhaps the most useful graph to show before detailing the model estimates is the spaghetti plots by group, as shown in Figure 4.5. This figure summarizes almost all of the important results. We can see what the fixed effects are via the heavy lines, and what the random effects are by comparing the thin lines to the heavy lines, and we get a useful idea of the magnitudes of both. Such a plot sets the scene for the formal tests of hypotheses. What this figure does not show is how well the model fits the raw data. Figure 4.4, with a separate data panel for each person in each group, fills in this missing information. The drawback is that it is likely to be considered too unimportant to include, given space limitation in journals. One solution is to present only a subset of panels; an example of this approach is provided in the example write-up.

The central part of most results sections is the presentation of parameter estimates and tests of significance. Although it is possible to present all of these in the text only, most multilevel model results will benefit from presentation in tabular form. When presenting regression or ANOVA results, the APA *Publication Manual* cites the use of canonical forms for such tables. In fact, the sixth edition of the manual now includes a sample multilevel model table (p. 147). The table is complex because it presents results of five separate models that are intended to be compared. The sample table we use in our write-up has a similar structure but considers one model only. It includes essentially the information reported in the SPSS output for fixed and random effects shown earlier. Another important way our table differs from that in the APA manual is that we present confidence intervals for all estimates.

To summarize, then, our example write-up for modeling the time course of intensive longitudinal data (1) omits equations altogether, (2) begins with figures, and (3) ends with a suggested canonical form of a multilevel output table. The next section is the write-up itself, formatted according to the sixth edition of the APA manual.

The Write-Up

We begin the write-up with a statement of the hypothesis to be tested, as it might appear at the end of an Introduction section of an APA-style empirical paper.

In summary, the major hypothesis to be tested is whether females in the treatment group showed greater increases in intimacy over time than did females in the control group.

METHOD

Participants

Fifty opposite-sex couples were randomized to treatment ($n = 25$) and control ($n = 25$) conditions. The mean age of male partners was 32.4 years ($SD = 4.6$). The mean age of female partners was 30.8 years ($SD = 3.4$). All couples were homogeneous in terms of race. The racial breakdown in order of size was white ($n = 32$, 64%), Asian ($n = 8$, 16%), Hispanic ($n = 6$, 12%), and black ($n = 4$, 8%). Although couples were recruited into the study, in this paper we focus on the data for the female partners only.

Measures

Intimacy (female). The six-item Reis and Shaver Intimacy Scale was used (Reis & Shaver, 1988). Raw scores were rescaled to a 0–10 interval, such that 0 was the lowest possible score and 10 was the highest possible score. Summary statistics for wives' intimacy over couples and time were: $M = 3.5$, $SD = 1.6$, range = 0–10.

Time. The 16 weeks of 1-hour therapy sessions were scaled such that 0 was the value for week 1 and 1 was the value for week 16, with the intervening 14 weeks spaced equally across the 0 to 1 interval. This scaling of time implies that a linear slope for time estimates the total change in intimacy over the complete therapeutic period.

Procedure

Heterosexual couples were recruited from a marital therapy clinic in a large Midwestern city. The standard therapy for distressed couples was a 1-hour session each week for 16 consecutive weeks. Couples seeking treatment were randomly assigned to a treatment group that received therapy immediately, or to a control group that remained on a waiting list over the same 16-week period. All couples completed web-based questionnaires once per week. In the case of the treatment group, the reports were obtained on the evening prior to the day of each therapy session. Analyses were conducted on data from wives only.

RESULTS

Descriptive Statistics

The analysis dataset consisted of 50 (couples) * 16 (weeks) = 800 observations. Inspection of person-by-person scatterplots indicated that the within-person change in intimacy over time was approximately linear. The plots did not reveal any outliers, and there were no missing data.

Multilevel Model of Intimacy Change

We specified and estimated a linear growth model for intimacy that allowed each wife to have her own initial level of intimacy and rate of change in intimacy. Because couples were randomized to treatment and control conditions, we hypothesized no group differences in average initial levels of intimacy. We predicted that both groups would show an increase in intimacy over the course of the study. Our key hypothesis was that wives in the treatment group would show a steeper rate of change in intimacy compared to those in the control group.

The results are presented in Table 1 and in Figures 1 and 2. Table

Table 1. Parameter Estimates for Linear Growth Model of Female Intimacy as a Function of Intervention Group

Fixed effects (intercept, slopes)	Estimate (SE)	$t(48)$	p^a	CI_{95} Lower	Upper
Intercept (level at week 1)	2.90 (0.21)	14.00	<.001	2.48	3.32
Time[b]	0.74 (0.35)	2.12	.039	0.04	1.43
Group[c]	−0.06 (0.29)	−0.19	.848	−0.65	0.53
Group by time	0.92 (0.49)	1.88	.067	−0.07	1.91

Random effects ([co-]variances)	Estimate (SE)	z	p	$CI_{95}{}^d$ Lower	Upper
Level 2 (between-person)					
Intercept	0.69 (0.22)	3.10	.001	0.40	1.46
Time	1.89 (0.62)	3.04	.001	1.09	4.09
Intercept and time	−0.52 (0.31)	−1.69	.092	−1.12	0.08
Level 1 (within-person)					
Residual	1.69 (0.09)	18.37	<.001	1.53	1.89
Autocorrelation	0.00 (0.04)	0.00	.999	−0.08	0.08

Note. $N = 50$.
[a]All p-values are two-tailed except in the case of variances, where one-tailed p-values are used (because variances are constrained to be non-negative).
[b]Time is coded 0 = week 1, 1 = week 16, with equal intervals for the intervening weeks.
[c]Group is coded 0 for the control group and 1 for the treatment group.
[d]Confidence intervals for variances were computed using the Satterthwaite method (see Littell, Milliken, Stroup, Wolfinger, and Schabenberger, 2006).

1 has two sets of parameter estimates. The first set, the fixed effects, can be thought of as the results for typical persons in the control and treatment groups, respectively. These fixed effects are represented by the heavy dark lines in Figure 1. The second set of effect estimates in Table 1 are the random effects. These describe variability at two levels of analysis: At the upper level they are the extent to which people vary from their group averages, and at the lower level they are the extent to which individual data points vary from the values predicted by the model. The upper-level random effects are represented in Figure 1 by the variability in individual regression lines from the group averages. The lower-level random effects are shown in Figure 2, which consists

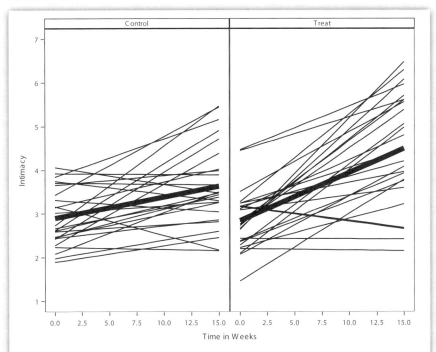

Figure 1. Spaghetti plot of average (thick) and subject-specific (thin) time courses for control (left) and treatment (right) groups.

of the raw data and fitted lines for a selection of five individuals from each group (about which, more details are to come).

The heavy black lines in Figure 1 show the central findings of the study, that the typical wife in the treatment group, who had similar levels of intimacy to the typical wife in the control group in week 1, showed a steeper rate of change and had a markedly higher level of intimacy by the end of the study at week 16. Of course, these graphical patterns do not necessarily imply that the results are statistically significant using standard criteria. We now turn to tests of significance on these fixed effects, listed in Table 1.

Recall that the control group was coded 0 and the treatment group, 1, and that time was coded 0 for week 1 and 1 for week 16, with equal intervals for the intervening weeks. Therefore, the model parameter

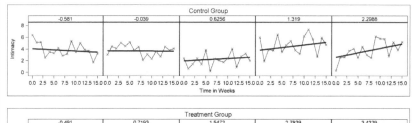

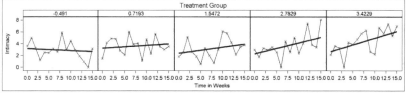

Figure 2. Raw and fitted time course for participants at the 5th, 25th, 50th, 75th, and 95th slope percentiles for the control (upper panel) and treatment (lower panel) groups.

estimates in Table 1 have the following interpretation: (1) the intercept is the level of intimacy at week 1 for the control group, (2) the group estimate is the intimacy difference (treatment minus control) at week 1, (3) the time estimate is the change in intimacy in the control group over the 16 weeks of the study, and (4) the time-by-group interaction is the difference in intimacy change between the treatment and control groups.

As we expected, and consistent with successful random assignment, there was no group difference in initial intimacy: Both groups showed an initial level of approximately 2.9 units on a 0–10 scale (control = 2.9; treatment = 2.90 + (–0.06) = 2.8). Over the 16 weeks of data collection, the control group showed a 0.7 unit increase in intimacy, whereas the treatment group showed a 0.74 + 0.92 = 1.6 unit increase in intimacy. The 0.9 unit slope difference due to group had a marginal p-value of .067. Its 95% confidence interval ranged from –0.1 to 1.9. Thus, although the best estimate of typical change in the treatment group change is that it is more than twice that of the control group, the uncertainty in the estimate does not allow us to rule out the possibility that the true difference is zero.

One reason for the uncertainty about differences in these typical patterns is that the between-persons random effects are substantial. The variability of the thin dark lines around their respective thick dark lines in Figure 1 is one way of illustrating this variability. These are model-based estimates of true growth patterns for the 50 individuals in the sample. The lower panel of Table 1 shows numerical values of the random effect parameters for the population. We can see that the variances for both intercept and rate of change are large relative to their standard errors, indicating that within the treatment and control groups there is substantial between-persons heterogeneity. The intercept variance, 0.69, corresponds to an SD of $\sqrt{0.69} = 0.8$, which indicates that 95% of the population vary between ±1.6 units of the typical intercept for their group. The predictions for the sample shown in Figure 1 broadly show this pattern. The slope variance is 1.89, which corresponds to an SD of $\sqrt{1.89} = 1.4$, which indicates that 95% of the population vary between ±2.8 units of the typical slope for its group. Again, the between-persons variability in the sample-predicted slopes in Figure 1 is consistent with these numbers.

To better understand the size of this heterogeneity for rates of change, it is useful to calculate how much overlap in the population it implies between distributions of the control and treatment groups (Cohen, 1988). With mean rates of change of 0.7 and 1.6 units, respectively, and a common SD of $\sqrt{1.89} = 1.4$ units, there is a 60% overlap between the distributions of the control and treatment groups. At the same time, there is appreciable between-groups separation: The patterns of means and standard deviations imply that 75% of persons in the treatment group had rates of change greater than the average for the control group (see Cohen, 1988, p. 22, for a table of these overlap values).

The second major reason for the uncertainty in the estimates of typical patterns is that the level-1 random effects (i.e., residuals from the level-1 fitted values) are large. Figure 2 shows examples of the fitted values and residuals at level 1 for five selected individuals in each group. Our choices were intended to show the range of slope estimates within and between each group. To do this, we first ordered the persons in each group by their slope magnitude and then chose persons corresponding approximately to the 5th, 25th, 50th, 75th, and 95th percentiles in each group. Notice that although there is a lot of variability in intimacy from week to week, a linear pattern of change is a reasonable summary of the data. Table 1 reports the population variance of the residuals from the fitted line as 1.69, which corresponds to an SD of $\sqrt{1.69} = 1.3$ units, and this, assuming that the residuals are normally distributed, implies that 95% of observed residuals should lie between ±2.6 units of their fitted values. The observed residuals in the selected participants are broadly consistent with this summary estimate. Finally, we note from the estimate reported at the bottom of Table 1 that there is no evidence of autocorrelation in the level-1 residuals.

4.4 CHAPTER SUMMARY

This completes the first and most basic empirical chapter of the book. Using as an example an intervention study with weekly diary assessments, we have illustrated how the time course of intensive longitudinal data can be displayed and analyzed. We believe an initial focus on the time course, with graphical displays for each subject, is desirable, whether or not the goal of the design is to model time trends. As we will see in the next chapter, even when time is not a focus, it remains an essential feature of the analysis model.

4.5 RECOMMENDED READINGS

Bollen, K. A., & Curran, P. J. (2006). *Latent curve models: A structural equation perspective.* Hoboken, NJ: Wiley.

This text provides a comprehensive and accessible introduction to growth curve modeling using a structural equation modeling framework.

Singer, J. D., & Willett, J. B. (2003). *Applied longitudinal data analysis: Modeling change and event occurrence.* New York: Oxford University Press.

The first half of this book is an excellent resource on modeling change over time in continuous outcomes using a regression-based multilevel framework.

Appendix to Chapter 4

SPSS CODE FOR PANEL PLOTS

A version of the panel plot depicted in Figure 4.4 can be accomplished using the following SPSS code with the Time Course dataset:

```
GGRAPH
  /GRAPHDATASET NAME="GraphDataset" VARIABLES= intimacy time id
  treatment
  /GRAPHSPEC SOURCE=INLINE INLINETEMPLATE=[].
BEGIN GPL
SOURCE: s=userSource( id( "GraphDataset" ) )
DATA: intimacy=col( source(s), name( "intimacy" ) )
DATA: time=col( source(s), name( "time" ) )
DATA: treatment=col(source(s), name("treatment"), unit.category() )
DATA: id=col( source(s), name( "id" ), unit.category() )
GUIDE: text.title( label( "Panel Plot by Treatment" ) )
GUIDE: axis( dim( 1 ), label( "time" ) )
GUIDE: axis( dim( 2 ), label( "intimacy" ) )
GUIDE: axis( dim( 3 ), label( "id" ), opposite() )
GUIDE: legend( aesthetic( aesthetic.shape.interior ), null() )
SCALE: linear( dim( 1 ), min( 0 ), max( 15 ) )
SCALE: linear( dim( 2 ), min( 0 ), max( 10 ) )
ELEMENT: point( position( time * intimacy * id ), shape.
interior(treatment), color(treatment) )
ELEMENT: line( position(smooth.linear( time * intimacy * id) ),
shape.interior(treatment), color(treatment))
  END GPL.
```

SPSS MIXED CODE FOR ANALYSIS

```
MIXED intimacy WITH time01 treatment
  /FIXED=time01 treatment time01*treatment | SSTYPE(3)
  /METHOD=REML
  /PRINT=G  SOLUTION TESTCOV
  /RANDOM=INTERCEPT time01 | SUBJECT(id) COVTYPE(UN)
  /REPEATED=time | SUBJECT(id) COVTYPE(AR1).
```

SAS PROC MIXED CODE FOR ANALYSIS

```
PROC MIXED covtest DATA=intimacy METHOD=reml cl;
CLASS id time;
MODEL intimacy=time01 treatment time01*treatment/solution cl
ddf=48,48,48,48
OUTP=intp outpm=intpm residual;
RANDOM int time01/SUBJECT=id TYPE=un s g gcorr;
REPEATED time/SUBJECT=id TYPE=ar(1);
ODS exclude SolutionR;
ODS output SolutionR = randpred;
RUN;
```

Mplus CODE FOR ANALYSIS

```
TITLE:    Chapter 4 Intimacy Intervention Example;
DATA:     FILE IS intimacy.dat;
VARIABLE: NAMES ARE id time time01 intimacy treatment;
          USEVAR ARE intimacy treatment time01;
          WITHIN =  time01;
          BETWEEN = treatment;
          CLUSTER = id;
ANALYSIS: TYPE = twolevel random;
          ESTIMATOR=ml;
MODEL:    %WITHIN%
          slope | intimacy on time01;
          %BETWEEN%
          intimacy slope on treatment;
          intimacy with slope;
OUTPUT:   cinterval;
```

5

Modeling the Within-Subject Causal Process

In this chapter, we move from modeling the time course of an intensive longitudinal outcome to modeling the underlying causal process for that outcome. Here the task is a much more demanding one, for not only must we grapple with a complex data structure (see Chapter 3), but we must also correctly specify and measure relevant causal factors. Nevertheless, if one wishes to test causal hypotheses *in situ*, a well-designed and theoretically driven intensive longitudinal study is, we believe, the best way to do so. Furthermore, research programs that combine experimental tests of causal hypotheses with non-experimental evidence that the causal processes occur naturally, can be especially compelling. Accordingly, our goal in this chapter is to illustrate how such a nonexperimental test can be conducted using an intensive longitudinal research design. We demonstrate also how, under certain reasonable assumptions, having missing data need not deter us from our modeling goals. Finally, we provide an example write-up of the analysis approach in a format suitable for publication.

5.1 CONCEPTUALIZING A WITHIN-SUBJECT CAUSAL PROCESS

Now that we have invoked the word *cause*, we have raised the stakes considerably. In contrast to the example in the previous chapter, intensive longitudinal data are often collected as part of a nonexperimental study design, and nonexperimental study designs are usually considered to be a poor way of assessing causal effects. What makes us so bold as to talk about understanding causes using a nonexperimental design? The answer is that by designing intensive longitudinal studies wherein the temporal measurement corresponds to when causes and effects change, one can model the causal relationship accurately as a temporal within-subject process. The analyst therefore has much greater leverage to assess cause than is possible in traditional nonexperimental designs. Make no mistake, though: For all their virtues, intensive longitudinal designs do not permit inferences anywhere near as strong as comparable experimental designs (assuming, of course, that such designs are feasible practically and ethically).

The most current view of causation in social science stresses what is often called a *counterfactual* or *potential outcomes* perspective (Neyman, 1923/1990; Rubin, 1974). In this view, causal analysis involves the within-subject manipulation (at least in principle) of putative causal variables in order to observe their effects. Discussions are usually framed in terms of treatment and control conditions, but it is usually conceded that the analysis issues can be applied to nonexperimental studies as well. There is, however, the fundamental problem that one cannot observe a given person (or other experimental subject) in both the experimental and control conditions at the same time, and therefore a pure assessment of a within-subject causal effect is impossible (Holland, 1986). It is for this reason that assessing a causal effect involves a counterfactual comparison. With random assignment of subjects to experimental conditions, however, one can assess what is called the *average causal effect*.

Intensive longitudinal designs do not qualify for this rigorous definition of cause because even though they allow within-subject comparisons, experimental conditions cannot but be experienced in a temporal order, thereby leaving open the possibility of (1) carryover effects from one condition to the next; (2) order effects, where the particular order in which a subject receives the condition moderates the experimental effect; or (3) expectancy effects, whereby the experience of one condition alters the meaning of subsequent conditions. As Gelman and Hill (2007) put it, researchers who use longitudinal designs need to carefully consider the extent to which their particular implementation is prone to these problems. However, even though *in situ* intensive longitudinal designs often do not involve manipulation of causal variables and do not permit pure within-subject comparisons, they more closely approximate the counterfactual ideal than traditional nonexperimental designs.

Adhering to the fundamental guidelines presented in Chapter 3 can be of particular help in strengthening causal inferences about within-subject processes. Our first guideline, distinguishing between-subjects from within-subject variations, is crucial for determining within-subject causal effects. Many key within-subject variables measured in intensive longitudinal studies (e.g., stressors, coping, emotions, symptoms) vary both between and within subjects. As already noted, between-subjects and within-subjects relationships can have very different magnitudes and even different signs, and can result in a conceptual error that is sometimes called an *ecological fallacy*, wherein relationships at the upper level of analysis are confused with those at the lower level (Robinson, 1950). Analyses that focus on within-subjects variation allow one to rule out between-subjects influences in results for a given independent variable. This is what is often referred to as *using the person as his or her own control*. It also allows us to treat the results as pertaining to the relationship between within-person changes in both X and Y (more on this below). Not a few analyses of intensive longitudinal data, including some of our own, have neglected to clearly separate these two sources of variation in a repeatedly measured predictor. In practical terms, between-subjects variation in a given X can be controlled by subtracting each subject's mean value on X from the subject's raw score on X.

Our second guideline is that elapsed time should always be included in the model because it is easily conceivable that it could be an important index of third variables that are unmeasured but closely linked to time. For example, if duration of the intensive longitudinal study is too long, participant fatigue could affect the levels of or interrelationships among variables. One can think of the growth curve analyses reported in the previous chapter as estimating a baseline model of time trends upon which one could add additional putative causal variables.

We will come across the additional guidelines from Chapter 3 in due course. There are, however, two issues that were not raised in Chapter 3 but that take center stage when causal inferences are one's goal: (1) specifying the correct causal lag, and (2) taking account of additional confounding variables. Specifying the correct causal lag is almost always a problem in nonexperimental analyses, and although intensive longitudinal designs are no exception, the frequency of repeated measurements provides more scope for investigating different lags than conventional designs. The importance of matching the actual time lag between cause and effect with the density and number of assessments taken of the putative cause and effect has been highlighted by Collins and Graham (2002) as a key design issue. The problem of additional confounding in within-subject variables is also a thorny one, and can only be considered in the context of each specific research question and intensive longitudinal design. We consider this issue in more detail in Chapter 6, when we specify causal factors in the occurrence of daily arguments.

5.2 EXAMPLE CAUSAL PROCESS DATASET

The example dataset in this chapter is, as in the previous one, simulated to correspond to datasets from actual intensive longitudinal studies with which we have been involved (Bolger, DeLongis, Kessler, & Schilling, 1989; Bolger, DeLongis, Kessler, & Wethington, 1989, 1990; Bolger, Stadler, Paprocki, & DeLongis, 2009; Kennedy, Bolger, & Shrout, 2002). We simulated a dataset to represent 28 consecutive daily reports of daily relationship conflicts and daily relational intimacy from 66 women in a cohabiting, intimate relationship. Sample data lines are shown in Figure 5.1. In this section of the chapter, we discuss the variables in their raw form; in the next section, we discuss transformations of the variables that will aid causal interpretation of the analysis results. As in previous chapters, *id* is

id	time	time7c $(\breve{T}_{ij})$	intimacy (Y_{ij})	conflict (X_{ij})	confc $(\breve{X}_{ij})$	confcb $(\breve{X}_{.j})$	confcw $(\breve{X}_{ij}) - (\breve{X}_{.j})$	relqual (W_j)
1	0	−1.93	4.78	0	−.221	−.114	−.107	1
1	1	−1.79	2.07	0	−.221	−.114	−.107	1
1	2	−1.64	3.80	0	−.221	−.114	−.107	1
.	.	.	.	.		.	.	.
1	25	1.64	5.18	1	.779	−.114	.893	1
1	26	1.79	6.16	0	−.221	−.114	−.107	1
1	27	1.93	2.68	0	−.221	−.114	−.107	1
2	0	−1.93	7.64	0	−.221	−.114	−.107	1
2	1	−1.79	8.12	0	−.221	−.114	−.107	1
2	2	−1.64	5.59	0	−.221	−.114	−.107	1
.	.	.	.	.		.	.	.
2	25	1.64	7.66	0	−.221	−.114	−.107	1
2	26	1.79	6.30	0	−.221	−.114	−.107	1
2	27	1.93	6.28	0	−.221	−.114	−.107	1
.	.	.	.	.		.	.	.
65	0	−1.93	5.21	0	−.221	−.186	−.036	0
65	1	−1.79	5.24	0	−.221	−.186	−.036	0
65	2	−1.64	1.83	0	−.221	−.186	−.036	0
.	.	.	.	.		.	.	.
65	25	1.64	4.45	0	−.221	−.186	−.036	0
65	26	1.79	6.35	0	−.221	−.186	−.036	0
65	27	1.93	5.47	0	−.221	−.186	−.036	0
66	0	−1.93	8.13	0	−.221	−.078	−.143	1
66	1	−1.79	3.40	0	−.221	−.078	−.143	1
66	2	−1.64	7.70	0	−.221	−.078	−.143	1
.	.	.	.	.		.	.	.
66	25	1.64	0.74	1	.779	−.078	.857	1
66	26	1.79	1.86	0	−.221	−.078	−.143	1
66	27	1.93	3.26	1	.779	−.078	.857	1

FIGURE 5.1. Structure of the causal process dataset.

a unique code that identifies each subject (i.e., person) in the study. The variable *time* indexes the ordinal time point (day) of the diary report (0 to 27). As in the previous dataset, we simulated scores on the Reis and Shaver Intimacy Scale (*intimacy*) to lie on a 0 to 10 interval, such that 0 was the lowest possible score and 10 was the highest possible score. The variable *conflict* was simulated such that 0 represented no conflict today, and 1 represented having at least one conflict today.

Finally, we simulated responses to a single-item, cross-sectional measure of how globally satisfied respondents felt about their intimate relationship. We simulated responses as follows (with *n*'s in parentheses): 5 = best I could ever imagine a relationship being (*n* = 10), 4 = extremely satisfied (*n* = 18), 3 moderately satisfied (*n* = 12), 2 = a bit dissatisfied (*n* = 19), 1 = very dissatisfied (*n* = 7). Note that for ease of exposition, relationship quality (*relqual*) is treated as a dichotomy of low- and high-quality relationships. A dichotomous (0, 1) version used in the analyses was created by combining codes 3, 4, and 5 into a high-relationship quality group (*n* = 40, 61%) and codes 1 and 2 into a low-relationship quality group (*n* = 26, 39%).

As with the previous chapter's dataset, we begin by examining the time course of the key variables. As has been emphasized, this is important even when the time course is not of direct interest. The key software commands for creating these plots are in the appendix to this chapter.

Figure 5.2 shows the resulting paneled data of daily intimacy for low-relationship quality (RQ) (upper panels) and high-RQ (lower panels) groups. Like the intimacy weekly outcome in the time course study (Chapter 4), we can see substantial change from one time point to the next, but unlike the earlier study, there are no overall linear increases or decreases with time for either group. There appear to be between-persons mean differences in intimacy; however, from the plots alone it is difficult to know if there are true between-groups differences.

Figure 5.3 shows paneled time plots for reports of daily conflict across groups. It is evident that people differ markedly in the frequency of reported conflicts. Visual inspection also provides some indication that conflicts are more frequent overall in the low-RQ

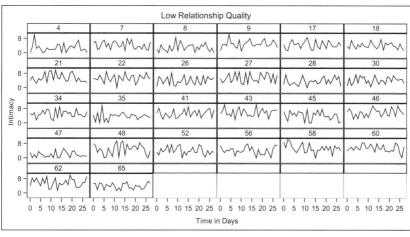

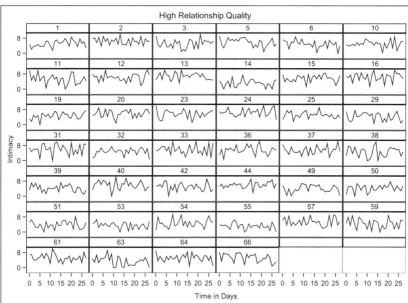

FIGURE 5.2. Panel plots of the 28-day time course of intimacy for each subject in the low- and high-relationship quality groups.

group. Sharp spikes indicate a 3-day *no-conflict* to *conflict* to *no-conflict* sequence. Across all participants this is the modal sequence. More blunted spikes show multiday conflict sequences; these appear to be common in the low-RQ group. Finally, there are four participants,

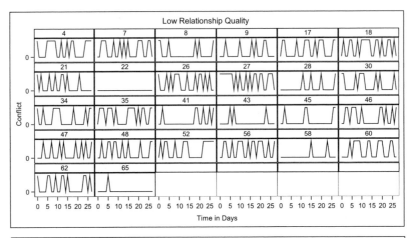

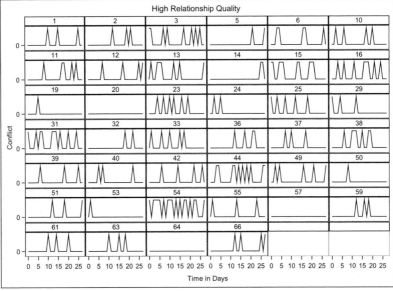

FIGURE 5.3. Panel plots of the 28-day time course of daily conflict for each subject in the low- and high-relationship quality groups.

one in the low group and three in the high group, who report no conflict over the entire 28-day period.

Having examined the separate time plots, a logical next step is to examine how they look when combined. However, we defer this step until later, because it will be particularly useful after we conduct a multilevel analysis of the data.

5.3 MULTILEVEL CAUSAL MODEL LINKING DAILY CONFLICT TO INTIMACY

We are now ready to specify a multilevel causal model where the onset of conflict on a particular day leads to lower intimacy at the end of that day, and where this process is most evident for those in low-quality relationships. We treat the moderation of a within-subject process as the central hypothesis of the study, but we could have treated the average within-subject conflict-to-intimacy effect as the central hypothesis and the moderation hypothesis as secondary. For didactic purposes, we have chosen to keep the causal model rather simple, to contain just one within-subject causal variable, one between-subjects moderating variable, and time, which we regard as a necessary component of all models of intensive longitudinal data. A more realistic model would include controls for other third variables such as external stressors, an indicator of weekdays versus weekend days, quality of sleep, etc. Also, one might take issue with our use of an analysis model where the X and Y were reports obtained at the same point in time. There is some justification for this approach, given that the X is a retrospection over the day about whether a relationship conflict had occurred on a given day, whereas Y is a momentary rating of end-of-day intimacy. This, we believe, is a reasonable causal lag for examining whether conflicts result in reduced end-of-day intimacy. (We present an example with an explicit morning-to-evening causal lag in the next chapter.)

Model specification for intensive longitudinal data usually requires some rescaling and recentering of the analysis variables (as noted in Chapter 3). Examples of these transformed variables are included (along with the raw versions) in Figure 5.1. The most complex transformation was required for the level-1 independent variable, *conflict*. Although *conflict* can be expected to vary within each subject over time (i.e., at level 1), it can also be expected to vary on average from subject to subject (i.e., at level 2). In this sense, it is very different from the focal level-1 independent variable from the previous chapter, *time*. In the intervention dataset, *time* varied within subjects only. To obtain correct estimates of the effect of within-subject variation in *conflict*, we needed to create separate between- and within-subject versions of this variable. We first subtracted the grand mean across subjects and time points ($M = 0.22$ conflicts) from the raw scores of conflict, which resulted in a variable called *confc* (algebraic form: $\check{X}_{ij}$, where the breve symbol "˘" indicates grand-mean centering). We then split *confc* into two (orthogonal) components: a between-subjects means component, *confcb* ($\check{X}_{\cdot j}$), and a within-subject deviations from those means component, *confcw* ($\check{X}_{ij} - \check{X}_{\cdot j}$). Also, we rescaled time such that 0 was the middle of the 28-day diary period (by subtracting 13.5) and a 1-unit difference corresponded to the passage of 1 week (by dividing by 7), resulting in *time7c* ($\check{T}_{ij}$).

As in the previous chapter, we first specify the model as separate level-1 and level-2 equations using the Raudenbush and Bryk (2002) statistical notation; we then respecify it in the single-equation mixed model form before presenting the results for our data example. The reader may wonder why we bother to employ both types of representation. We do so because each representation serves an important function. The former multilevel form is useful because it is very commonly used in research papers that specify models for intensive longitudinal data. It is also very helpful in deciding what degrees of freedom to use in statistical tests. In Chapter 3 we recommended the use of a conservative approach to tests of significance, such that degrees of freedom for *t*- and *F*-tests be based on the number of subjects in the study, N, rather than the total number of observations, $N * T$. As we illustrate below, the level-2 equations provide a key to determining degrees of freedom. Also, the level-1 and level-2 multilevel model representation facilitates an understanding of the indexing of parameters. The single-equation form serves an important function in that it is the form that is used in the SPSS and SAS software implementations provided in this book, and it therefore facilitates identifying and tabling relevant results.

The level-1 equation specifies the analysis of end-of-day intimacy rating of subject j ($j = 1, 2, \ldots, N$) at time point i ($i = 1, 2, \ldots, T$), Y_{ij}, into a series of components. Y_{ij} is the sum of (1) an intercept that is specific to each subject j, β_{0j}, that represents her predicted level of intimacy for a day that is average for her in terms of conflict exposure and is midway through the diary period; (2) a term for subject j's conflict deviation (from her own average) for time point i, with a coefficient, β_{1j}, that is specific to each subject j; (3) a term for elapsed time that has a coefficient, β_{2j}, that potentially varies across

subjects; and (4) a random residual term that is specific to each subject j and time point i (we assume that the residuals potentially have
a first-order autoregressive structure that was described in the previous chapter):

$$Y_{ij} = \beta_{0j} + \beta_{1j}(\check{X}_{ij} - \check{X}_{.j}) + \beta_{2j}\check{T}_{ij} + \varepsilon_{ij} \tag{5.1}$$

There are three level-2 equations, one for each coefficient in
the level-1 equation. Equation 5.2 specifies that the subject-specific
intercepts differ depending on each woman j's relationship quality,
her average level of conflict, the interaction of these variables, and a
random residual component specific to her, as follows:

$$\beta_{0j} = \gamma_{00} + \gamma_{01}W_j + \gamma_{02}\check{X}_{.j} + \gamma_{03}W_j\check{X}_{.j} + u_{0j} \tag{5.2}$$

We are now in a position to specify appropriate degrees of freedom
for tests of significance of the fixed effects in this equation. Given
that there are $j = 1, 2, \ldots, N$ subjects and there are four fixed-
effect parameters to be estimated $(\gamma_{00}, \gamma_{01}, \gamma_{02}, \gamma_{03})$, the appropriate
degrees of freedom for tests of these parameters is $N - 4$.

Equation 5.3 specifies that the subject-specific intimacy reactivity is the sum of an intercept, a term reflecting the influence of relationship quality, and a random residual component specific to each
subject, as follows:

$$\beta_{1j} = \gamma_{10} + \gamma_{11}W_j + u_{1j} \tag{5.3}$$

Degrees of freedom for tests of significance for each of the two fixed
effect parameters $(\gamma_{10}, \gamma_{11})$ are $N - 2$.

Equation 5.4 specifies that although the time slope potentially
varies across subjects, it is, in fact, a constant,

$$\beta_{2j} = \gamma_{20} \tag{5.4}$$

Degrees of freedom for tests of significance for the single fixed effect
parameter (γ_{20}) are $N - 1$.

Substitution of the level-2 Equations 5.2 through 5.4 into the
level-1 Equation 5.1 results in a single mixed-model Equation 5.5.

As we saw in the previous chapter, the mixed model form facilitates distinguishing fixed from random effects:

$$Y_{ij} = \gamma_{00} + \gamma_{01}W_j + \gamma_{02}\check{X}_{\cdot j} + \gamma_{03}W_j\check{X}_{\cdot j} \tag{5.5}$$

$$+ \gamma_{10}(\check{X}_{ij} - \check{X}_{\cdot j}) + \gamma_{11}W_j(\check{X}_{ij} - \check{X}_{\cdot j}) + \gamma_{20}\check{T}_{ij}$$

$$+ u_{0j} + u_{1j}(\check{X}_{ij} - \check{X}_{\cdot j}) + \varepsilon_{ij}$$

The first seven terms contain the fixed effects, and the remaining three terms contain the random effects. Given that we have just provided formal interpretations of these terms for the multilevel equations, we will not repeat ourselves here. For readers who find this section heavy going, relief is at hand: All of these terms will be given concrete, substantive interpretations when we examine the actual results.

The SPSS commands to conduct the analysis of the causal process example dataset are:

```
MIXED intimacy WITH time7c confcw confcb relqual
  /FIXED=time7c confcw confcb relqual confcw*relqual
      confcb*relqual | SSTYPE(3)
  /METHOD=reml
  /PRINT=g solution testcov
  /RANDOM=INTERCEPT confcw | SUBJECT(id) COVTYPE(un)
  /REPEATED=time | SUBJECT(id) COVTYPE(ar1).
```

The SAS commands to conduct this same analysis are:

```
PROC MIXED covtest DATA=conflict METHOD=reml cl;
CLASS id time;
MODEL intimacy=time7c confcw relqual confcw*relqual
    confcb confcb*relqual /solution cl DDF=65, 64,
    62, 62, 62, 62;
RANDOM intercept confcw/SUBJECT=id TYPE=un g gcorr cl;
REPEATED time/SUBJECT=id TYPE=ar(1);
```

Finally, we also provide the Mplus code to conduct this analysis. (Please note that we defer a more detailed discussion of the Mplus analysis approach until Chapter 6 and beyond):

```
TITLE: Ch. 5 Daily conflict and intimacy example;

DATA: FILE IS process.dat;

VARIABLE: NAMES ARE id time time7c intimacy conflict
    confc confcb confcw relqual;

USEVAR ARE time7c intimacy confcw confcb relqual
    confcbrq;

WITHIN = confcw time7c;

BETWEEN = relqual confcb confcbrq;

CLUSTER = id;

DEFINE: confcbrq=confcb*relqual;

ANALYSIS: TYPE = twolevel random;

ESTIMATOR=ml;

MODEL: %WITHIN%

confslp | intimacy ON confcw;

intimacy ON time7c;

%BETWEEN%

intimacy WITH confslp;

intimacy ON confcb confcbrq;

intimacy confslp ON relqual;

OUTPUT: sampstat cinterval;
```

For both SPSS and SAS, note that two versions of the elapsed time variable are used in model specification: (1) the version *time7c* is used to adjust for the linear effects of time and is represented algebraically as $\breve{T}_{ij}$ in Equation 5.1; (2) the version *time* (which can be thought of as an index variable for $i = 1, 2, \ldots, T$) is used to keep track of the ordinal position of observations, and is necessary to correctly estimate the autoregressive error parameter ρ. The DDF = option in SAS allows one to specify degrees of freedom for tests of fixed effects. We used it to implement the conservative approach to degrees of freedom recommended in Chapter 3. This degree of control is not available in the current version of SPSS MIXED (IBM SPSS 19). Mplus, because of the type of maximum likelihood estimation it employs, uses a z-distribution for tests of fixed effects; this effectively assumes a sample size sufficiently large that the t- and z-distributions are undistinguishable (see Chapter 3 for more discussion of this issue). It should also be noted that the current version of Mplus

(6.12) cannot estimate an autocorrelated error structure in a TYPE = TWOLEVEL RANDOM model. However, because there is essentially no autocorrelation in the data, the estimates from the Mplus analysis differ only slightly from those of SPSS and SAS. (The Mplus results can be seen on the website for this book.)

As previously, we first examine the results visually before turning to the numerical estimates and hypotheses about them. We begin with a paneled plot of the estimated conflict–intimacy relationship (see Figure 5.4). Each panel has four elements: the raw data for that subject, the multilevel model-predicted regression line (adjusting for all the effects in the model), a line representing the upper bound of the 95% confidence interval, and one representing the lower bound of that interval. Also, within each relationship quality group, we order the panels by the size of the model-predicted slope. The exact value of the slope is noted at the top of each panel. The commands to accomplish this paneling need not concern us now; we present them in the appendix to this chapter.

In interpreting these paneled plots, it is important to remember that the model-predicted regression line for a given subject need not be the same as the simple (i.e., ordinary least squares [OLS]) regression line for that subject, because the model controls for the within-subject variable of time, and the fitted lines combine information from the particular subject as well as from that subject's group. To the extent that a subject's data are lacking, the model uses the group data in arriving at an estimate (known as *shrinkage* in Raudenbush and Bryk [2002] terminology). Extreme cases are the single subject in the low-RQ group and the three subjects in the high-RQ group who have no conflict days. These subjects, therefore, cannot contribute to estimating the fixed effect of conflict, and as we will see, the degrees of freedom need to be adjusted accordingly. Yet the model can estimate an intercept for all subjects and, using data from the other subjects, estimates a slope for each of them. Thus, bear in mind that although we display the raw data for a given subject in each panel—and the fitted lines are, for the most part, consistent with those data—these lines also draw on additional information.

It is visually apparent from Figure 5.4 that the 26 subjects in the low-RQ group show more negative slopes than the 40 in the

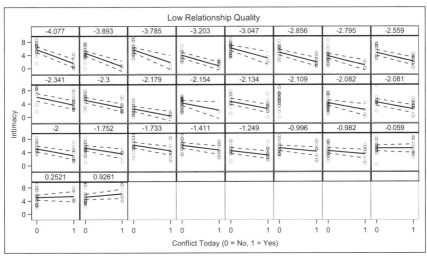

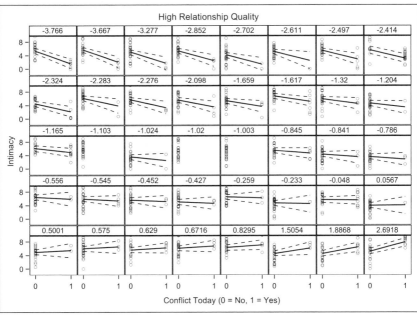

FIGURE 5.4. Intimacy as a function of daily conflict: Panel plots of raw data and model-predicted regression lines for each subject in the low- and high-relationship quality groups. Pairs of dashed lines show 95% confidence intervals.

high-RQ group. It is also apparent from the confidence limit lines (the thin dashed lines) that the slopes are better estimated in the low group. This is because those in the low-RQ group experience more conflicts on average, thereby making the estimates of the effects of conflict more precise. Thus, this visual evidence supports the central hypothesis we posed earlier: that conflict reactivity would differ by relationship quality.

We now turn to a second and arguably more effective way of examining the results visually, the spaghetti plot (Figure 5.5). The left-hand panel of the plot shows the low-RQ group: The single thick dark line is the group average slope, and the many thin lines are the slopes for particular subjects. The right-hand panel shows the equivalent for the high-RQ group. In this more compact form, it is possible to see that typical subjects in both groups are similar in their level of intimacy on no-conflict days. On conflict days, typical subjects in

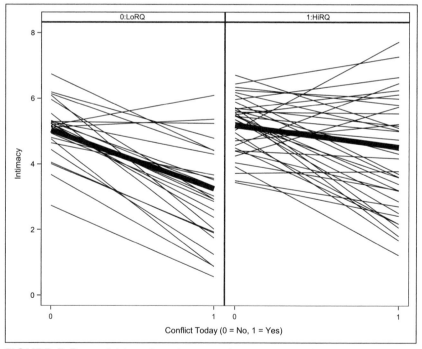

FIGURE 5.5. Model-based predictions of intimacy as a function of daily conflict: Spaghetti plots of average (thick) and subject-specific (thin) regression lines for the low- (left) and high- (right) quality relationship groups. (This figure has been duplicated as Figure 1 of the example write-up.)

the low-RQ group show noticeably lower intimacy. Finally, there is considerable between-subjects variability in intercepts and slopes in both groups.

It is now time to examine the numerical output of IBM SPSS MIXED in Tables 5.1 and 5.2 to determine to what extent the visual evidence is supported by estimates and hypothesis tests. Results for the corresponding model conducted in SAS PROC MIXED are essentially the same in terms of estimates, standard errors, and t-values; there are only slight differences in p-values resulting from our use of the SAS option of specifying conservative degrees of freedom. As noted above, Mplus also produced very similar results.

We consider first the fixed effect parameter estimates as shown in Table 5.1. The intercept is the predicted value of intimacy when the values of all variables in the model are zero, and as the reader is well

TABLE 5.1. Fixed Effects Output for Causal Process Example from SPSS (top) and SAS (bottom)

						95% Confidence Interval	
Parameter	Estimate	Std. Error	df	t	Sig.	Lower Bound	Upper Bound
Intercept	4.532200 ($\hat{\gamma}_{00}$)	.221262	63.092	20.483	.000	4.090056	4.974344
relqual	.647261 ($\hat{\gamma}_{01}$)	.282056	63.077	2.295	.025	.083631	1.210891
confcb	-.840931 ($\hat{\gamma}_{02}$)	1.103658	62.603	-.762	.449	-3.046689	1.364827
relqual * confcb	2.527340 ($\hat{\gamma}_{03}$)	1.680882	62.461	1.504	.138	-.832202	5.886882
confcw	-2.010616 ($\hat{\gamma}_{10}$)	.371079	52.144	-5.418	.000	-2.755192	-1.266040
relqual * confcw	1.016407 ($\hat{\gamma}_{11}$)	.492962	57.524	2.062	.044	.029462	2.003352
time7c	-.027881 ($\hat{\gamma}_{20}$)	.037071	649.216	-.752	.452	-.100675	.044913

Estimates of Fixed Effects[a]

a. Dependent Variable: intimacy.

Solution for Fixed Effects								
Effect	Estimate	Standard Error	DF	t Value	Pr > |t|	Alpha	Lower	Upper
Intercept	4.5322 ($\hat{\gamma}_{00}$)	0.2213	62	20.48	<.0001	0.05	4.0899	4.9745
relqual	0.6473 ($\hat{\gamma}_{01}$)	0.2820	62	2.29	0.0251	0.05	0.08346	1.2111
confcb	-0.8410 ($\hat{\gamma}_{02}$)	1.1036	62	-0.76	0.4488	0.05	-3.0456	1.3637
relqual*confcb	2.5273 ($\hat{\gamma}_{03}$)	1.6808	62	1.50	0.1377	0.05	-0.8325	5.8872
confcw	-2.0106 ($\hat{\gamma}_{10}$)	0.3711	64	-5.42	<.0001	0.05	-2.7519	-1.2693
relqual*confcw	1.0164 ($\hat{\gamma}_{11}$)	0.4929	64	2.06	0.0434	0.05	0.03105	2.0018
time7c	-0.02788 ($\hat{\gamma}_{20}$)	0.03707	65	-0.75	0.4548	0.05	-0.1020	0.04622

TABLE 5.2. Random Effects Output for Causal Process Example from SPSS (top) and SAS (bottom)

Estimates of Covariance Parameters[a]

Parameter		Estimate	Std. Error	Wald Z	Sig.	95% Confidence Interval	
						Lower Bound	Upper Bound
Repeated Measures	AR1 diagonal	3.579187 ($\hat{\sigma}^2$)	.122075	29.320	.000	3.347746	3.826629
	AR1 rho	-.045757 ($\hat{\rho}$)	.025102	-1.823	.068	-.094806	.003513
Intercept + confcw [subject = id]	UN (1,1)	.811845 ($\hat{\tau}_{00}$)	.166782	4.868	.000	.542757	1.214341
	UN (2,1)	.400675 ($\hat{\tau}_{10}$)	.242269	1.654	.098	-.074164	.875514
	UN (2,2)	2.711130 ($\hat{\tau}_{11}$)	.666437	4.068	.000	1.674603	4.389234

a. Dependent Variable: intimacy.

Covariance Parameter Estimates

Cov Parm	Subject	Estimate	Standard Error	Z Value	Pr Z	Alpha	Lower	Upper
UN(1,1)	id	0.8118 ($\hat{\tau}_{00}$)	0.1668	4.87	<.0001	0.05	0.5633	1.2710
UN(2,1)	id	0.4008 ($\hat{\tau}_{10}$)	0.2422	1.65	0.0980	0.05	-0.07393	0.8756
UN(2,2)	id	2.7107 ($\hat{\tau}_{11}$)	0.6663	4.07	<.0001	0.05	1.7645	4.6918
AR(1)	id	-0.04576 ($\hat{\rho}$)	0.02510	-1.82	0.0683	0.05	-0.09496	0.003442
Residual		3.5792 ($\hat{\sigma}^2$)	0.1221	29.32	<.0001	0.05	3.3515	3.8311

aware, we took special effort to scale the included predictor variables such that zero had a useful interpretation. Given the coding of these variables, then, the intercept ($\hat{\gamma}_{00}$) estimates the predicted level of daily intimacy for the typical woman in a low-quality relationship for days that are in the middle of the diary period and that are typical in terms of conflict exposure across all women in the sample. In other words, the intercept characterizes a typical day for a typical woman in a low-quality relationship. Its estimate is roughly 4.5 units on a 0–10 scale, and the 95% confidence interval (CI_{95}) is 4.1–5.0.

The coefficient for relationship quality ($\hat{\gamma}_{01}$) estimates how much higher or lower is the intimacy of women in high-quality relationships compared to those in low-quality relationships, for days that are typical in conflict across all women in the sample. It is 0.65 units with a CI_{95} ranging from 0.08 to 1.21 units. It is a statistically significant difference, $t(62) = 2.30$, $p = .025$, but, given the range of the scale, it is not a large difference.

The next two fixed effects reflect upper-level, between-subjects associations between conflict and intimacy. For reasons already discussed in Chapter 3, we feel that they are not as interpretable or as interesting as the within-subject associations. The coefficient for *confcb* ($\hat{\gamma}_{02}$) estimates between-subjects association between conflict and intimacy for women in the low-RQ group (i.e., do women with higher average conflict across the 28-day diary period also tend to have lower average daily intimacy?). The coefficient for *relqual * confcb* ($\hat{\gamma}_{03}$) estimates whether the between-subjects association between conflict and intimacy differs for the low- and high-RQ groups. Neither is statistically significant, and we do not discuss them further.

By contrast, the coefficient for *confcw* ($\hat{\gamma}_{10}$) is of focal interest: It estimates the difference in intimacy between no-conflict and conflict days for the typical woman in the low-RQ group. Its value is substantial, approximately –2.0 units, and it has a CI_{95} that ranges from –2.8 to –1.3 units, $t(64) = -5.42$, $p < .001$. Our specific coding of relationship quality, where the low group was coded 0 and high group was coded 1, is the reason that the coefficient for *confcw* estimates the simple slope for the low group. To obtain the equivalent simple slope for the high group, one simply needs to reverse the coding for relationship conflict, re-estimate the model, and read off the new result for *confcw*. The simple slope for the high group was –1.0 units, $CI_{95} = -1.6, -0.3$, $t(64) = 3.06$, $p = .003$. (The necessary code for accomplishing this, together with the associated output, can be found on the book's website.)

Given the centrality of the relationship quality moderation hypothesis, the coefficient for *relqual*confcw* ($\hat{\gamma}_{11}$) is the single most important coefficient: It estimates the difference in the conflict reactivity between a typical woman in the low-RQ group and a typical woman in the high-RQ group. Its value is roughly 1.0, but it has a CI_{95} that ranges from 0 to 2.0 units, $t(64) = 2.06$, $p = .044$. It is statistically significant, but barely. A fair assessment of these results is that relationship quality is probably a moderator of conflict reactivity, but one cannot rule out the possibility that its effect is too small to be of practical importance.

The final fixed effect is for *time7c*, and it confirms what was clear from the visual evidence already discussed: There are no linear time trends in intimacy over the 28-day diary period, $\hat{\gamma}_{20} = -.03$, $CI_{95} = -0.10, 0.04$, $p = .45$.

As the spaghetti plots in Figure 5.5 showed, there was substantial between-subjects variability in slopes and intercepts in both the low- and high-RQ groups. Table 5.2 presents numerical estimates and statistical tests of this variability. The intercept variance estimate, $\hat{\tau}_{00}$, is 0.8, with a CI_{95} that ranges from 0.6 to 1.3 units. As a standard deviation, this random effect estimate is approximately $\sqrt{0.8}$ = 0.9 units, and given the assumption that it has a normal distribution, the 95% prediction interval (PI_{95}), that is, the model-implied 95% between-subjects range in intercepts is approximately ±2 * 0.9 = ±1.8 units. This interval can be used to deepen our understanding of the heterogeneity that is present within the two groups. Specifically, the model-implied range of intercepts for the low-RQ group is 4.5 ± 1.8 = 2.7 to 6.3 units. The equivalent range for the high-RQ group intercepts is 4.5 + 0.6 ± 1.8 = 3.3 to 6.9 units. One can conclude from these results that, although relationship quality can account for some of the between-subjects differences in average intimacy levels (as we saw, its fixed effect was approximately 0.6 units), there are large between-persons differences in intercepts left unexplained (the 95% interval is 3.6 units).

Expressed as a standard deviation, the variation for the conflict slopes is $\sqrt{2.7}$ = 1.6 units, which, assuming a normal distribution in the population, implies that 95% of the population is within ±2 * 1.6 = ±3.2 units of the typical value for their group. Thus the PI_{95} for conflict reactivity for the low-RQ group is –2.0 ± 3.2 = –5.2 to 1.2 units; for the high-RQ group it is (–2.0 + 1.0) ± 3.2 = –4.2 to 2.2 units. When we compare the fixed effect of relationship quality on conflict reactivity, –2.0 units on a 0–10 scale, with the remaining 95% interval of variability in reactivity, 6.8 units, we can see that relationship quality is important in explaining variability in slopes, whereas we saw above that it was unimportant in explaining variability in intercepts (compare a ratio of explained to unexplained of 1:6 for intercepts and 1:3 for slopes). Note that the table for the example write-up at the end of this chapter (Table 5.3) contains a full reporting of the fixed and random effects for the analysis model.

5.4 MODELING A PROCESS WITH MISSING REPEATED MEASUREMENTS

Up to this point, we have worked on examples that have no missing data. As anyone who has used intensive longitudinal methods will

TABLE 5.3. Estimates for Multilevel Model of Intimacy as a Function of Daily Conflict and Relationship Quality (This table has been duplicated as Table 1 of the example write-up.)

Fixed effects (intercept, slopes)	Estimate	(SE)	t^a	p^b	CI_{95} Lower	Upper
Intercept	4.53	(0.22)	20.48	<.001	4.09	4.97
Time (per 7 days)	−0.03	(0.04)	−0.75	.45	−0.10	0.05
Within conflict	−2.01	(0.37)	−5.42	<.001	−2.75	−1.27
Relationship quality[c]	0.65	(0.28)	2.29	.025	0.83	1.21
Within conflict by RQ	1.02	(0.49)	2.06	.044	0.03	2.00
Between conflict	−0.84	(1.10)	−0.76	.45	−3.05	1.49
Between conflict by RQ	2.53	(1.68)	1.50	.14	−0.83	5.89

Random effects ([co-]variances)	Estimate	(SE)	z	p	$CI_{95}{}^d$ Lower	Upper
Level 2 (between-person)						
Intercept	0.81	(0.17)	4.87	<.001	0.56	1.27
Within conflict	2.71	(0.67)	4.07	<.001	1.76	4.69
Intercept and within conflict	0.40	(0.24)	1.65	.098	−0.07	0.88
Level 1 (within-person)						
Residual	3.58	(0.12)	29.32	<.001	3.35	3.83
Autocorrelation	−0.046	(0.025)	−1.82	.068	−0.095	0.003

Note. N = 66 persons, 28 days, 1,848 observations.

[a]We took a conservative approach to specifying degrees of freedom, such that these were based on the number of subjects (N = 66) rather than the total number of observations (N = 1,848).

[b]All p-values are two-tailed except in the case of variances, where one-tailed p-values are used (because variances are constrained to be non-negative).

[c]Relationship quality (RQ) is coded 0 for those in low-quality relationships and 1 for those in high-quality relationships.

[d]Confidence intervals for variances were computed using the Satterthwaite method (see Littell et al., 2006).

admit, it is unrealistic to expect to have no missing data. The typical scenario is that many participants will have a modicum of measurement occasions missing. Nevertheless, analysis of intensive longitudinal data with missing data entries on some occasions is tractable in many real-world situations.

In our experience with diary studies, the majority of missing data occur because a participant fails to complete an entire diary entry. Thus, for diary studies at least, it is typically the case that both predictors and outcomes are missing for that occasion. We now turn to an example where the same analysis just conducted and discussed in this chapter is rerun with the same diary dataset, only this time containing missing measurement occasions.

We produced a dataset with missing data by taking the intimacy and daily conflict dataset and, using a random number generation procedure, deleted approximately 20% of the 1,848 diary days. This resulted in 1,502 remaining rows of daily diary entries. Then we reran the analyses using the same SAS PROC MIXED syntax detailed earlier this chapter. The model results are presented in Table 5.4. First, note that the parameter estimates are very similar to those for the full dataset. Second, notice that the standard errors for parameter estimates are the same or larger for the analysis with missing data, reflecting that there are fewer data being analyzed. Third, the statistical decisions for all inferential tests are the same across both sets of results. Thus, the findings remain unchanged.

The comparison of findings with and without missing data are based on the assumption that the data are missing at random (Schafer & Graham, 2002). This assumption refers to the situation in which missingness can be systematic, but so long as one has measured the variables that predict missingness and included them in the analysis model, unbiased estimates can be obtained. Although this assumption is one that unfortunately cannot be tested, it is one that sometimes can be realistic to make in a longitudinal data context (Graham, 2009) and renders valid inferences when estimates are obtained using maximum likelihood estimation procedures (as is the case when using SPSS MIXED, SAS PROC MIXED, or Mplus). In cases where it is not reasonable to regard the missing data as missing due to a random process, then more complex analyses are usually required (see Enders, 2010; Graham, 2009; Little & Rubin, 2002; Schafer & Graham, 2002).

TABLE 5.4. Estimates for Multilevel Model of Intimacy as a Function of Daily Conflict and Relationship Quality with Randomly Selected Diary Days Missing

Fixed effects (intercept, slopes)	Estimate	(SE)	t^a	p^b	CI_{95} Lower	Upper
Intercept	4.54	(0.22)	21.14	<.001	4.11	4.97
Time (per 7 days)	−0.001	(0.04)	−0.19	.85	−0.09	0.08
Within conflict	−2.12	(0.39)	−5.41	<.001	−2.91	−1.33
Relationship quality[c]	0.62	(0.27)	2.27	.03	0.08	1.17
Within conflict by RQ	1.26	(0.52)	2.41	.019	0.21	2.30
Between conflict	−0.93	(1.04)	-0.89	.38	−3.01	1.16
Between conflict by RQ	2.15	(1.60)	1.35	.18	−1.04	5.35

Random effects ([co-]variances)	Estimate	(SE)	z	p^b	$CI_{95}{}^d$ Lower	Upper
Level 2 (between-person)						
Intercept	0.76	(0.17)	4.63	<.001	0.50	1.16
Within conflict	2.88	(0.73)	3.92	<.001	1.74	4.74
Intercept and within conflict	0.34	(0.25)	1.33	.18	−0.16	0.83
Level 1 (within-person)						
Residual	3.54	(0.14)	26.22	<.001	3.29	3.82
Autocorrelation	−0.035	(0.032)	−1.08	.28	−0.097	0.028

Note. N = 66 persons, 1,502 diary days.

[a]We took a conservative approach to specifying degrees of freedom, such that these were based on the number of subjects (N = 66) rather than the total number of observations (N = 1,502).

[b]All p-values are two-tailed except in the case of variances, where one-tailed p-values are used (because variances are constrained to be non-negative).

[c]Relationship quality (RQ) is coded 0 for those in low-quality relationships and 1 for those in high-quality relationships.

[d]Confidence intervals for variances were computed using the Satterthwaite method (see Littell et al., 2006).

5.5   WHEN THE INTERVALS BETWEEN MEASUREMENTS ARE UNEQUAL

In the example process model for continuous outcomes, although there was a cross-sectional or same-day relationship between daily X and Y, there was a longitudinal relationship between the unexplained portion of Y on a given day (i.e., its error) and the unexplained portion on adjacent days. Estimating this autocorrelation parameter is facilitated by having equal intervals between measurements, as there typically are in daily diary designs. What happens in the case of intensive longitudinal designs, such as experience sampling designs, where the interval between measurements varies across time and subjects? The length of time between one occasion of measurement and the next in the same experience sampling study can vary from hours to minutes to seconds. Clearly, the standard first-order autoregressive AR(1) error structure is inappropriate in variable-interval intensive longitudinal designs.

There is a solution to this problem, at least for the case of AR(1) errors, but to our knowledge it is only available in SAS's PROC MIXED. It works on the same principle as equal-interval AR(1), namely that the autocorrelation shows an exponential decay such that Y errors one time unit apart are correlated ρ (rho), those two time units apart are correlated ρ^2 (rho-squared), those three time units apart are correlated ρ^3, etc. In the unequal-interval case, the solution is to use the exact time interval between measurements— for example, 0.5, 1.6, and 3.2 days—to estimate what the autocorrelation would have been had the interval been 1.0 days.

We are now ready to discuss how the problem would be solved in the case of an unequal-interval daily conflict dataset. Conveniently, the solution can be illustrated with the missing data version of the dataset, where the missingness potentially creates idiosyncratic unequal intervals between measurements. Although by default PROC MIXED adjusts for the unequal intervals without requiring any changes to the syntax (as we did in the previous section), we can be more explicit about the adjustment by making two changes to this syntax. First, the variable called *time* must be removed from the CLASS statement, and second, the REPEATED statement must be substituted, with the following version containing the option for a spatial power structure:

```
REPEATED /SUBJECT=id TYPE=sp(pow)(time);
```

When the model is rerun in this way, PROC MIXED treats the variable *time* as continuous, such that, if for a given person day 3 is followed by day 6, the program estimates an autocorrelation parameter that effectively adjusts the observed correlation to reflect what it would have been had the interval been a single day. In fact, the program uses all the observed intervals to arrive at a single overall estimate of the rho, ρ, parameter.

To summarize, when one has unequal intervals due to missing data (planned or unplanned) in an otherwise equal-interval design, the standard approaches for SAS and SPSS can be used (assuming, of course, that the data are missing at random). When one has unequal intervals due to a fundamental randomness that is part of the intensive longitudinal research design, one can use the spatial power error structure approach we have described, which, unfortunately, can be used only in SAS. For a more fully developed account of the SAS approach to handling unequal intervals of data for continuous outcomes, see the chapter by Schwartz and Stone (2007) on analyzing data from Ecological Momentary Assessment designs.

5.6 EXAMPLE WRITE-UP OF CAUSAL PROCESS DATA

Almost all of the advice we provided for writing up the time course dataset applies to the causal process dataset as well. Thus far in the chapter, we have presented far more results than need or can be included in the typical journal article. What information is essential to report? Again, we recommend no equations, one table, and two graphs. The table should be a combination of the fixed and random effects tables from SPSS or SAS presented above. The first graph should be the spaghetti plot shown in Figure 5.5. The second graph should be a heavily abridged form of the paneled plots, one that shows five subjects from each RQ group. As shown in Figure 5.6, these individuals represent the 5th, 25th, 50th, 75th, and 95th percentiles in each group in terms of conflict slope negativity.

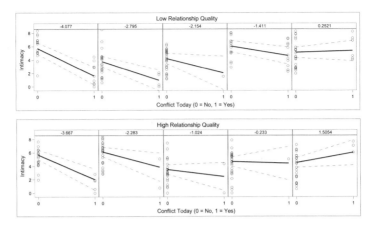

FIGURE 5.6. Intimacy as a function of daily conflict: Raw data and fitted regression lines for participants at the 5th, 25th, 50th, 75th, and 95th slope percentiles for the low- and high-relationship quality groups. Pairs of dashed lines show 95% confidence intervals. (This figure has been duplicated as Figure 2 of the example write-up.)

The Write-Up

As in Chapter 4, we begin the write-up with a statement of the hypothesis to be tested, as it might appear at the end of an Introduction section of an APA-style empirical paper.

In sum, the key hypothesis to be tested is whether global relationship quality is a moderator of the impact of daily conflicts on intimacy.

METHOD

Sample

The sample consisted of 66 women in a cohabiting intimate relationship. Fifty-eight of these were in an opposite-sex relationship and eight were in a same-sex relationship. The women had a mean age of 26.2 years ($SD = 3.1$). The racial breakdown in order of size was white ($n = 38$, 58%), Asian ($n = 12$, 18%), Hispanic ($n = 8$, 12%), and black ($n = 8$, 12%).

Measures

Daily conflict. Conflict was measured each day by the following diary question: "Did you experience any tension or disagreement with your partner today?" A "No" answer was coded 0, and a "Yes" answer was coded 1. To facilitate interpretation of the intercept in the analyses, we grand-mean centered scores on this variable by subtracting the mean conflict across subjects and time points ($M = 0.22$) from each score. In addition, because conflict varied both between- and within-subjects and because we wished to focus on within-subjects variation, we created a between-subjects and within-subjects version of the variable, *between conflict* and *within conflict*, respectively.

Daily intimacy. The six-item Reis and Shaver Intimacy Scale was used (Reis & Shaver, 1988). Raw scores were rescaled to a 0–10 interval, such that 0 was the lowest possible score and 10 was the highest possible score. Summary statistics for intimacy over participants and time were $M = 4.8$, $SD = 2.3$, range = 0–10.

Relationship quality. Participants completed the single-item measure of how globally satisfied they felt about their relationship. The question was "Overall, how satisfied are you with your relationship with [intimate partner]?" The response options were (with n's in parentheses): 5 = best I could ever imagine a relationship being ($n = 10$), 4 = extremely satisfied ($n = 18$), 3 = moderately satisfied ($n = 12$), 2 = a bit dissatisfied ($n = 19$), 1 = very dissatisfied ($n = 7$). A dichotomous (0, 1) version used in the analyses was created by combining codes 3, 4, and 5 into a high-RQ group ($n = 40$, 61%) and codes 1 and 2 into a low-RQ group ($n = 26$, 39%).

Procedure

Participants were recruited using flyers on a university campus. They responded to the flyers by e-mail or phone. Following recruitment, they completed an online background questionnaire and online nightly diaries for 28 consecutive days. Research assistants verified via time-date stamps that daily entries were indeed completed each evening.

RESULTS

Preliminary Analyses

The analysis dataset consisted of 66 (subjects) × 28 (days) = 1,848 observations. Inspection of scatterplots, subject by subject, indicated that four of the subjects did not report any relationship conflicts on any of the 28 diary days. These subjects, therefore, could not contribute to the estimation of within-subject reactivity to conflicts nor to relationship quality differences in this within-subject relation. The scatterplots did not reveal any outliers in the dataset. Although there were no apparent time trends in the data, we included in the model a centered version of day (divided by 7 to put the units in weeks). We observed no missing data. Finally, although there were too few same-sex couples to examine them separately, when the analyses reported below were rerun with women in opposite-sex couples only, the results were substantively unchanged.

Main Analyses

We analyzed our data using a multilevel model that specified a within-subject process of reactivity to daily conflicts that we predicted would be stronger for those in low-quality as opposed to high-quality relationships. The results are presented in Figure 1 and Table 1. Figure 1 shows fitted regression lines for each subject in the low- and high-RQ groups together with thick fitted lines for the average subject in each group. Visual inspection of the thick lines suggests that our hypothesis was

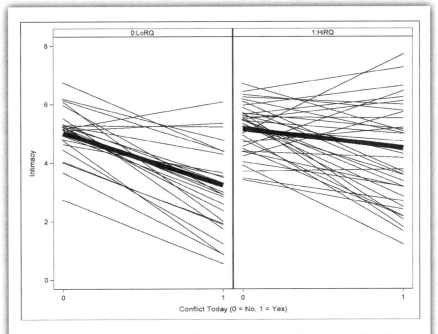

Figure 1. Spaghetti plots of average (thick) and subject-specific (thin) regression lines for female daily intimacy as a function of conflict for low- (left) and high- (right) relationship quality (RQ) groups.

supported: The slope for the high-RQ group is less steep than it is for the low-RQ group.

For a statistical test of the hypothesis, we turn to the upper panel of Table 1, labeled *fixed effects*, and to the results for the RQ by *within-conflict* interaction. Note that because the analysis model included time in weeks, and because the within- and between-subjects forms of conflict were also included, results for the focal moderation hypothesis cannot be artifacts of temporal changes or between-subjects differences in average number of conflicts over the diary recording period. The estimate of 1.02 units means that the women in the high-RQ group were 1 unit (on a 0–10 scale) less reactive to (within-person variation in)

Table 1. Parameter Estimates for Multilevel Model of Female Daily Intimacy as a Function of Daily Conflict and Relationship Quality

Fixed effects (intercept, slopes)	Estimate	(SE)	t^a	p^b	CI_{95} Lower	Upper
Intercept	4.53	(0.22)	20.48	<.001	4.09	4.97
Time (per 7 days)	−0.03	(0.04)	−0.75	.45	−0.10	0.05
Within conflict	−2.01	(0.37)	−5.42	<.001	−2.75	−1.27
Relationship quality^c	0.65	(0.28)	2.29	.025	0.83	1.21
Within conflict by RQ	1.02	(0.49)	2.06	.044	0.03	2.00
Between conflict	−0.84	(1.10)	−0.76	.45	−3.05	1.49
Between conflict by RQ	2.53	(1.68)	1.50	.14	−0.83	5.89

Random effects ([co-]variances)	Estimate	(SE)	z	p^b	$CI_{95}{}^d$ Lower	Upper
Level 2 (between-person)						
Intercept	0.81	(0.17)	4.87	<.001	0.56	1.27
Within conflict	2.71	(0.67)	4.07	<.001	1.76	4.69
Intercept and within conflict	0.40	(0.24)	1.65	0.098	−0.07	0.88
Level 1 (within-person)						
Residual	3.58	(0.12)	29.32	<.001	3.35	3.83
Autocorrelation	−0.046	(0.025)	−1.82	0.068	−0.095	0.003

Note: $N = 66$ persons, 28 days, 1,848 observations.
^{a}We took a conservative approach to specifying degrees of freedom, such that these were based on the number of subjects ($N = 66$) rather than the total number of observations ($N = 1,848$).
^{b}All p-values are two-tailed except in the case of variances, where one-tailed p-values are used (because variances are constrained to be non-negative).
^{c}Relationship quality (RQ) is coded 0 for those in low-quality relationships and 1 for those in high-quality relationships.
^{d}Confidence intervals for variances were computed using the Satterthwaite method (see Littell et al., 2006).

daily conflicts than women in the low-RQ group, $t(62) = 2.06$, $p = .044$, $CI_{95} = 0.03, 2.00$.

Important ancillary hypotheses are tests of the simple slopes for daily conflict for the low- and high-RQ groups. Given the coding of relationship quality, and given the presence of the conflict-by-relationship quality interaction term in the model, for the low group this is the coefficient for *within conflict*. It is -2.01 units, $t(62) = -5.42$, $p < .001$, $CI_{95} = -2.75, -1.27$. For the high group the simple slope is half that amount: $-2.01 + 1.04 = -0.97$ units, $t(62) = 3.06$, $p = .003$, $CI_{95} = -1.6$, -0.3. (Note that this coefficient was obtained by rerunning the analysis model with the 0,1 coding of relationship quality reversed and reading off the coefficient for *within conflict*.)

As we saw in Figure 1, there was substantial between-subjects variability in slopes and intercepts in the both the low- and high-RQ groups. The lower panel of Table 1 presents numerical estimates and statistical tests of this variability. These are reported as variances and covariances. Expressed as a standard deviation, the variation for the conflict slopes is $\sqrt{2.7} = 1.6$ units, which, assuming a normal distribution in the population, implies that approximately 95% of the population are within $\pm 2 * 1.6 = \pm 3.2$ units of the typical value for their relationship-quality subpopulation. Accordingly, the low-RQ group is predicted to have a 95% range of slopes of $-2.0 \pm 3.2 = -5.2$ to 1.2. The high-RQ group is predicted to have an equivalent range from $-1.0 \pm 3.2 = -4.2$ to 2.2.

Missing from Figure 1 are the raw data that were used to obtain the fitted lines for each person. Figure 2 shows the raw data and the fitted lines for five subjects selected from each RQ group. These subjects represented the 5th, 25th, 50th, 75th, and 95th percentiles for the conflict reactivity slopes for their group. Also shown are the 95% confidence intervals for each slope. Not surprisingly, the slopes for the low-RQ group are more negative than those for the high-RQ group. However, it can also be seen that because those in the high-RQ group experience fewer conflicts, the uncertainty as to their true slope is greater than it is for those in the low-RQ group. (This difference in uncertainty is

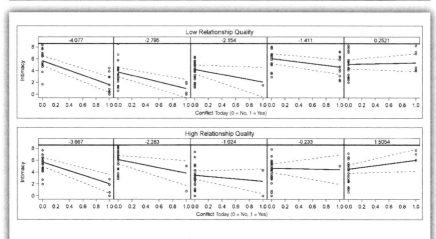

Figure 2. Intimacy as a function of daily conflict: Raw data and fitted regression lines for participants at the 5th, 25th, 50th, 75th, and 95th percentiles for the low- and high-relationship quality groups. Pairs of dashed lines show 95% confidence intervals.

balanced out by the greater number of people in the high-RQ group [40 vs. 26], such that the uncertainty about the typical person in the high group is very similar to that of the low group [*SE* of 0.33 for the high vs. 0.37 for the low].)

At the bottom of Table 1 is an estimate of the size of the residual variance at level 1 (also known as the level-1 random effect). This represents the deviations of the actual intimacy scores at level 1 from the predicted values obtained from the model. A common value is assumed for conflict and no-conflict days and for all subjects. Finally, as shown by the size and *p*-value of the coefficient, there is no evidence of auto-correlation in the level-1 (within-subject) residuals.

5.7 CHAPTER SUMMARY

Testing a causal hypothesis is difficult under any circumstances, but it is especially difficult when one wishes to observe a process unfold naturally *in situ*. Yet without such *in situ* investigations how can one be confident that a particular causal process—perhaps one previously established in laboratory research—actually occurs in nature? We believe a well-designed, theoretically driven intensive longitudinal study is the best way to test causal hypotheses *in situ*. We hope that this chapter's example research question on the effects of daily conflicts on daily intimacy has given readers a sense of how to design, analyze, and write up such a study. More complex research designs and causal hypotheses will follow in subsequent chapters.

5.8 RECOMMENDED READINGS

Enders, C. K. (2010). *Applied missing data analysis.* New York: Guilford Press.

> This clearly written book provides an excellent review of state-of-the-art as well as traditional methods for handing missing data in social and behavioral science research.

Hox, J. J. (2010). *Multilevel analysis: Techniques and applications* (2nd ed.). New York: Routledge.

> There are now many introductory books on multilevel modeling. In its treatment of missing data problems this one is up to date and written in an accessible style.

Schafer, J. L., & Graham, J. W. (2002). Missing data: Our view of the state of the art. *Psychological Methods, 7,* 147–177.

> This article is a very readable overview of assumptions and issues to consider when dealing with missing data.

Appendix to Chapter 5

IBM SPSS ANALYSIS CODE

```
MIXED intimacy WITH time7c confcw confcb relqual

  /FIXED=time7c confcw confcb relqual confcw*relqual
   confcb*relqual | SSTYPE(3)

  /METHOD=REML

  /PRINT=G  SOLUTION TESTCOV

  /RANDOM=INTERCEPT confcw | SUBJECT(id) COVTYPE(UN)

  /REPEATED=time | SUBJECT(id) COVTYPE(AR1).
```

SAS PANELING AND ANALYSIS CODE

```
PROC SGPANEL DATA=conflict NOAUTOLEGEND;

  PANELBY id/COLUMNS=6 ROWS=5 novarname;

  SERIES x = time y = intimacy /LINEATTRS =
    (pattern = 1 color = black);


PROC MIXED covtest DATA=conflict METHOD=reml cl;

CLASS id time;
```

```
MODEL intimacy=time7c confcw relqual confcw*relqual
   confcb confcb*relqual /solution cl DDF=65, 64,
   62, 62, 62, 62;

RANDOM intercept confcw/SUBJECT=id TYPE=un g gcorr cl;

REPEATED time/SUBJECT=id TYPE=ar(1);
```

Mplus ANALYSIS CODE

```
TITLE:     Ch. 5 Daily conflict and intimacy example;

DATA:      FILE IS process.dat;

VARIABLE: NAMES ARE id time time7c intimacy conflict
                    confc confcb confcw relqual;

           USEVAR ARE time7c intimacy confcw confcb
                    relqual confcbrq;

           WITHIN = confcw time7c;

           BETWEEN = relqual confcb confcbrq;

           CLUSTER = id;

DEFINE:    confcbrq=confcb*relqual;

ANALYSIS: TYPE = twolevel random;

           ESTIMATOR=ml;

MODEL:     %WITHIN%

           confslp | intimacy ON confcw;

           intimacy ON time7c;

           %BETWEEN%

           intimacy WITH confslp;

           intimacy ON confcb confcbrq;

           intimacy confslp ON relqual;

OUTPUT:    sampstat cinterval;
```

6

Modeling Categorical Outcomes

Thus far we have discussed analysis methods suitable for intensive longitudinal outcomes that are measured on a continuum—measures such as feeling states and evaluations. However, some of the most important and interesting features of people's lives are fundamentally categorical: events, experiences, and activities that have a clear onset, duration, and offset. In daily life people can experience positive events such as receiving a compliment, watching a funny movie, having sex, and seeing their sports team win. They can experience negative events such as rejection, arguments, and bad headaches. We have already encountered variables such as these implicated in causal processes, as in Chapter 5, where we examined the effect of daily arguments on end-of-day intimacy. In this chapter, we consider them as outcomes of other within-subject causes.

Unlike the case of continuous outcomes, we do not first cover how to model the time course of categorical outcomes. However, as in causal models of continuous outcomes, we do include time as a predictor in the model, and it will be possible to interpret its coefficient as the effect of time net of the effects of the other factors. Readers interested in the effect of time without taking other factors into account will be able to do so by simply omitting the other variables from the analysis model. Before discussing the modeling per se, it is useful to introduce the example dataset.

6.1   EXPLORING THE CATEGORICAL OUTCOMES DATASET

The dataset is from a daily diary study of couples during what was for them a typical 4-week period. Each day both partners in each couple provided reports in the morning, within an hour of rising, and in the evening, within an hour of going to bed. In the morning, each partner reported his or her momentary (i.e., "right now") emotional states as well as sleep quality and duration. In the evening, each partner again reported on momentary states and on events that had occurred during the day. Analyses based on this dataset have already appeared in several publications (see Gleason, Iida, Bolger, & Shrout, 2003; Gleason, Iida, Shrout, & Bolger, 2008; Kennedy et al., 2002). The current analyses are based on a subset of 61 heterosexual couples from the original dataset.

Here we examine evening reports of conflict from the point of view of the male partners to see if the anger/irritability of the female partner at the beginning of a given day increased the risk of such conflicts later in the day. As is always the case with intensive longitudinal data, we allow for between-subjects differences (i.e., random effects), which in this case are between-couples differences, in the occurrence of conflict and in the anger–conflict relationship.

Figure 6.1 presents an abbreviated view of the data structure. The variable names are, in order, a couple ID number (*id*), diary day (*time*), the male partner's evening report of the occurrence of a conflict that day (*pconf*), and the female partner's morning report of anger/irritability (*amang*). Conflict is coded 0 on days when the male partner did not report a conflict and 1 on days on which he did. Anger is a mean of three anger items and is scaled to range from 0 (no anger) to 10 (maximal anger). Figure 6.2 presents scatterplots of *pconf* by *amang* separately for each couple. The key SAS code used to produce these is presented below.

```
PROC SGPANEL DATA=categorical NOAUTOLEGEND;
PANELBY id/COLUMNS=6 ROWS=11 NOVARNAME;
SCATTER x = amang y = pconf/MARKERATTRS =
    SYMBOL=circlefilled COLOR = black);
```

id	time	pconf (Y_{ij})	amang (X_{ij})
1	1	0	0.0
1	2	0	0.4
1	3	0	0.0
1	4	0	0.0
1	5	0	0.0
1	6	1	0.0
1	7	0	0.0
1	8	0	0.0
.	.	.	.
.	.	.	.
1	25	0	0.0
1	26	0	0.0
1	27	0	0.0
1	28	0	0.0
3	1	0	0.0
3	2	0	0.0
3	3	0	0.0
.	.	.	.
.	.	.	.
3	26	0	0.0
3	27	0	0.4
3	28	0	0.0
5	1	0	2.5
5	2	0	2.1
5	3	0	2.5
.	.	.	.
.	.	.	.
102	26	0	0.0
102	27	0	0.0
102	28	0	0.0

FIGURE 6.1. Structure of the categorical outcomes dataset.

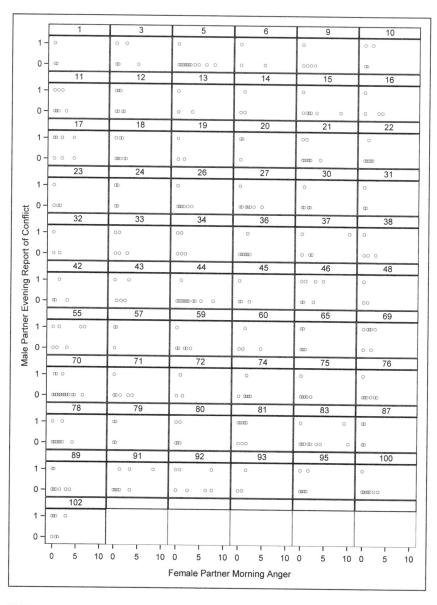

FIGURE 6.2. Male partner's evening report of conflict as a function of female partner's morning anger: Panel plots of raw data for 61 couples.

```
ROWAXIS MIN=0 MAX=1 LABEL='Male Partner Evening Report
    of conflict Today' VALUES=(0 1);

COLAXIS MIN=0 MAX=10 LABEL='Female Partner Morning
    Anger' VALUES=(0 5 10);

RUN;
```

Figure 6.2 shows what has been found in previous diary studies of couples (e.g., Bolger, DeLongis, Kessler, & Schilling, 1989): that conflicts with partners were not a daily occurrence. For the average couple on the average day, the probability of the male partner reporting a conflict was 0.16, which corresponds to slightly more than 1 conflict per week. In terms of between-couples differences, the incidence varied from a low of once a month (0.04) to a high of 3–4 days a week (0.50). Morning anger for female partners is also a relatively rare occurrence in most couples. On a 0–10 scale, the average level across couples is a mere 0.50 units, with a low of .04 units in one couple and a high of 2.10 units in another.

If morning anger predicts later reports of conflict, we should observe that relatively high levels of morning anger predict conflicts that evening. Of course, even if female anger predicts later conflict, it may not play a causal role; it could simply be a reflection of a conflict the previous day that has continued into a second day. It also could be the product of the male's morning anger, which is the real cause of the argument later. A full causal analysis would also need to consider whether the female partner agreed that a conflict took place later that day. Since our goal in this book is not to present new substantive findings but to show relatively straightforward examples of models, we do not take all of these possibilities into account. We will, however, consider a very compelling one: the prior day's (i.e., lagged) conflict (*lpconf*) as a confounding variable.

Intensive longitudinal categorical outcomes present the same analytic issues that occur for their equivalent continuous outcomes. For example, if the goal is to investigate causal processes at the within-subject level, it is important to distinguish between-subjects from within-subjects variation in putative causal X's; likewise, it is important to take account of time T as a potential third variable. Categorical outcomes, however, also present unique problems. As we will see, they require the use of nonlinear models where the outcome is not modeled directly, but rather indirectly, through its probability.

Those wishing to carry out statistical modeling of categorical intensive longitudinal data have a bewildering array of options from which to choose: from the relatively basic and easily implemented stratified logistic regressions (Allison, 2005) and generalized estimating equations (Diggle, Heagerty, Liang, & Zeger, 2002), to the relatively complex generalized mixed models (Raudenbush & Bryk, 2002) and nonlinear mixed models (Littell, Milliken, Stroup, Wolfinger, & Schabenberger, 2006). Our choices in this chapter were based on two considerations. The first was to choose an approach that allowed for between-subjects heterogeneity in a within-subject process. The second consideration was that the approach would ideally allow for serial correlation in residuals at the level of the repeated measurements. We settled on two implementations of generalized mixed models: GLIMMIX in SAS (SAS Institute Inc., 2011) and GENLINMIXED in IBM SPSS (IBM Inc., 2010). A third consideration was that the approach would allow an expansion of the model to include mediating variables. For mediation analysis at the level of the repeated measurements, Mplus is the only software option of which we are aware. Mplus lacks the capacity, however, to easily model serial correlation, and it does not have the option of using restricted maximum likelihood (the default approach in SAS and IBM SPSS for continuous outcomes). We return to these limitations later.

6.2 A LONGITUDINAL MULTILEVEL MODEL LINKING MORNING ANGER TO THE INCIDENCE OF DAILY CONFLICT IN COUPLES

We are now ready to specify the causal model to be estimated using the diary data. The model is simple in the sense that it specifies a purely within-subjects causal process linking a focal causal variable X to a binary outcome Y (in this case, the subject is the couple). Between-subjects differences enter the picture as random effects and as controls for mean X; there are no measured between-subjects variables. The general approach, therefore, is an example of research that seeks to identify a within-subject causal process, document between-subjects differences, if any, and leave the explanation of any between-subjects differences to a later investigation with the same or a different dataset.

In the remainder of this section, we lay out the precise statistical model and specify the data used to estimate the model. As in the previous chapter, key variables were transformed so that they would provide the most interpretable hypothesis tests. Figure 6.3 shows an expanded view of the dataset with the transformed variables. To keep the presentation simple, unlike previous chapters, we do not provide the multilevel formulation of the model before proceeding to the single-equation formulation.

The dependent variable, Y_{ij} (*pconf*), is the male partner in couple j's report of a conflict with the female partner on a given day i, where $Y_{ij} = 1$ when he reports a conflict and $Y_{ij} = 0$ when he does not. As noted, we do not model Y_{ij} directly but indirectly, through its probability. Also, because the probability is a bounded variable, confined to the interval 0 to 1, we cannot use a linear function to predict it; instead, we use an exponential function known as the *logit*. Thus, as shown in Equation 6.1, we can express the underlying probability that a conflict will be reported, that is, $p(Y_{ij} = 1)$, as an exponential function of an underlying propensity to report conflicts, η_{ij}, which can vary across couples j and time points i.

In our model, we specify all the independent variables to be in grand-mean deviated form, which, as before, we signify in the equations by putting a breve accent (" ˇ ") above each variable. The exception is morning anger; here, in addition to grand-mean centering, we also use group-mean centering, which involves decomposing *amang* into its between- and within-subjects components. With the independent variables defined in this way, in Equation 6.2 η_{ij} is composed of an intercept γ_{00}, a quantity we can interpret as a grand mean across all observations; a component for between-couples differences in the female partner's average anger, $\gamma_{01}\check{X}_{j}$ (*amangcb*; the original variable name *amang* with c for centered and b for the between-subjects component); a component for within-couple variation in the female partner's (j's) anger in the morning of day, i, $\gamma_{10}(\check{X}_{ij} - \check{X}_{j})$ (*amangcw*, where w stands for the within-subjects component); a component for centered yesterday's conflict report, $\gamma_{20}Y_{i-1j}$ (*lpconfc*); a component for the passage of time in weeks, $\gamma_{30}\check{T}_{i}$ (*time7c*); and a random component unique to each couple j, u_{0j}. The u_{0j} term represents how much

id	time	time7c	pconf	lpconfc	amang	amangc	amangcb	amangcw
		$(\breve{T}_i)$	(Y_{ij})	$(\breve{Y}_{ij-1})$	(X_{ij})	$(\breve{X}_{ij})$	$(\breve{X}_{.j})$	$(\breve{X}_{ij} - \breve{X}_{.j})$
1	1	–	–	–	–	–	–	–
1	2	–1.88	0	–.157	0.4	–.07	–.47	.40
1	3	–1.73	0	–.157	0.0	–.49	–.47	–.02
1	4	–1.58	0	–.157	0.0	–.49	–.47	–.02
1	5	–1.43	0	–.157	0.0	–.49	–.47	–.02
1	6	–1.28	1	–.157	0.0	–.49	–.47	–.02
1	7	–1.13	0	.843	0.0	–.49	–.47	–.02
1	8	–0.99	0	–.157	0.0	–.49	–.47	–.02
.	.	.	.	.	.	.	.	.
.	.	.	.	.	.	.	.	.
1	25	1.53	0	–.157	0.0	–.49	–.47	–.02
1	26	1.68	0	–.157	0.0	–.49	–.47	–.02
1	27	1.83	0	–.157	0.0	–.49	–.47	–.02
1	28	1.98	0	–.157	0.0	–.49	–.47	–.02
3	1	–	–	–	–	–	–	–
3	2	–1.88	0	–.157	0.0	–.49	–.22	–.26
3	3	–1.73	0	–.157	0.0	–.49	–.22	–.26
.	.	.	.	.	.	.	.	.
.	.	.	.	.	.	.	.	.
3	26	1.68	0	–.157	0.0	–.49	–.22	–.26
3	27	1.83	0	–.157	0.4	–.07	–.22	.15
3	28	1.98	0	–.157	0.0	–.49	–.22	–.26
5	1	–	–	–	–	–	–	–
5	2	–1.88	0	–.157	2.1	1.60	1.61	–.02
5	3	–1.73	0	–.157	2.5	2.01	1.61	.40
.	.	.	.	.	.	.	.	.
.	.	.	.	.	.	.	.	.
102	26	1.68	0	–.157	0.0	–.49	–.22	–.26
102	27	1.83	0	–.157	0.0	–.49	–.22	–.26
102	28	1.98	0	–.157	0.0	–.49	–.22	–.26

FIGURE 6.3. Categorical outcomes dataset: Original and constructed variables.

higher or lower a given couple's male conflict report is compared to the grand mean. Equation 6.3 states that these couple-specific components are assumed to be normally distributed with a mean of 0 and a variance of τ_{00}.

$$p(Y_{ij}) = 1/(1 + e^{-\eta_{ij}}) \tag{6.1}$$

$$\eta_{ij} = \gamma_{00} + \gamma_{01}\check{X}_{\cdot j} + \gamma_{10}(\check{X}_{ij} - \gamma_{01}\check{X}_{\cdot j}) + \gamma_{20}\check{Y}_{i-1j} + \gamma_{30}\check{T}_i + u_{0j} \tag{6.2}$$

$$u_{0j} \sim N(0, \tau_{00}) \tag{6.3}$$

Equations 6.1, 6.2, and 6.3 are standard equations for a multilevel binary outcome with a random intercept (e.g., see Fitzmaurice, Davidian, Verbeke, & Molenberghs, 2009). One way in which these equations differ from those for continuous outcomes is that they are missing a separate term for random variation at the lower, within-subject, level of analysis. This is because for a binary outcome, once we know the mean, we automatically know the variance: If the mean is $p(Y_{ij})$, then the variance is simply $p(Y_{ij})$ multiplied by $1 - p(Y_{ij})$ (see Agresti, 2007). Therefore, if our model is correct, the residual variation implied by the model should match the residual observed variation in $p(Y_{ij})$. There are reasons to think that this should not be the case for intensive longitudinal data, if, as commonly occurs, there is unexplained autocorrelation in the data. Fortunately, the SAS and SPSS analysis software we use allows for residual autocorrelation while also providing an index of the model's adequacy in accounting for binomial variation. In our annotation of the SAS output, we flag the autocorrelation parameter as ρ and the deviation from binomial variance parameter as ϕ, where $\phi = 1$ represents exact binomial variation, $\phi < 1$ represents less variation than would be expected (termed *underdispersion*), and $\phi > 1$ represents more variation than would be expected (termed *overdispersion*).

The model specifies that only one of the possible four coefficients (i.e., intercept; within-subjects morning anger, $\check{X}_{ij} - \check{X}_{\cdot j}$; lagged conflict, $\check{Y}_{i-1j}$; and time, $\check{T}_i$), show random effects, namely, the intercept. This is an empirical rather than a theoretically driven specification. In preliminary analyses, we investigated the other possibilities but found no evidence in their favor. Also, in the case of the control variable, lagged conflict, we saw no compelling reason to split it into its between- and within-subjects components. What follows is a detailed treatment of the analysis and results using SAS; we then shift to SPSS and Mplus and point out any differences or limitations one encounters when using them.

6.3 IMPLEMENTATION IN SAS PROC GLIMMIX

To implement this model, we use PROC GLIMMIX in SAS (SAS Institute, 2011). The syntax is as follows:

```
PROC GLIMMIX DATA=categorical;
CLASS id time;
MODEL pconf(EVENT="1")=amangcw amangcb lpconfc
   time7c/LINK=logit
DIST=binary DDF=60,59,60,60 SOLUTION CL;
RANDOM intercept/SUBJECT=id TYPE=un g SOLUTION CL;
RANDOM time/SUBJECT=id TYPE=ar(1) RESIDUAL;
```

The MODEL statement above specifies the fixed effects predictor variables in Equation 6.2. As was the case with PROC MIXED in earlier chapters, the software allows us to specify the degrees of freedom to use for all fixed effects other than that of the intercept. Following the rules for degrees of freedom used in previous chapters, we specify $N - 2 = 59$ degrees of freedom for the between-subjects predictor *amangcb*, and $N - 1 = 60$ degrees of freedom for the remaining coefficients. As with PROC MIXED, the software itself specifies degrees of freedom $(N - 2)$ for the intercept, a feature that cannot be overridden. There are two RANDOM statements. The first specifies a between-subjects random intercept (u_{0j} in Equations 6.2 and 6.3). The second RANDOM statement specifies that, having taken account of the fixed effects and upper-level random effect, the daily outcome variable shows extrabinomial variation (as discussed above) and an AR(1) pattern. This statement is the equivalent of the REPEATED statement in PROC MIXED.

Before we examine the numerical output, let us look at Figure 6.4, which shows what the estimated model predicts in our sample.

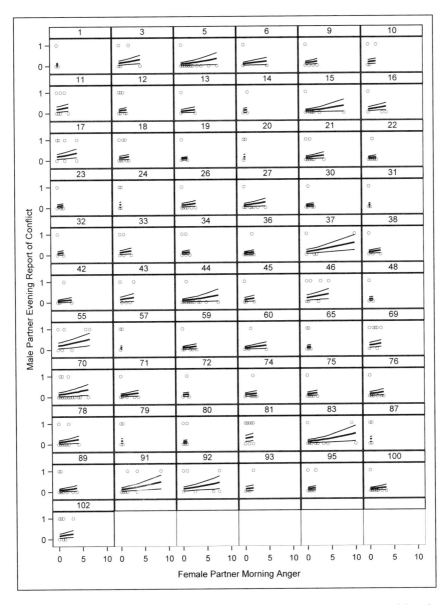

FIGURE 6.4. Male partner's evening report of conflict as a function of female partner's morning anger. Panel plots of raw data and model-predicted regression lines for 61 couples. Pairs of thin lines show 95% confidence intervals.

(We provide the syntax for producing Figure 6.4 on the website for this book.) Figure 6.4 is an overlay of (1) the scatterplot of anger and conflict from Figure 6.2 and (2) predicted values and confidence limits based on the model. The figure again draws attention to the limited variability in morning anger shown by many of the female partners and the relatively few days on which male partners reported conflict. The model appears to show a modest positive relationship between the two variables.

The key numerical output provided by SAS is reproduced in Table 6.1. The estimate of the average intercept, $\hat{\gamma}_{00}$, was −1.87, with a standard error of 0.10. The meaning of this coefficient comes from its role in Equation 6.1: It is the model-predicted log odds of the male partner's report of conflict when all the other variables in the model are zero, which, given the coding we used, is their typical value. In other words, it is the predicted log odds of male-partner-reported conflict for the typical couple on the typical day. To make this more meaningful, we transform it into a probability metric. We substitute for $\hat{\gamma}_{00}$ for η_{ij} in Equation 6.1 and calculate $\hat{p} = 1/(1 + e^{-\hat{\gamma}_{00}})$, which

TABLE 6.1. Partial Output from PROC GLIMMIX (SAS Institute, Inc.) for Multilevel Logistic Regression with Random Intercept and Fixed Slope for Female Partner's Morning Anger as a Predictor of Male Partner's Evening Report of Conflict

Covariance Parameter Estimates			
Cov Parm	Subject	Estimate	Standard Error
UN(1,1)	Id	0.2125 ($\hat{\tau}_{00}$)	0.1019
AR(1)	Id	-0.09492 ($\hat{\rho}$)	0.05631
Residual		0.9730 ($\hat{\phi}$)	0.03968

Solutions for Fixed Effects								
Effect	Estimate	Standard Error	DF	t Value	Pr > |t|	Alpha	Lower	Upper
Intercept	-1.8652 ($\hat{\gamma}_{00}$)	0.09708	59	-19.21	<.0001	0.05	-2.0595	-1.6710
amangcw	0.2076 ($\hat{\gamma}_{10}$)	0.06551	59	3.17	0.0024	0.05	0.07656	0.3386
amangcb	-0.1839 ($\hat{\gamma}_{01}$)	0.2035	59	-0.90	0.3699	0.05	-0.5911	0.2233
lpconfc	0.8630 ($\hat{\gamma}_{20}$)	0.1799	59	4.80	<.0001	0.05	0.5031	1.2229
time7c	-0.1676 ($\hat{\gamma}_{30}$)	0.06415	59	-2.61	0.0113	0.05	-0.2959	-0.03933

gives a value of 0.155. To calculate a 95% confidence interval for γ_{00}, we use the formula

$$\hat{\gamma}_{00} \pm t_{(.975, 59)} \times SE(\hat{\gamma}_{00}) \qquad (6.4)$$

which, for this example, gives

$$(-1.87) \pm 2.00 \times 0.10 \qquad (6.5)$$

This CI_{95} is −2.06 to −1.67 in the log-odds metric (as shown in Table 6.1) and from 0.13 to 0.19 in a probability metric. (The commands for these calculations are included in the software-specific command files for this chapter.)

The estimate of greatest substantive interest in Table 6.1 is $\hat{\gamma}_{10}$, the slope for *amangcw*, which is the within-couple effect for female partner's morning anger. Its value on a log-odds scale is 0.21, $SE = 0.07$, $t(60) = 3.17$, $p = .0024$, $CI_{95} = 0.08, 0.34$, which indicates that morning anger predicts an increase in partner reports of conflict. To aid interpretation, it is common to convert log-odds coefficients to an odds scale by exponentiating the coefficient. Doing so for $\hat{\gamma}_{10}$ gives $e^{0.21} = 1.24$, which is the odds ratio of a conflict corresponding to a one-unit increase in morning anger ($CI_{95} = 1.08, 1.40$).

We can get an even better grasp of what these numbers mean if we use the fitted model to create predicted probabilities of conflict for the average couple as a function of particular values of morning anger. Specifically, when we used $\hat{\gamma}_{00}$ and $\hat{\gamma}_{10}$ to generate predicted values for $X_{ij} = 0.0, 2.5, 5.0, 7.5,$ and 10.0, we obtained 0.12, 0.19, 0.28, 0.40, and 0.53, respectively. Thus, when the typical female partner reports no anger in the morning, the probability of the male partner reporting a conflict that evening is about 10%. When she reports a maximal level of anger in the morning, the probability of a male partner reporting a conflict that evening is about 50%. Viewed as a causal effect of traversing the complete range of the anger scale, this finding is noteworthy but not dramatic.

Figure 6.5 fills out this picture by representing the predicted probability of conflict as a continuous function of morning anger for the typical couple. Overlaid on this graph are the raw scores on morning anger and conflict. Although the raw scores are a bivariate scatterplot, whereas the fitted function is based on a multivariate model, we include them to give the reader a broad sense of where the data are relatively dense versus sparse. Plotted also are the 95% confidence limits for the predicted values. The reader will notice that there is much more uncertainty for predictions where the raw data are sparse—namely, days on which high levels of anger are reported by female partners.

We have so far neglected to discuss the random effect parameter estimate in the model. This is $\hat{\tau}_{00}$, an estimate of between-subjects variance in u_{0j}, namely, in how much male partners differ across couples in their average reports of conflict. Because we are assuming that the u_{0j} are normally distributed, we can now use this assumption to calculate the PI_{95}, the predicted interval of log-odds values that include 95% of the population. The relevant equation is

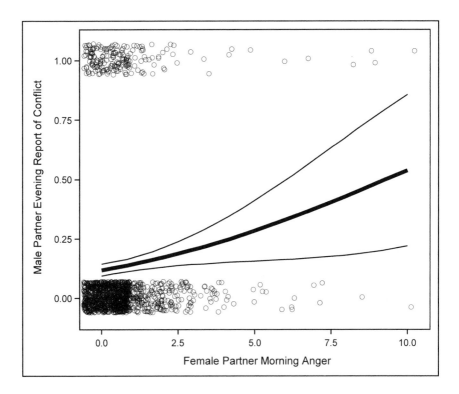

FIGURE 6.5. Male partner's evening report of conflict as a function of female partner's morning anger. Raw data and model-predicted regression line for the typical couple. Upper and lower thin lines show 95% confidence intervals. Data points have been randomly jittered to increase their visibility.

$$\hat{\gamma}_{00} \pm z_{.975}(\hat{\tau}_{00})^{1/2} \qquad (6.6)$$

which, when we substitute values, becomes

$$-1.87 \pm 1.96(0.21)^{1/2})$$

which gives a range of -2.77 to -0.97. In probability metric the range is from 0.06 to 0.38. At the low end, we have couples in which the male partner reports a conflict on 1 day in 20, whereas at the high end we have male partners reporting conflict on 8 days in 20. This range should not be confused with the CI_{95}, the 95% confidence interval for $\hat{\gamma}_{00}$ shown earlier. In the earlier case we were concerned with a fixed effect, the average intercept, and we wanted to know how much sampling variation there was in the estimate. In the current case we are concerned with a random effect of couple-specific intercepts, and from its estimate we want to know how much couples in the population differ from one another in their intercepts.

Finally, we examine the results testing the assumptions about residual variance in the outcome. The AR(1) coefficient, $\hat{\rho}$, is slightly negative but small in absolute value ($-.095$). It is less than twice its standard error (0.056), and therefore not statistically significant if one computes its z-value ($z = -0.095/0.056 = 1.70$, $p = .092$). There is little evidence of underdispersion or overdispersion. The value of $\hat{\phi}$ is 0.97, and given that its standard error is 0.04, it is not significantly different from the default value of 1.0 ($CI_{95} = 0.90, 1.05$).

6.4 IMPLEMENTATION IN IBM SPSS GENLINMIXED

To estimate the same model in SPSS GENLINMIXED, the following syntax is required.

```
GENLINMIXED
/DATA_STRUCTURE SUBJECTS=id REPEATED_MEASURES=time
COVARIANCE_TYPE=AR1
/FIELDS TARGET=pconf OFFSET=none
/TARGET_OPTIONS DISTRIBUTION=binomial LINK=logit
    REFERENCE=0
```

```
/FIXED EFFECTS= amangcw amangcb lpconfc time7c
    USE_INTERCEPT=true

/RANDOM USE_INTERCEPT=true SUBJECTS=id
    COVARIANCE_TYPE=unstructured.
```

The syntax is similar in many respects to GLIMMIX in SAS. The main difference is that the error structure for the repeated measurements is not given on its own command line. Another difference is that the dependent variable has its own command line, and it is referred to as a TARGET. Table 6.2 shows relevant output. It can be seen that the results for both fixed and random effects are essentially identical to those from GLIMMIX.

6.5 IMPLEMENTATION IN Mplus

As we saw in Chapter 5 on continuous outcomes, the Mplus implementation of multilevel models has radically different syntax from

TABLE 6.2. Partial Output from SPSS GENLINMIXED in Tabular Form for Multilevel Logistic Regression with Random Intercept and Fixed Slope for Female Partner's Morning Anger as a Predictor of Male Partner's Evening Report of Conflict

Model term	Coefficient (*SE*)	*t*	*p*	CI_{95} Lower	Upper
Intercept	−1.87 (0.10)	−19.21	<.001	−2.06	−1.68
amamgcw	0.21 (0.07)	3.17	.002	0.08	0.34
amangcb	−0.18 (0.20)	−0.90	.37	−0.58	0.22
lpconfc	0.86 (0.18)	4.80	<.001	0.51	1.22
time7c	−0.17 (0.06)	−2.61	.009	−0.29	−0.04

Random effect covariances	Estimate (*SE*)	*z*	*p*	CI_{95} Lower	Upper
Level-2 (between persons)					
Intercept	0.21 (0.10)	2.085	.037	0.08	0.54
AR1 diagonal	0.97 (0.04)	24.519	<.001	0.90	1.05
AR1 rho	−0.10 (0.06)	−1.686	.09	−0.20	0.02

that of SAS and IBM SPSS. For example, between-subjects and within-subject variables are explicitly distinguished using the WITHIN = and BETWEEN = commands. For the current example, a categorical dependent variable is identified in the CATEGORICAL = command, and when used in conjunction with ESTIMATOR = ml, the software models this outcome using a logistic function (see Muthén & Muthén, 1998–2010, chap. 3). The %WITHIN% and %BETWEEN% model commands are used to specify the within-subject and between-subjects levels of the model, and, through syntax conventions, which elements are fixed and random. As in the case of the SAS and SPSS implementations, a random-intercept-only model is specified. The exact Mplus syntax is as follows:

```
TITLE: Analysis for categorical chapter;
DATA: FILE IS categorical.dat;
VARIABLE: NAMES ARE id time time7c pconf lpconf
    lpconfc amang amangc amangcb amangcw;
USEVAR ARE pconf amangcw amangcb lpconfc time7c;
CATEGORICAL = pconf;
WITHIN = amangcw lpconfc time7c;
BETWEEN = amangcb;
CLUSTER = id;
ANALYSIS: TYPE = twolevel random;
ESTIMATOR=ml;
ALGORITHM = integration;
MODEL: %WITHIN%
pconf ON amangcw lpconfc time7c;
%BETWEEN%
pconf ON amangcb;
OUTPUT: cinterval;
```

Partial output from this Mplus analysis is provided in Table 6.3. There is a reasonably close correspondence between the parameters of interest and those found using SAS and SPSS. For morning anger, *amangcw*, the estimates are essentially in agreement: Mplus reports

0.22 with an *SE* of 0.07; SAS\SPSS report 0.21 with an *SE* of 0.07. For the random intercept variance, there is more of a divergence: Mplus reports 0.26 with an *SE* of 0.12; SAS\SPSS reports 0.21 with an *SE* of 0.10.

The fixed effect of the intercept is similar in size but opposite in sign: Mplus reports 1.9 with an *SE* of 0.1; SAS\SPSS reports –1.9 with an *SE* of 0.1. We believe that this sign difference is due to how Mplus codes the dependent variable. A much more serious divergence can be seen for the coefficient of the lagged dependent variable, *lpconfc*: Mplus reports 0.31 with an *SE* of .21, whereas SAS\SPSS reports 0.86 with an *SE* of 0.18. The difference can be explained by how the programs handle the level-1 residual variance. Recall that, for intensive longitudinal data at least, Mplus is essentially unable to incorporate

TABLE 6.3. Partial Output from Mplus of Multilevel Logistic Regression with Random Intercept and Fixed Slope for Female Partner's Morning Anger as a Predictor of Male Partner's Evening Report of Conflict

MODEL RESULTS				
				Two-Tailed
	Estimate	S.E.	Est./S.E.	P-Value
Within Level				
PCONF ON				
AMANGCW	0.216	0.068	3.191	0.001
TIME7C	-0.193	0.071	-2.703	0.007
LPCONFC	0.314	0.211	1.492	0.136
Between Level				
PCONF ON				
AMANGCB	-0.225	0.226	-0.992	0.321
Thresholds				
PCONF$1	1.902	0.110	17.256	0.000
Residual Variances				
PCONF	0.255	0.124	2.051	0.040

adjustments to the residual structure at level 1: It cannot allow for residual autocorrelation; and for categorical outcomes, it cannot handle departures from binomial dispersion (i.e., underdispersion or overdispersion; see Agresti, 2007). When the SAS and SPSS programs were rerun without adjustments to level-1 residuals, the coefficient for lagged Y became similar to that in Mplus: a coefficient of 0.30 with an SE of 0.21.

6.6 CHAPTER SUMMARY

As we have seen, even in the relatively simple case of a binary outcome, a generalized linear mixed model was necessary for the analysis. For cases where the longitudinal outcome has more than two categories, it would be necessary to use a multilevel generalization of multinomial logistic regression (as described in Hedeker, 2003, 2008). In cases where one is interested in the timing of onset, duration, and offset of categorical outcomes, one would need to use a multilevel generalization of survival analysis. For an introduction to these models, we suggest reading Hox's text on multilevel modeling (Hox, 2010, chap. 8) and a recent chapter by Hedeker and Mermelstein (2011).

In summary, this chapter has explored a causal analysis of changes in an intensively assessed categorical outcome. We used intensive longitudinal data from couples to estimate the effect of the female partner's morning anger on the male partner's report of interpersonal conflict later that day. This chapter differs from most earlier chapters in presenting analyses of a real dataset. We saw through graphical inspection that there was large between-subjects variation in the range of the putative causal variable. Having fitted a multilevel model, we saw that only a minority of couples had female partners with greater than minimal levels of morning anger. The chapter therefore illustrates another source of heterogeneity in intensive longitudinal data, and it illustrates the value of subject-specific graphical displays to fully grasp the importance of the various types of heterogeneity.

6.7 RECOMMENDED READINGS

Agresti, A. (2007). *An introduction to categorical data analysis* (2nd ed.). Hoboken, NJ: Wiley.

This book provides an overview of the theoretical and practical issues of modeling categorical outcomes in single- and multilevel data.

McCulloch, C. E., Searle, S. R., & Neuhaus, J. M. (2008). *Generalized, linear, and mixed models* (2nd ed.). New York: Wiley.

Focusing on both normally and non-normally distributed data, this book provides comprehensive coverage of both fixed and mixed effects models.

Rabe-Hesketh, S., & Skrondal, A. (2009). Generalized linear mixed-effects models. In G. M. Fitzmaurice, M. Davidian, G. Verbeke, & G. Molenberghs (Eds.), *Longitudinal data analysis* (pp. 79–106). Boca Raton: CRC Press.

The authors introduce the statistical theory underlying generalized linear mixed models and present an analysis of longitudinal data on an ordinal dependent variable.

Appendix to Chapter 6

IBM SPSS CODE FOR ANALYSIS

```
GENLINMIXED

/DATA_STRUCTURE SUBJECTS=id REPEATED_MEASURES=time

COVARIANCE_TYPE=ar1

/FIELDS TARGET=pconf OFFSET=none

/TARGET_OPTIONS DISTRIBUTION=binomial LINK=logit
    REFERENCE=0

/FIXED  EFFECTS= amangcw amangcb lpconfc time7c
    USE_INTERCEPT=true

/RANDOM USE_INTERCEPT=true SUBJECTS=id
    COVARIANCE_TYPE=unstructured
```

SAS PROC GLIMMIX CODE FOR ANALYSIS

```
PROC GLIMMIX DATA=categorical;

CLASS id time;

MODEL pconf(EVENT="1")=amangcw amangcb lpconfc
    time7c/LINK=logit

DIST=binary DDF=60,59,60,60 SOLUTION CL;
```

```
RANDOM intercept/SUBJECT=id TYPE=un g SOLUTION CL;

RANDOM time/SUBJECT=id TYPE=ar(1) RESIDUAL;
```

Mplus CODE FOR ANALYSIS

```
TITLE:     Analysis for categorical chapter;

DATA:      FILE IS categorical.dat;

VARIABLE: NAMES ARE id time time7c pconf lpconf
                    lpconfc amang amangc amangcb
                    amangcw;

           USEVAR ARE pconf amangcw amangcb lpconfc
                    time7c;

           CATEGORICAL = pconf;

           WITHIN = amangcw lpconfc time7c;

           BETWEEN = amangcb;

           CLUSTER = id;

ANALYSIS: TYPE = twolevel random;

           ESTIMATOR=ml;

           ALGORITHM = integration;

MODEL:    %WITHIN%

           pconf ON amangcw lpconfc time7c;

           %BETWEEN%

           pconf ON amangcb;

           OUTPUT:  cinterval;
```

7

Psychometrics of Intensive Longitudinal Measures of Emotional States

All researchers know that bad measures can ruin an otherwise well-designed study. Intensive longitudinal studies are surely no exception. Guidance on measurement, however, has been almost completely absent from the diary and experience sampling methods literature. This is surprising given that these and related intensive longitudinal methods are purported to provide a window on processes involving thoughts and feelings that may be qualitatively different from those assessed by traditional measurement strategies (Bolger, Davis, & Rafaeli, 2003). It is also surprising given that a major focus of intensive longitudinal research is on within-subject change, an aspect of measurement that has traditionally been viewed as difficult to assess reliably (Cronbach & Furby, 1970; Lord, 1963).

We begin this chapter by reviewing traditional principles of measurement for assessing between-subjects differences reliably. We then introduce generalizability theory as a framework for assessing the reliability of between-subjects differences and within-subjects changes. This leads to an application of the framework to assessing the reliability of within-subject changes in diary data on emotional states. We finish by showing an alternative approach to analyzing the same data, one rooted in latent variable structural equation modeling.

7.1 BASIC IDEAS ABOUT RANDOM MEASUREMENT ERROR

Even if you are already very familiar with the basics of measurement, we think it is useful to repeat them in this chapter. More extensive treatments of this material can be found in Crocker and Algina (1986) and more recently in Raykov and Marcoulides (2011). Measurement errors are usually classified into two kinds: random errors, which are treated under the name of *reliability*, and systematic errors, which are treated under the name of *validity*. To be clear at the outset, we cover the issue of measurement reliability only. Validity is, we believe, an equally important aspect of measurement error and we refer those readers interested in evaluating validity for measures from experience sampling and diary studies to Shrout and Lane (2012a).

To start, imagine a sample of people whose heights you want to measure using a standard measuring tape. Now consider a single person from the sample, and consider what would result if you measured that person many times over an interval of time sufficiently small that no true change in height were likely. The measurements would tend to cluster around a single value, the true height of the person. In mathematical terms, each of the k measurements of Y, Y_k, can be thought of as being composed of a person's true score, P, plus an error component, v_k, specific to each measurement k, as follows:

$$Y_k = P + v_k \tag{7.1}$$

Few researchers are interested in measures on just one person, of course. To study the heights of a population of persons, we have to expand the equation as follows:

$$Y_{jk} = P_j + v_{jk} \tag{7.2}$$

where Y_{jk} stands for the k measurements taken on person j, P_j stands for each person j's true score, and v_{jk} stands for the specific error in each of k measurements taken on person j. Assume further that the true scores are normally distributed, as are the deviations of the individual measurements from their respective true scores. A useful visual image is to think of a series of small normal distributions arrayed along a line representing height, where each small distribution corresponds to height measurements of one individual in the population. The total variability in potential height scores is a combination of the variability between the means of these distributions, that is, the true differences in heights, and the variability of actual scores around each person's true score, that is, the measurement error variability (Lord & Novick, 1968). That is,

$$\sigma_Y^2 = \sigma_P^2 + \sigma_v^2 \tag{7.3}$$

To repeat, the variance in height measurements across the population, σ_Y^2, is a sum of the true between-persons variability in heights, σ_P^2, and measurement error, σ_v^2. By taking the ratio of the true variability to the total variability, we can calculate what is known as the reliability of our measure of height in the population, the most famous of which is Cronbach's alpha (Cronbach, 1951). A measure of reliability, then, is an estimate of what proportion of the observed variability is true variability. Following Lord and Novick (1968), we use the formula below:

$$\rho_{YY} = \frac{\sigma_P^2}{\sigma_Y^2} \tag{7.4}$$

Notice that the formula is a ratio of variances rather than the more easily interpretable standard deviations. This is because of the mathematical property that variances can be added to compute the total variance, whereas standard deviations cannot be added to compute the total standard deviation. Thus,

$$\sigma_Y \neq \sigma_P + \sigma_v \tag{7.5}$$

To increase the reliability of a measure, one can increase the true score variance, decrease the error variance, or both. Perhaps the most common way of decreasing error variance is to take multiple measurements of the same person and to average them. It has long been known that the precision of measurement is improved by averaging (Stigler, 1986).

How much improved? Let us continue to use the model described above, where the v_{jk}'s are normally distributed around the true value for each person, and let us, for the time being, consider the precision of a single measurement. One way of quantifying the precision of a single measurement is to assess how far, on average, one would expect it to be from the mean. Such a quantity, the standard error of measurement (*SE*), would simply be the standard deviation (*SD*) of the distribution of v_{jk}. Now, if instead of one you took, say, four measurements and averaged them, the *SE* of the estimate of the true score (mean) would be halved—that is, it would be $SD/\sqrt{4} = 0.5\ SD$. Note that this calculation relies on the formula for the standard error of a mean (e.g., see Ferguson & Takane, 1989).

The implications of averaging for our visual representation is that the greater the number of repeated measurements that go into the average, the narrower the width of the small bell-shaped curves will be. The narrower these are, the bigger the share of the total variance is due to true score variance, and the greater the reliability.

7.2   MAKING USE OF GENERALIZABILITY THEORY

Classical test theory (Crocker & Algina, 1986), of which we have given just the briefest of summaries, considers just one source of measurement error. The approach we advocate for intensive longitudinal data involves multiple sources because these data typically show multiple sources of influence. As we will see, generalizability theory (see Brennan, 2001; Cronbach, Gleser, Nanda, & Rajaratnam, 1972; Shavelson & Webb, 1991), which we henceforth shorten to G theory, provides an elegant way to answer a key measurement question: Can within-subject (i.e., within-person) changes in a particular psychological construct be measured reliably? Details on the application of G theory for assessing the reliability of diary measures can be found in Cranford et al. (2006) and Shrout and Lane (2012a). Below, we provide a summary and sample application.

To answer the question of whether within-subject changes in a particular construct can be assessed reliably, G theory requires us to specify the dimensions of generalizability that are possible for a given intensive longitudinal study. In a typical intensive longitudinal study, there are at least three: time points, persons, and items. To conduct a G theory analysis one must specify a random effects ANOVA model with factors corresponding to these dimensions of generalizability. After estimating such a model for a particular measure and dataset, it is possible to decompose the variability in the scores into components based on variability across time, across persons, across items, and across higher-order interactions of these factors. Finally, based on such an analysis, one can make predictions about which specific types of research designs would lead to reliable measures of a given construct. This would involve issues such as how many items would be needed for a particular construct, how many time points would be necessary, and how many persons to sample.

At this point, we follow the Cranford et al. (2006) and Shrout and Lane (2012a) G theory approach to assessing the reliability of multi-item daily diary mood scales. We apply their approach to an example dataset of 50 breast cancer patients, who completed a 10-day diary soon after diagnosis and treatment, and evaluate the reliability of a four-item scale of momentary positive affect. Like their example datasets, our example dataset contains variability over the dimensions of time, persons, and items. The first step is to specify a three-way, crossed random effects ANOVA model (i.e., Time * Person * Item). For a person j, responding at time point (day) i to mood item k, the model for mood Y_{ijk} is

$$Y_{ijk} = \mu + T_i + P_j + I_k + (TP)_{ij} + (TI)_{ik} + (PI)_{jk} + (TPI)_{ijk} + v_{ijk} \quad (7.6)$$

The overall mean for all mood ratings of this type is μ. It is the lone fixed effect in the model. The remaining terms represent levels of random effects and their interactions. T_i reflects the tendency of each time point i to have higher or lower scores across all persons and items; P_j reflects the equivalent effect of each person j over all time points and items; and I_k is the equivalent effect of each item k across time points and persons. $(TP)_{ij}$ is an effect specific to time point i and person j over all days; $(TI)_{ik}$ is an effect specific to time point i and item k over all persons; and $(PI)_{jk}$ is an effect specific to person j and item k over all time points. The final two terms, $(TPI)_{ijk}$ and v_{ijk}, describe effects specific to time point i for person j and item k. The first of these terms represents a systematic measurement effect to do with time point i for person j and item k, and the second represents a random variable that captures all remaining influences on Y_{ijk}. In our design, these two terms cannot be distinguished.

In the case of a completely balanced dataset, where each person provides scores for each item for each time point, it is a remarkable fact that the variances associated with each of the random effects sum to the total variance. Thus,

$$\sigma^2_{Y_{ijk}} = \sigma^2_{T_i} + \sigma^2_{P_j} + \sigma^2_{I_k} + \sigma^2_{(TP)_{ik}} + \sigma^2_{(TI)_{ik}} + \sigma^2_{(PI)_{jk}} + \left[\sigma^2_{(TPI)_{ijk}} + \sigma^2_{v_{ijk}} \right] \quad (7.7)$$

The final two variances are bracketed to indicate that only their sum can be estimated.

Although it is may seem strange to readers that random effects ANOVA variances can be used for measurement purposes, a key linking idea is that random effects can also be thought of as latent variables. Consider $\sigma^2_{P_j}$. This can be thought of as a latent variable that reflects differences between persons in positive mood that are temporally stable and that are common to all measurement items. This is positive mood considered as a trait. Analogously, $\sigma^2_{T_j}$ can be thought of as a latent variable that reflects day-to-day changes in positive mood that is common across items and persons.

$\sigma^2_{(TP)_{ij}}$ is of particular interest because it is a latent variable representing the extent to which people differ in how they change over time (averaging across items). We saw earlier that a major justification for intensive longitudinal research is that it can examine within-subject changes. Are these within-subject changes measured reliably? It turns out that the variance component $\sigma^2_{(TP)_{ij}}$ is crucial to answering this question. If we can (1) conclude that this variance is substantial and (2) through averaging across items create a scale that reflects it reliably, then we are in a good position to proceed to estimate models where we examine within-subject changes in the scale, and between-subjects differences in within-subject changes.

When estimating the variances in the first step, we treated all possible sources of variation as random. This provides the most flexibility at the second step, where in calculating reliabilities, the analyst has the choice of whether to treat any or all factors as fixed or random. We return to this issue in a moment.

We obtained estimates of the variance components associated with Equation 7.7 using software that conducts variance decompositions, such as the VARCOMP procedure of SAS (SAS Institute Inc., 2011) and VARCOMP in SPSS (IBM Inc., 2010). Had there been no days with missing data, this procedure would produce exactly the same estimates as would be obtained from an analysis of the expected mean squares from the three-way, mixed model ANOVA design (e.g., see Winer, 1971). The VARCOMP software uses the MIVQUE estimation method (Rao, 1971) to make use of information from the respondents who missed one or more days in the diary procedure.

Before we proceed, it will be useful to look at the example dataset and the necessary data structure for conducting the variance decomposition analysis. Figure 7.1 consists of the 10 days of data for the first three participants for four positive mood items. The entire dataset is available on the website for this book and consists of 50 (persons) * 10 (days) = 500 rows of data. Specifically, Item1, Item2, Item3, and Item4 refer to "interested," "determined," "enthusiastic," and "inspired," respectively. Ratings of each item were made on a scale from 1 (not at all) to 5 (extremely), and missing values are represented by –999. Although this is the format for longitudinal data that is most typical for data analysis, restructuring of the dataset is necessary before a G theory analysis can be performed.

The variance components procedure assumes that we are working with a three-level dataset, one that has a separate data line for each person, for each day, for each item. The resulting restructured dataset consists of stacking the items on top of each other in separate rows. For the example in this chapter, the dataset consists of 50 (persons) * 10 (days) * 4 (items) = 2,000 rows. A unique code is required for each level of each variable. The variable Y is simply the score on a particular positive mood item for a particular person on a

person	time	item1	item2	item3	item4
301	1	2	2	3	4
301	2	2	3	3	2
301	3	3	3	2	2
301	4	4	3	3	3
301	5	2	2	2	2
301	6	2	2	1	2
301	7	2	2	1	2
301	8	2	2	2	2
301	9	2	3	2	2
301	10	3	3	3	3
309	1	3	3	−999	1
309	2	3	3	3	3
309	3	3	3	3	1
309	4	3	1	3	1
309	5	1	1	1	1
309	6	3	1	1	1
309	7	1	1	3	1
309	8	1	1	1	1
309	9	1	1	1	1
309	10	1	1	1	1
319	1	3	2	2	2
319	2	−999	−999	−999	−999
319	3	3	2	2	2
319	4	3	3	3	2
319	5	−999	−999	−999	−999
319	6	2	1	2	2
319	7	2	1	1	1
319	8	2	2	2	2
319	9	−999	−999	−999	−999
319	10	3	3	3	3

FIGURE 7.1. Structure of the measurement dataset in wide form (for three subjects).

particular day of the diary study. Figure 7.2 is the restructured version of the example data displayed in Figure 7.1.

The SAS code for the VARCOMP analysis is presented below:

```
PROC VARCOMP;
CLASS time person item;
MODEL y = time|person|item;
```

The CLASS statement specifies that time, person, and item are categorical variables. The MODEL statement specifies that all main effects and higher-order interactions are to be estimated. All three factors are treated as random effects. The corresponding SPSS code is as follows:

```
VARCOMP y BY time person item
/RANDOM=time person item
/METHOD= minque(1)
/DESIGN=time person item time*person time*item
    person*item.
```

It is worth noting that the same variance decomposition can be conducted using a multilevel modeling approach, as shown in Shrout and Lane (2012a). Below we give the relevant SPSS code:

```
MIXED y BY time item
/FIXED=time item time*item | SSTYPE(3)
/METHOD=REML
/RANDOM=INTERCEPT time item | SUBJECT(person).
```

Table 7.1 presents the relevant variance components estimates for positive mood for the breast cancer dataset. Cranford et al. (2006) considered four different measures of reliability; in this chapter we consider only the one that we see as the most crucial for intensive longitudinal studies: the reliability of within-subject change. In the calculations to be discussed, the only factors we treated as random were person and all higher-order interactions involving person. This implies that the reliabilities calculated are estimates that refer to the population of persons. By contrast, we treated the four mood items

person	time	item	y
301	1	1	2
301	1	2	2
301	1	3	3
301	1	4	4
301	2	1	2
301	2	2	3
301	2	3	3
301	2	4	2
.	.	.	.
.	.	.	.
.	.	.	.
309	1	1	3
309	1	2	3
309	1	3	−999
309	1	4	1
309	2	1	3
309	2	2	3
309	2	3	3
309	2	4	3
.	.	.	.
.	.	.	.
.	.	.	.
319	1	1	3
319	1	2	2
319	1	3	2
319	1	4	2
319	2	1	−999
319	2	2	−999
319	2	3	−999
319	2	4	−999
.	.	.	.
.	.	.	.
.	.	.	.
319	10	4	3

FIGURE 7.2. Structure of the measurement dataset in long form (for three subjects).

TABLE 7.1. Variance Partitioning of Positive Mood Items in the Example Dataset

Source of variance	Symbol	Variance (%)
Time	$\hat{\sigma}^2_T$	0.000 (0.0)
Person	$\hat{\sigma}^2_P$	0.362 (31.2)
Item	$\hat{\sigma}^2_I$	0.049 (4.2)
Time * Person	$\hat{\sigma}^2_{TP}$	0.256 (22.1)
Time * Item	$\hat{\sigma}^2_{TI}$	0.005 (0.1)
Person * Item	$\hat{\sigma}^2_{PI}$	0.190 (16.4)
Error	$\hat{\sigma}^2_{ERROR}$ [a]	0.299 (25.8)
	Total	1.162 (100)

[a]This component is the sum of σ^2_{TPI} and σ^2_v in Equation 7.7.

per scale and the 10 measurement days as fixed, meaning that we kept our inferences to potential studies that used the same set of items and days.

The focal reliability measure, R_C, assesses whether there are reliable within-subject differences in change over time. Specifically, if we were to conduct an intensive longitudinal study of a sample of persons over the fixed set of 10 equally spaced time points and create scales from the fixed set of indicators of the latent variable of positive mood, would there be adequate systematic time*person variance in the resulting scores? The formula, omitting the *ijk* subscripts, is

$$R_C = \frac{\sigma^2_{TP}}{\sigma^2_{TP} + \left[\sigma^2_{TPI} + \sigma^2_v\right]/k} \qquad (7.8)$$

The numerator contains only one component, the time by person variance, σ^2_{TP}. The denominator contains the same variance component plus the error variance component, divided by the number of items k (note that the error variance component is the sum of

$\sigma^2_{TPI} + \sigma^2_v$). Substituting the appropriate estimates of variance components from Table 7.1 in Equation 7.8, we find that R_C is .77, which suggests that the four-item measure of positive mood in the 10-day diary study can assess within-person change reliably.

7.3 MAKING USE OF MULTILEVEL CONFIRMATORY FACTOR ANALYSIS

We now turn to an alternative method of gauging the reliability of multi-item scales for assessing within-person change: multilevel confirmatory factor analysis (MCFA; Muthén, 1994; Muthén & Asparouhov, 2011). MCFA allows for the specification of separate within-subjects and between-subjects parts of a confirmatory factor model. The within-subjects part of the model specifies factor loadings for the within-subjects variation in a set of items that have been repeatedly measured. Shrout and Lane (2012a) showed how a reliability index that comes from a factor analytic tradition can be calculated from the estimates of confirmatory factor analysis (CFA) conducted separately on each participant's set of data from a diary study. This statistic is known as coefficient omega (ω), and it has the following formula (McDonald, 1999, Eq. 6.20b, p. 89):

$$\omega = \frac{\left(\Sigma\lambda_k\right)^2}{\left(\Sigma\lambda_k\right)^2 + \Sigma\psi^2_k} \tag{7.9}$$

The numerator of omega is the squared sum of the estimated factor loadings λ of each item k. The denominator adds to this quantity the sum of the error variances Ψ^2 of each item; this sum is equal to the total variance of all items. In essence, this formula reflects the classical test theory conceptualization of reliability where the numerator reflects true score variance and the denominator reflects the total variance.

When coefficient omega is calculated on the basis of estimated factor loadings and variances from the within-person part of a multilevel CFA, it roughly corresponds to the G theory R_C coefficient. However, there are two important features worth noting about coefficient omega that may make it a more appropriate choice over R_C. Notice that in the formula above, the item loadings and error variances are allowed to vary across items k. Whereas R_C specifies that all items are equally related to the underlying construct being measured, such that they have identical factor loadings (of 1.0) and identical error variances, omega allows each of the items to have unique loadings and error variances.

Below is the Mplus syntax for conducting an MCFA of the four positive affect items from our example dataset:

```
TITLE:      Ch7 Psychometrics example;
DATA:       FILE IS psychometrics.dat;
VARIABLE:   NAMES ARE person time item1 item2 item3 item4;
            USEVAR = item1 item2 item3 item4 time;
            WITHIN = time;
            CLUSTER = person;
            missing are all (-999);
ANALYSIS:   TYPE = TWOLEVEL ;
            PROCESSORS=4;
MODEL:      %WITHIN%
               PAw by
               item1* (a)
               item2 item3 item4 (b-d);
               item1 item2 item3 item4 (e-h);
               PAw@1;
               item1 item2 item3 item4 on time;
            %BETWEEN%
               PAb by
               item1*
               item2 item3 item4 ;
               PAb@1;
               item1 item2 item3 item4 ;
            MODEL CONSTRAINT:
               new (omega);
               omega=((a+b+c+d)**2)/((a+b+c+d)**2 + (e+f+g+h));
OUTPUT:     sampstat;
```

Note that Mplus can read data in the wide format shown in Table 7.1. The within-person part of the MCFA model is specified on the set of lines following the %WITHIN% statement. PAw is the name of the within-person positive affect factor. The following line, item1* (1), specifies that positive affect Item 1 loads on PAw with a loading that is estimated from the data and assigned the label of 1. (This label and the ones that follow are used in the calculation of coefficient omega at the end of the code segment.) The next line specifies that Items 2 through 4 load on the PAw factor. The line item1 item2 item3 item4 (5-8) gives the labels 5, 6, 7, and 8 to the error variances of Items 1, 2, 3, and 4, respectively. PAw@1 fixes the variance of the factor to be 1.0.

The code under MODEL CONSTRAINT uses estimates of the labeled parameters to calculate omega for the within-person part of the model. For our example data, the resulting omega value is .794, which is very close to the R_C estimate shown earlier. Based on these results, therefore, we can conclude that, for the particular items and particular days chosen in our example diary study of breast cancer patients, it is possible to reliably distinguish people in terms of their patterns of change over time. This is an especially useful finding, given the potential value of intensive longitudinal designs for studying how people change, as we have stressed already.

7.4 CHAPTER SUMMARY

With the publication of Cranford et al. (2006) and Shrout and Lane (2012a), it is now possible with intensive longitudinal datasets to conduct a psychometric analysis of latent constructs as they are revealed in multiple indicator variables. In this chapter, we illustrated this psychometric approach by calculating the reliability of within-person changes in daily positive mood assessed with multiple items from a daily diary study of 50 subjects on 10 consecutive days. Our emphasis in this chapter on the psychometrics of within-subject changes should not be surprising given our overall emphasis in the book on within-subject changes rather than between-subject differences.

7.5 RECOMMENDED READINGS

Cranford, J. A., Shrout, P. E., Iida, M., Rafaeli, E., Yip, T., & Bolger, N. (2006). A procedure for evaluating sensitivity to within-person change: Can mood measures in diary studies detect change reliably? *Personality and Social Psychology Bulletin, 32,* 917–929.

This article is the first we know of to describe and apply a G-theory analysis for the purposes of assessing the reliability of multi-item scales in an intensive longitudinal study.

Shrout, P. E., & Lane, S. P. (2012a). Psychometrics. In M. R. Mehl & T. S. Conner (Eds.), *Handbook of research methods for studying daily life* (pp. 302–320). New York: Guilford Press.

This chapter provides an excellent introduction to the psychometrics of intensive longitudinal data.

Shrout, P. E., & Lane, S. P. (2012b). Reliability. In H. Cooper, P. M. Camic, D. L. Long, A. T. Panter, D. Rindskopf, & K. J. Sher (Eds.), *APA handbook of research methods in psychology: Vol. 1. Foundations, planning, measures and psychometrics* (pp. 643–660). Washington, DC: American Psychological Association.

This chapter provides an accessible overview of measurement reliability in psychological research.

Design and Analysis
of Intensive Longitudinal Studies
# of Distinguishable Dyads

Thus far we have focused on intensive longitudinal studies of individuals, and we have shown how intensive longitudinal data can be used to trace changes over time and to model a causal process. The daily lives of individuals are rarely spent in isolation from others, however, and arguably the most important context of daily life is the one defined by close dyadic relationships (Reis, Collins, & Berscheid, 2000). These relationships include ones with spouses, friends, roommates, siblings, and parents. Although intensive longitudinal studies of larger group associations are possible (e.g., families), in this chapter we focus on dyads.

As we hope will become clear in this chapter, dyadic intensive longitudinal data allow investigators to ask important new questions that cannot be addressed in intensive longitudinal studies of individuals. With these new questions come new challenges of modeling dyadic interdependence at multiple levels. In this chapter we illustrate interdependence in dyads where members can be distinguished on some important characteristic such as gender (male, female), role (therapist, patient), or age (older sibling, younger sibling). Our analysis model enables us to answer the same types of questions that can be asked of intensive longitudinal data where the subject is a single individual, such as whether work stressors affect a subject's view of his or her relationship partner at home. What is new about the analysis model is that it treats the data from dyad partners as a paired longitudinal series where the pairing is modeled (1) at each time point in the series, such that, for example, at time points where one partner is especially dissatisfied, the other partner is also; and (2) at the level of the statistical parameters for each series, such that, for example, if one partner has a relatively steep work-stress-to-dissatisfaction slope, the other partner is likely to have one also.

8.1 MOTIVATION FOR STUDYING THE EVERYDAY LIVES OF DYADS

Researchers who study close relationships have traditionally used a variety of research methodologies, including long-interval (e.g., yearly) longitudinal assessments of couple functioning, surveys of couple/family members across various community and social contexts, and laboratory-based observation of dyadic interactions (Berscheid, 1999). Intensive longitudinal methods are increasingly being used to complement these more traditional approaches (Laurenceau & Bolger, 2005). As noted in the introductory chapter, one of the early applications of intensive longitudinal methods was to the study of marriage by Wills et al. (1974), who examined the link between daily spouse behaviors and ratings of global satisfaction in seven couples over 14 days.

We view the role of intensive longitudinal methods as complementing traditional relationship research methodologies. As argued by Reis (1994), global self-report methods, controlled observation of laboratory interactions, and intensive longitudinal methods each often provide unique, at times discrepant, and important perspectives on close relationship and family phenomena. We believe that the most persuasive programs of research draw from two or all three methodological perspectives. For example, in their study of mother–preschooler dyads, Repetti and Wood (1997) combined (1) daily diary reports of job stress; (2) behavioral observation of parent–child interactions; and (3) global self-report measures of trait anxiety, depression, and Type A personality to examine the effects of daily stress on parent–child interactions. The researchers found that daily work stress leads to greater mother withdrawal at the end of the day and that this effect was stronger for mothers with high, versus low, Type A personality traits. In the example dataset for this chapter, we draw on Repetti's (1989) intensive longitudinal design where daily reports were obtained at the end of the workday as well as later in the evening.

8.2 METHODOLOGICAL AND DESIGN ISSUES IN INTENSIVE LONGITUDINAL STUDIES OF DISTINGUISHABLE DYADS

Note that although there are three distinct units in dyadic intensive longitudinal data—the dyad, the person in the dyad, and the repeated observations of the person in the dyad—the fundamental, independent sampling unit is the dyad. Dyads are assumed to be independently sampled, but once a dyad is sampled, the persons and observation within each dyad are treated as nonindependent. Although this chapter focuses on *distinguishable dyads*, the methods and analytic strategies described can be readily extended to distinguishable triads (e.g., mother, father, child) and larger groups such as work teams with distinguishable roles (Kenny, Kashy, Cook, 2006; Kenny, Mannetti, Pierro, Livi, & Kashy, 2002). Distinguishability is typically determined conceptually by identifying some important characteristic (e.g., gender, age, role) that may differentiate partners, but it can also be determined empirically (Ackerman, Donnellan, & Kashy, 2011).

Why Not Analyze Dyad Members Separately?

Upon collecting dyadic intensive longitudinal data, one solution to dealing with the problem of nonindependence in dyads is to analyze the data from each member of the couple separately. Thus, one could model end-of-the-day relationship conflict in male partners in a multilevel model that is separate from the equivalent multilevel model for female partners. Although it circumvents the nonindependence problem, such an approach rules out the investigation of important questions such as within-dyad covariation in negative mood for male and female partners and whether certain processes (e.g., child behavior problems) can explain this covariation. In addition, one cannot examine covariation between dyads in average levels of male and female negative mood and whether certain individual (e.g., personality) or dyadic (e.g., number of kids at home, length of relationship) factors can explain this covariation. In general, the approach of analyzing each set of partners with separate models is not recommended because it neglects the interdependencies that make dyadic intensive longitudinal data interesting and informative.

There are, however, some situations in which modeling the *outcomes* of only one partner in the couple is theoretically justified. An example is studying daily social support processes in couples where there are distinct roles each partner takes in the process being studied. Bolger, Zuckerman, and Kessler (2000) studied the effects of emotional social support on daily distress in heterosexual couples here one partner was studying for an impending bar examination (i.e., the examinee). In this work, the authors were specifically interested in the roles that examinee reports of receiving daily support and partner reports of providing daily support played in predicting examinees' experience of daily distress. Although examinee distress was modeled as the sole outcome in this example, the upper-level sampling unit should still be considered the couple because there is only one examinee in each couple and variables from both partners were used as predictors (for a related example, see Thompson & Bolger, 1999). This type of model differs from one in which the daily process for each partner is modeled simultaneously and in parallel. This would mean, in the case of the support example, modeling distress outcomes for both the male and female partners in each couple as a function of both partners' provision and receipt of support. We refer to this type of model as a multilevel model for dyadic intensive longitudinal data.

Dyadic Intensive Longitudinal Data Analysis Model:
Two or Three Levels?

Considering that intensive longitudinal data from distinguishable dyads have three levels of analysis, it may seem obvious that such data should be analyzed using a three-level statistical model. In fact, as pointed out by Kenny and Kashy (2011), this is rarely, if ever, a good idea in the distinguishable dyads context. This is because a central idea underlying multilevel models is that there be random variability at each level of analysis, and with distinguishable dyads there cannot be random variability at the person level. Note that we are not denying that there are three conceptual levels of analysis in dyadic data, merely that there are not three levels with random variability that need to be modeled.

To explain our thinking, let us start with the case of indistinguishable dyads. Figure 8.1 compares a three-level model of dyadic intensive longitudinal data with a three-level model of classrooms, children within classrooms, and longitudinal assessments of children within classrooms (see Raudenbush & Bryk, 2002, chap. 8). In the latter context, classrooms (level 3) are presumed to be randomly sampled from a population, or if not, then in the context of one's statistical model there are between-classrooms differences that behave as if they were the result of random factors (see Snijders & Bosker, 2012, for a discussion of this issue). Upon sampling classrooms, children (at level 2) can be sampled from each classroom, or if all children are studied, then in the context of one's statistical model, there are between-children differences within a classroom that behave as if they were the result of random factors. Finally, each child is repeatedly assessed, and again either a random sampling model is applied, or more likely, within-child variation is attributed in part to random factors.

A similar three-level sampling model can be specified for indistinguishable dyads: At level 3, dyads can be either sampled or modeled as if some of the between-dyads variability is due to random factors. At level 2, one can at least imagine sampling a person from the dyad or otherwise regarding between-persons differences within a dyad as reflecting random factors. At level 1, at least some part of

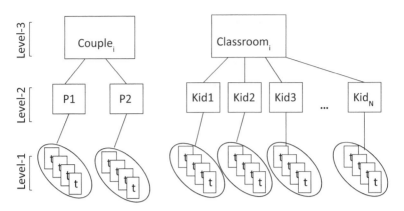

FIGURE 8.1. Three-level structure of intensive longitudinal data from indistinguishable dyads (left) and children in classrooms (right).

the within-person variation can be random due to sampling (as in experience sampling designs), or if fixed assessments are used (as in daily diary designs), random due to the action of factors that can be modeled as random (e.g., weather effects).

Let us now turn to the case of distinguishable dyads. Unlike the case of indistinguishable dyads, it is not possible to have random variability at level 2: Once role within the dyad (e.g., wife vs. husband, mother vs. child) is included as a variable in a statistical model, there can be no estimate of additional variability at the middle level. The model is said to be saturated at the middle level, and a conceptual three-level model can be represented by a model with only two levels showing random variation (see Diggle et al., 2002, p. 65, for a discussion of this problem in the context of longitudinal data analysis).

In addition to the features described above, another feature of the dyadic longitudinal designs covered in this chapter is that time as a factor is fully crossed within each dyad. This means that observations are made at the same time points for both partners. (This is not an assumption made about individuals from different dyads.) This crossed design is depicted in Figure 8.2 by the double-headed arrows that connect the same time points for male and female partners within a couple. Therefore, it is possible (and very likely) that there will be a within-couple correlation between outcomes for male and female partners for any given time point. Within the context of a model for intensive longitudinal dyadic data, these within-couple links can either be (1) modeled by measured variables included in the model or (2) modeled by residual correlations at each time point, that is, correlations that reflect the interdependence of partner outcomes within a time point above and beyond what is accounted for by the predictors in the model.

8.3   THE MULTILEVEL MODEL FOR INTENSIVE LONGITUDINAL DATA FROM DISTINGUISHABLE DYADS

In this section we detail the setup and analysis of what we call the *multilevel model for intensive longitudinal data from distinguishable dyads*. For the reasons described in the previous section, this model represents the three conceptual levels of dyadic intensive longitudinal data as a statistical model with two levels of analysis. The lower, within-couple level represents a two-equation multivariate system, where one equation specifies a longitudinal process linking within-subject variation in X to within-subject variation in Y for the male

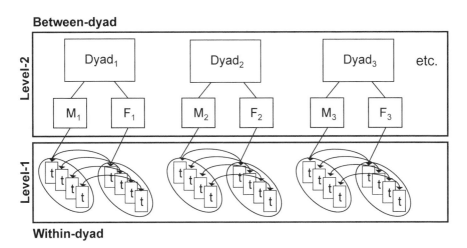

FIGURE 8.2. Two-level structure of intensive longitudinal data from distinguishable dyads.

partner, and the other equation specifies an equivalent process for the female partner. These level-1 equations are linked in the sense that each time point in the male equation has a corresponding time point in the female equation, and the male residuals and female residuals at any given time point are allowed to correlate. In this way, any nonindependence due to omitted contemporaneous influences can be quantified. The upper level represents between-couples differences in the random intercept and random slopes for the male level-1 equation and for the female level-1 equation. Nonindependence at this level of analysis is quantified by the sign and degree of correlation between corresponding male and female random effects.

As depicted in Figure 8.2, the multilevel model for dyadic intensive longitudinal data has male and female processes represented in parallel. This kind of multilevel model was first described by Raudenbush and colleagues (Barnett, Marshall, Raudenbush, & Brennan, 1993; Raudenbush, Brennan, & Barnett, 1995) as a multivariate hierarchical linear model and later by MacCallum, Kim, Malarkey, and Kiecolt-Glaser (1997) as a multivariate change model. The ideas presented below also draw on work by Kenny and Zautra (1995) as well as Gonzalez and Griffin (2000). A version of this model that incorporates dependency in errors between dyad members at each time point and within dyad members across time can be found in Bolger and Shrout (2007) and Kennedy et al. (2002). This last approach is advanced in this chapter.

Example Dyadic Process Dataset on Daily Work Stressors and Daily Relationship Dissatisfaction

We now describe the example dataset to be used in this chapter. The design and variables are motivated by the work of Rena Repetti and focus on the phenomenon of work–home stress spillover (Repetti, 1989). The data were simulated to represent 100 dual-career heterosexual couples where each partner provided diary reports twice daily over the course of 21 consecutive days. We simulated the first diary report to be at the end of each workday and to include the number of stressors that occurred over the course of the workday and current (i.e., end-of-workday) work dissatisfaction. We simulated the second diary report to be at the end of the waking day (within an hour of bedtime) and to include a rating of current relationship dissatisfaction. Note that, to keep the dataset at simple as possible, we simulated the data such that each partner worked each day of the diary period. Clearly this is unrealistic, but we hope it is a feature that the reader can overlook, given that the goal of the simulation was to create a pedagogically uncomplicated dataset rather than a realistic one.

There are two sets of questions that we examine using this dataset. The first set asks questions of the sort asked in earlier chapters with causal process models for individuals. Thus we examine whether number of daily work stressors, rated at the end of the workday, predicts ratings of relationship dissatisfaction at the end of the waking day. Moreover we examine the size of this effect for the typical male partner and the typical female partner (fixed effects) and whether there is heterogeneity in the strength of the effect across male partners in couples, and similarly whether there is heterogeneity in the strength of the effect across female partners in couples.

The second set of questions can only be examined with the dyadic longitudinal model. We have already described them as level-1 and level-2 nonindependence. In the context of our specific dataset, level-1 nonindependence is whether, over and above any similarity due to explanatory variables included in the model, a male partner's relationship dissatisfaction on a given day is correlated with a female partner's relationship dissatisfaction. For our dataset, an example of level-2 nonindependence would be the presence of correlated intercepts and work stress slopes between males and females. Positively correlated intercepts would mean that if, adjusting for work stressors and time, a male in a given couple shows a relatively high level of dissatisfaction, the female in the couple would also show a relatively high level of dissatisfaction.

Figure 8.3 shows the stacked data structure needed for estimating a multilevel model for dyadic intensive longitudinal data (in SPSS and SAS); specifically, it shows the first 7 days from the 21-day diary recording period for male and female partners in a single dyad. *coupleid* is a uniquely identifying number for each couple. *personid* uniquely identifies each partner in the dataset. *time* indexes the day of the diary recording period. *time7c* is a version of time that has been centered on the middle day of the diary period and then divided by 7, which puts time on a metric where one unit is a week. *gender* is an

coupleid	personid	time	time7c	gender	female	male	reldis	wrkstrs	wrkstrsc	wrkstrscb	wrkstrscw
1	1	0	-1.50	0	0	1	4.46	3	.010	-.133	.143
1	1	1	-1.36	0	0	1	4.88	3	.010	-.133	.143
1	1	2	-1.21	0	0	1	4.58	3	.010	-.133	.143
1	1	3	-1.07	0	0	1	4.49	1	-1.990	-.133	-1.857
1	1	4	-.93	0	0	1	5.04	3	.010	-.133	.143
1	1	5	-.79	0	0	1	4.87	3	.010	-.133	.143
1	1	6	-.64	0	0	1	5.63	2	-.990	-.133	.857
.	.	.	.	.	.	.	.	.	.	.	.
1	2	0	-1.50	1	1	0	3.03	3	.010	-.324	.333
1	2	1	-1.36	1	1	0	4.62	3	.010	-.324	.333
1	2	2	-1.21	1	1	0	2.85	3	.010	-.324	.333
1	2	3	-1.07	1	1	0	6.40	4	1.010	-.324	1.333
1	2	4	-.93	1	1	0	2.54	1	-1.990	-.324	-1.667
1	2	5	-.79	1	1	0	5.16	2	-.990	-.324	-.667
1	2	6	-.64	1	1	0	2.70	3	.010	-.324	.333
.	.	.	.	.	.	.	.	.	.	.	.

FIGURE 8.3. Structure of the dyadic dataset (first 7 days for one couple).

indicator variable that is 1 for female data rows and 0 for male data rows. The variables *female* and *male* are indicator variables where *male* is 0 for the female rows of data and 1 for the male rows of data and *female* is 0 for male rows of data and 1 for female rows of data.

The outcome variable for this analysis is a measure of relationship dissatisfaction, *reldis*, that has been scaled to range from 0 to 10. The first seven rows of data for each couple show the male *reldis* scores, and the second seven rows represent the female *reldis* scores. The substantive predictor of interest is *wrkstrs*, which is a count variable, ranging from 0 to 7, representing the number of stressors that took place at work. Again, the first seven rows of data show the male *wrkstrs* scores and the second seven the female scores.

Figure 8.4 is a panel plot of the time course of daily relationship dissatisfaction for 25 of the 100 couples in the dataset (every fourth couple). Within each couple's panel, the time course for males is shown in gray and the time course for females is shown in black. (This plot was made using SAS SGPANEL, and this code as well as a similar code for constructing this plot in IBM SPSS is provided on the website for this book.) Like intimacy in the time course study described in Chapter 4, we can see substantial variability from one time point to the next for each partner in a couple, but unlike the earlier study, there are no overall monotonic increases or decreases with time. Although there are mean-level differences in relationship dissatisfaction between dyad members in some couples, there is also a lot of variability in the size and direction of these differences across couples.

Data Transformation of Independent Variables Prior to Modeling

Before specifying the precise statistical model, we need to discuss two data transformations: (1) the overall centering of the predictors and (2) their separation into components reflecting within and between male partners variation, and within and between female partners variation. First, the overall centering: *wrkstrsc*, shown in column 10 of Figure 8.3, is a grand-mean centered version of *wrkstrs* that was created by subtracting the mean level of *wrkstrs* across all partners and time points (i.e., across all 4,200 observations) from

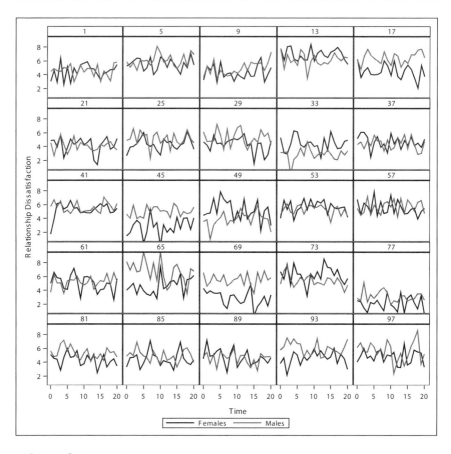

FIGURE 8.4. Panel plots of the 21-day time course of evening relationship dissatisfaction for male and female partners in 25 dyads.

the individual daily scores for all male and female partners (the actual mean level was 3.0 stressors). Thus a value of zero on *wrkstrsc* indicates a day that is typical in terms of work stress across male and female partners across all diary days. The other level-1 predictor, *time7c* (shown in column 4 of Figure 8.3), is centered so that zero is midway through the 10th diary day (the temporal center of the diary period), and it is scaled such that one unit represents the passage of 1 week. Thus the range of *time7c* is from –1.5 to +1.5.

Second, the separation of variation by levels of analysis: The key to this next step is to center *wrkstrsc* (the putative causal *X* variable) person by person, not dyad by dyad, and to stack the resulting between-person means into a *wrkstrscb* column and the within-person deviations into a *wrkstrscw* column. Thus, the reader will see that in Figure 8.3 *wrkstrscb* has a constant value of −.133 for the seven data lines for the male partner (*personid* 1 in *coupleid* 1) but a different constant value of −.324 for the seven data lines for the female partner (*personid* 2 in *coupleid* 1). The *wrkstrscw* column is simply the deviation of each person's *wrkstrsc* score at a particular time point from their own person-mean score. Therefore, the first seven lines of *wrkstrscw* contain these deviations for the male partner and the second seven for the female partner. Although the logic of this stacking and centering may currently be unclear to readers, it will become more apparent (we hope) in the next section where we describe the formal statistical model to be used in the data analysis.

Modeling of Within-Dyad Processes

In the following multilevel analysis, we want to know, separately for male and female partners, whether the number of work stressors on a particular day predicts greater relationship dissatisfaction that day and whether there are between-couples differences in these effects. We have already shown in Figure 8.3 how the putative causal variable at the daily level, *wrkstrscw*, is in a stacked form where the first 21 observations are for each male partner in each dyad and the second 21 observations are for each female partner in each dyad. Given that there are 100 dyads, this means that there are 4,200 data lines. *reldis* is a similarly stacked variable containing 21 observations for male partners and a further 21 observations for female partners. We continue with the approach used in Chapters 4 and 5 where we first show the model at level 1 (in this case, within male partners, within female partners) and level 2 (between male partners, between female partners). Equations 8.1 and 8.2 are the paired level-1 equations for the male and female partners in each dyad:

$$Y M_{ij} = \beta_{0jM} + \beta_{1jM}(\check{X}M_{ij} - \check{X}M_{.j}) + \beta_{2jM}\check{T}_{ij} + \varepsilon M_{ij} \tag{8.1}$$

$$Y F_{ij} = \beta_{0jF} + \beta_{1jF}(\check{X}F_{ij} - \check{X}F_{.j}) + \beta_{2jF}\check{T}_{ij} + \varepsilon F_{ij} \tag{8.2}$$

Equation 8.1 can be thought of as describing data from the first 21 observations within a dyad; 8.2 is the equivalent for the remaining 21 observations. Thus Equation 8.1 specifies that the relationship dissatisfaction of the male partner at time i in dyad j, $Y M_{ij}$, is a function of a male intercept specific to dyad j, β_{0jM}; a male slope specific to dyad j representing the effect of within-subject variation in work stress, β_{1jM}; a male slope representing the passage of time, β_{2jM}; and a residual specific to time i for dyad j, εM_{ij}. Equation 8.2 specifies that the relationship dissatisfaction of the female partner at time i in dyad j, $Y F_{ij}$, is a function of a female intercept specific to dyad j, β_{0jF}; a female slope specific to dyad j representing within-subject variation in work stress, β_{1jF}; a female slope representing the passage of time, β_{2jF}; and a residual specific to time i for dyad j, εF_{ij}.

Central to our modeling approach is Equation 8.3, which describes the structure of nonindependence of the level-1 residuals in each dyad. On the left-hand side of the equation is a column vector with 42 rows, of which the first 21 represent the male residuals in a given dyad, and the second 21 represent the female residuals in that dyad. The $Cov[.]$ operator calculates a 42×42 covariance matrix of the level-1 residuals. If all of the residuals were linearly independent of one another, there would be variances along the main diagonal of the covariance matrix and zeroes everywhere else. In fact, the right-hand side of Equation 8.3 specifies that there can be dependency between residuals. One source of dependency is shown by the elements σ_{MF} and σ_{FM} in the small 2×2 covariance matrix: namely, that male and female residuals within any given day can be correlated. The second source of dependency is shown by the 21×21 covariance matrix that represents a first-order autoregressive process linking the residuals within the male partner and within the female partner. In other words, these component matrices of the large 42×42 covariance matrix capture within-dyad (i.e., male–female) dependence within a given day (e.g., due to common experiences that day that are not captured by the predictor variables), and within-partner dependence between days (e.g., due to experiences specific to male or female partners that are not captured by the predictor variables). Bolger and Shrout (2007) provide a more detailed discussion of these two distinct sources of nonindependence.

$$
Cov\left(\begin{bmatrix} \begin{bmatrix} \varepsilon M_1 \\ \varepsilon M_2 \\ \vdots \\ \varepsilon M_{21} \\ \varepsilon F_1 \\ \varepsilon F_2 \\ \vdots \\ \varepsilon F_{21} \end{bmatrix}_{42\times1} \end{bmatrix}\right) = \begin{bmatrix} \sigma_M^2 & \sigma_{MF} \\ \sigma_{FM} & \sigma_F^2 \end{bmatrix}_{2\times2} \otimes \begin{bmatrix} 1 & \rho & \rho^2 & \cdots & \rho^{20} & \rho^{21} \\ \rho & 1 & \rho & \ddots & & \rho^{20} \\ \rho^2 & \rho & 1 & \ddots & \ddots & \vdots \\ \vdots & \ddots & \ddots & \ddots & \rho & \rho^2 \\ \rho^{20} & & \ddots & \rho & 1 & \rho \\ \rho^{21} & \rho^{20} & \cdots & \rho^2 & \rho & 1 \end{bmatrix}_{21\times21} \tag{8.3}
$$

Equations 8.4 through 8.9 are the level-2 equations that specify between-dyads variations in the coefficients of the level-1 equations. Thus, for example, Equation 8.4 specifies that between-dyads variations in male intercepts are a function of an intercept, an effect of between-dyads differences in male work stress, and a residual component specific to each dyad. Equation 8.5 is the equivalent for females. Equation 8.7 specifies that between-dyads variations in female work stress slopes are a function of an intercept and a residual component specific to each dyad. Equation 8.6 is the equivalent for males. Equation 8.8 specifies that although the level-1 notation allows for between-dyads variation in the time slopes for males, there is in fact no actual variation, merely a constant value. Equation 8.9 is the equivalent for females.

$$\beta_{0jM} = \gamma_{00M} + \gamma_{01M}\check{X}M_{\cdot jM} + u_{0jM} \tag{8.4}$$

$$\beta_{0jF} = \gamma_{00F} + \gamma_{01F}\check{X}F_{\cdot jF} + u_{0jF} \tag{8.5}$$

$$\beta_{1jM} = \gamma_{10M} + u_{1jM} \tag{8.6}$$

$$\beta_{1jF} = \gamma_{10F} + u_{1jF} \tag{8.7}$$

$$\beta_{2jM} = \gamma_{20M} \tag{8.8}$$

$$\beta_{2jF} = \gamma_{20F} \tag{8.9}$$

Another central feature of our modeling approach is that we allow between-dyads differences in level-2 residuals to correlate. In Equation 8.10 U is a column vector that contains the four residual terms just discussed: the residuals for male intercepts, female intercepts, male work stress slopes, and female work stress slopes. τ is a 4×4 covariance matrix of these residual random effects. Of interest are not only the variances along the main diagonal (e.g., how much do dyads differ from one another in terms of male intercepts?), but the covariances elsewhere (e.g., do male intercepts covary with female intercepts, as shown by covariances τ_{00FM}, τ_{00MF}?; do male slopes covary with female slopes, as shown by covariances τ_{11FM}, τ_{11MF}?).

$$U = \begin{bmatrix} u_{0jM} \\ u_{0jF} \\ u_{1jM} \\ u_{1jF} \end{bmatrix}_{4\times 1} \quad Cov(U) = T = \begin{bmatrix} \tau_{00MM} & \tau_{00MF} & \tau_{01MM} & \tau_{01MF} \\ \tau_{00FM} & \tau_{00FF} & \tau_{01FM} & \tau_{01FF} \\ \tau_{10MM} & \tau_{10MF} & \tau_{11MM} & \tau_{11MF} \\ \tau_{10FM} & \tau_{10FF} & \tau_{11FM} & \tau_{11FF} \end{bmatrix}_{4\times 4} \quad (8.10)$$

Finally, Equations 8.11 and 8.12 are the mixed model equations obtained by substituting the relevant level-2 equations into the level-1 equations. Given that by discussing the level-1 and level-2 equations, we have already effectively discussed each of the terms in the mixed model equations, we can now proceed to the software code that enables these equations to be estimated.

$$YM_{ij} = \gamma_{00M} + \gamma_{01M}\check{X}M_{\cdot j} + \gamma_{10M}(\check{X}M_{ij} - \check{X}M_{\cdot j}) + \gamma_{20M}\check{T}_{ij} \quad (8.11)$$

$$+ u_{0jM} + u_{1jM}(\check{X}M_{ij} - \check{X}M_{\cdot j}) + \varepsilon M_{ij}$$

$$YF_{ij} = \gamma_{00F} + \gamma_{01F}\check{X}F_{\cdot j} + \gamma_{10F}(\check{X}F_{ij} - \check{X}F_{\cdot j}) + \gamma_{20F}\check{T}_{ij} \quad (8.12)$$

$$+ u_{0jF} + u_{1jF}(\check{X}F_{ij} - \check{X}F_{\cdot j}) + \varepsilon F_{ij}$$

SAS and SPSS Software

The following PROC MIXED code allowed us to estimate the model:

```
PROC MIXED DATA=ild.dyads COVTEST METHOD=reml CL;
CLASS coupleid gender time;
```

```
MODEL reldis=male female male*time7c female*time7c
   male*wrkstrscw

female*wrkstrscw male*wrkstrscb
   female*wrkstrscb/NOINT S CL

DDF=98,98,99,99,99,99,98,98;

RANDOM male female male*wrkstrscw female*wrkstrscw /
   SUBJECT=coupleid

TYPE=un S G GCORR;

REPEATED gender time /SUBJECT=coupleid TYPE=un@ar(1);
```

Although the statistical model above has parallel level-1 equations (and mixed model equations) for male and female partners, the MODEL statement in the above code has only a single equation. To understand how, nonetheless, distinct male and female equations are estimated, it is important to see that each of the substantive variables, *wrkstrscw*, *wrkstrscb*, and *time7c*, appears in interaction terms with the dummy variables *male* and *female*. The function of these dummy variables is to select certain portions of the data matrix. For example, *male* selects the male rows only, thereby allowing a submodel with male-specific intercepts and slopes; similarly *female* selects the female rows only, allowing for a female-specific submodel. The reader may be surprised that both male and female dummies can be included in the same regression equation. This is indeed a nonstandard use of dummy codes, and for the approach to work, the overall regression intercept needs to be removed (by including the NOINT option on the MODEL statement).

The complex level-1 error covariance structure shown in Equation 8.10 is specified on the REPEATED statement, and in particular by the TYPE=un@ar(1) option. The UN part specifies the 2×2 covariance matrix of male and female variances and covariances in Equation 8.10. The AR(1) part specifies a first-order autoregressive structure for the 21×21 within-partner error covariance matrix shown in Equation 8.3.

The IBM SPSS MIXED code for estimating this model is

```
MIXED reldis WITH male female time7c wrkstrscw
   wrkstrscb

/FIXED=female male male*time7c female*time7c
   male*wrkstrscw
```

```
female*wrkstrscw male*wrkstrscb female*wrkstrscb |
    NOINT SSTYPE(3)

/METHOD=REML

/PRINT= G TESTCOV SOLUTION

/RANDOM=female male male*wrkstrscw female*wrkstrscw
    | SUBJECT(coupleid)

COVTYPE(UN)

/REPEATED=time | SUBJECT(coupleid*gender)
    COVTYPE(ar1).
```

The SPSS code is very similar to SAS, with one exception. It is not possible to allow for contemporaneous within-dyad error correlations (the UN part of the UN@AR(1) option in SAS). It is, however, possible to allow for the AR(1) part using the COVTYPE(ar1) on the REPEATED statement.

Results

Before we turn to the numerical results, we first examine Figure 8.5, which shows the raw data with *reldis* on the Y-axis and *wrkstrs* on the X-axis as well as the fitted regression lines from the multilevel model. Broadly speaking, one can see that as work stressors increase, relationship dissatisfaction increases. We can see that this trend is evident for both male and female partners, and we can also see that there is considerable between-dyad heterogeneity in these relationships. Figure 8.6 shows a spaghetti plot of the same results. The figure highlights the large differences in intercepts and the noticeable but relatively smaller differences in slopes.

Table 8.1 presents excerpts of the output from SAS PROC MIXED, the available software that best took account of dyadic interdependence. One of the processes of substantive interest is the extent to which work stressors can spill over to affect one's close relationships at home. Thus we were interested in the link between number of stressors that occur at work on a given day and end-of-the-day relationship dissatisfaction. To consider this link for typical male and typical female partners, we examine the fixed effects in Table 8.1. Controlling for any systematic linear change over time, work significantly predicted levels of relationship dissatisfaction

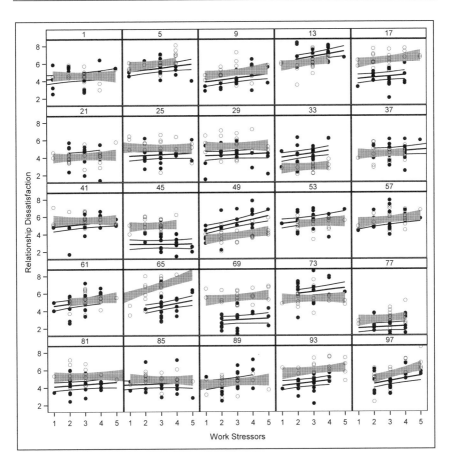

FIGURE 8.5. Evening relationship dissatisfaction as a function of work stressors: Panel plots of raw data and model-predicted regression lines for male and female partners in 25 of 100 dyads. Data points for males are white (unfilled) circles; 95% confidence bounds for regression lines for males are indicated by gray bands; data points for females are black (filled) circles; 95% confidence bounds for females are indicated by upper and lower thin lines surrounding the fitted lines.

later that evening for both husbands and wives: $\hat{\gamma}_{10M} = 0.1091$, $SE = 0.026$, $t(99) = 4.27$, $p < .0001$, and $\hat{\gamma}_{10F} = 0.1599$, $SE = 0.025$, $t(99) = 6.37$, $p < .0001$, respectively. Thus, for every one unit increase in work stressors during the workday above one's average, there is a corresponding 0.11 and 0.16 unit increase in relationship dissatisfaction later in the evening for males and females, respectively. The

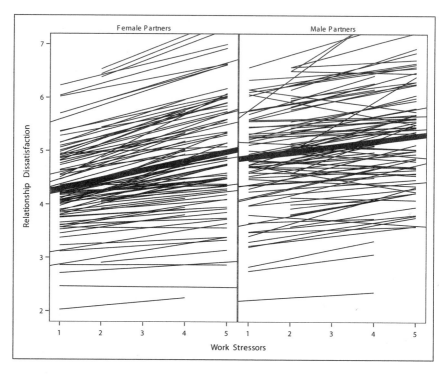

FIGURE 8.6. Model-based predictions of evening relationship dissatisfaction as a function of work stressors: Spaghetti plot of average (thick) and subject-specific (thin) regression lines for female (left) and male (right) partners in 100 dyads. (This figure has been duplicated as Figure 1 of the example write-up.)

results of our model clearly indicate a work stress–family life spill-over effect.

Although there is an average effect of work stressors predicting greater relationship dissatisfaction, we might also expect that male and female partners across dyads will vary from each other in the degree to which work stress spills over. To evaluate the existence of these between-dyads random effects, we examine the variance terms for the *male * wrkstrscw* and *female * wrkstrscw* slopes. In the bottom panel of Table 8.1, with the header Random Effects, we find that the male partner random effect ($\hat{\tau}_{11MM}$) was 0.02833, SE = 0.009138, p = .001, and the female partner random effect ($\hat{\tau}_{11FF}$) was 0.01551, SE = 0.008659, p = .035. Thus there is evidence of significant variability. We discuss other important results in the next section of the chapter.

TABLE 8.1. Excerpted SAS Output for the Multilevel Model for Distinguishable Dyads

Fixed Effects							
Effect	Estimate	SE	DF	t Value	Pr > |t|	Lower	Upper
male	5.0857 ($\hat{\gamma}_{00M}$)	0.1038	98	48.98	<.0001	4.8796	5.2917
female	4.6475 ($\hat{\gamma}_{00F}$)	0.09893	98	46.98	<.0001	4.4512	4.8438
male*wrkstrscb	−0.1432 ($\hat{\gamma}_{01M}$)	0.4389	98	−0.33	0.7450	−1.0141	0.7278
female*wrkstrscb	0.6206 ($\hat{\gamma}_{01F}$)	0.4280	98	1.45	0.1502	−0.2287	1.4700
male*wrkstrscw	0.1091 ($\hat{\gamma}_{10M}$)	0.02553	99	4.27	<.0001	0.05847	0.1598
female*wrkstrscw	0.1599 ($\hat{\gamma}_{10F}$)	0.02511	99	6.37	<.0001	0.1101	0.2098
male*time7c	0.01150 ($\hat{\gamma}_{21M}$)	0.02243	99	0.51	0.6092	−0.03300	0.05600
female*time7c	−0.02483 ($\hat{\gamma}_{21F}$)	0.02553	99	−0.97	0.3330	−0.07548	0.02581

Random Effects						
Cov Parm	Estimate	SE	Z Value	Pr Z	Lower	Upper
UN(1,1)	1.0313 ($\hat{\tau}_{00MM}$)	0.1526	6.76	<.0001	0.7871	1.4103
UN(2,1)	0.2566 ($\hat{\tau}_{00FM}$)	0.1072	2.39	0.0167	0.04655	0.4667
UN(2,2)	0.9208 ($\hat{\tau}_{00FF}$)	0.1384	6.66	<.0001	0.7001	1.2659
UN(3,1)	0.03050 ($\hat{\tau}_{10MM}$)	0.02676	1.14	0.2543	−0.02194	0.08294
UN(3,2)	−0.00294 ($\hat{\tau}_{10MF}$)	0.02594	−0.11	0.9098	−0.05378	0.04790
UN(3,3)	0.02833 ($\hat{\tau}_{11MM}$)	0.009138	3.10	0.0010	0.01643	0.06012
UN(4,1)	0.000965 ($\hat{\tau}_{10FM}$)	0.02719	0.04	0.9717	−0.05233	0.05426
UN(4,2)	0.05767 ($\hat{\tau}_{10FF}$)	0.02569	2.25	0.0248	0.007322	0.1080
UN(4,3)	0.01056 ($\hat{\tau}_{11FM}$)	0.006711	1.57	0.1156	−0.00259	0.02371
UN(4,4)	0.01551 ($\hat{\tau}_{11FF}$)	0.008659	1.79	0.0367	0.006586	0.07006
gender UN(1,1)	0.7612 ($\hat{\sigma}_{M}^{2}$)	0.02471	30.81	<.0001	0.7150	0.8121
UN(2,1)	0.06392 ($\hat{\sigma}_{MF}$)	0.01988	3.21	0.0013	0.02494	0.1029
UN(2,2)	0.9974 ($\hat{\sigma}_{F}^{2}$)	0.03237	30.81	<.0001	0.9369	1.0640
time AR(1)	0.01016 ($\hat{\rho}$)	0.01689	0.60	0.5477	−0.02295	0.04326

8.4 EXAMPLE WRITE-UP OF DYADIC PROCESS STUDY DATA

As in earlier chapters, we have presented more results than can—
or need be—included in a typical journal article. Which results,
then, are crucial to report? For models of dyad intensive longitudinal data, we recommend no equations, one table, and two
graphs. The table should be a combination of the fixed and random effects tables from the final SPSS MIXED\SAS PROC MIXED
runs presented above. The first graph should be the spaghetti plot
shown in Figure 8.6, which depicts the variability across male and
female intercepts and slopes. The second graph, shown in Figure
8.7, depicts the random effects showing the correlation of male and
female intercepts and slopes.

The Write-Up

As in Chapters 4 and 5, we begin the write-up with a statement of
the hypothesis to be tested, as it might appear at the end of an Introduction section of an APA-style empirical paper.

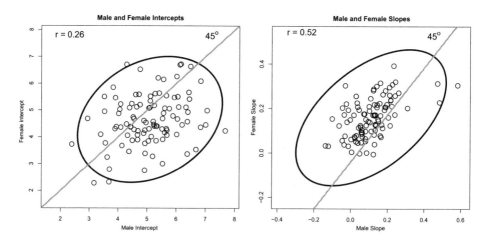

FIGURE 8.7. Dyad-level interdependence of male and female partners: Ninety-
five percent confidence ellipses for bivariate normal distribution of male and
female intercepts (left) and slopes (right). Small circles are empirical Bayes predictions from the dyadic longitudinal model. (This figure has been duplicated as
Figure 2 of the example write-up.)

In summary, the major hypothesis to be tested is whether the number of daily stressors at work predicts degree of end-of-the-day relationship dissatisfaction for both husbands and wives.

METHOD

Design

Couples were recruited using advertisements in local newspapers. Each partner completed an initial set of background questionnaires and then completed two online daily diaries for each of 21 consecutive days. The first diary was completed within an hour of the end of the workday and assessed experiences in the workplace, including the number of work stressors experienced that day. The second diary was completed later that day, within an hour of going to bed, and assessed feelings of dissatisfaction and tension in the relationship with the partner.

Sample

The sample consisted of male and female partners from 100 dual-career married or cohabiting heterosexual couples from a metropolitan city who volunteered to participate in a study of "work and family experiences." Male partners were, on average, 30.9 years old (SD = 5.1) and female partners were, on average, 29.4 years old (SD = 4.7). Sample composition: 54.2% were European American, 28.3% were Hispanic American, 9% were African American, 5.4% were listed in other categories (e.g., Caribbean descent), and 2.1% were Asian American and Pacific Islanders. Couples were cohabiting for an average of 5.2 years (SD = 4.4). The median number of children in the home was two.

Measures

Relationship dissatisfaction. Feelings of dissatisfaction and tension in the relationship were measured at the end of each day using five of the highest loading items from a well-established measure of marital tension (Kurdek, 1994). Raw scores for each item were combined to form a composite and rescaled to a 0–10 scale, such that 0 was the lowest possible score (no tension) and 10 was the highest possible score (extreme tension). Summary statistics for dissatisfaction averaged over persons and time were $M = 5.08$, $SD = 1.35$, range = 0–10 for male partners, and $M = 4.64$, $SD = 1.40$, range = 0–10 for female partners.

Work stressors. Participants were asked the following as part of the end-of-workday diary: "Take a moment to think about the stressful events that you experienced at work today. Please check all on the following list that apply." Examples included "transportation problem," "demand from coworker," "demand from supervisor," and "missed a deadline." Summary statistics for number of work stressors aggregated over persons and time were $M = 3.01$, $SD = 1.03$, and range = 0–7 for male partners, and $M = 2.97$, $SD = 1.03$, range = 0–6 for female partners.

RESULTS

Data Structure and Preliminary Analyses

The analysis dataset consisted of 100 (couples) × 2 (persons) × 21 (days) = 4,200 observations. Scatterplots of the daily relationship dissatisfaction and work stressors did not reveal any outliers, and there were no visually apparent time trends. Scatterplots for each partner within each couple are available upon request from the authors.

Statistical Model

Before presenting the central aspects of the model, it is useful to first note any scaling of variables that affects interpretation of results. A crucial feature of our analyses is that we created within- and between-subjects versions of the work stressors variable, separately for male and female partners. Although there were no obvious time trends in the data, elapsed time in days was also included as a control. Its original scale was 0 to 20, but to aid interpretation of the intercept in the model, it was centered on the middle of the time span, that is, day 10.5, and then divided by 7 so that one unit on the time variable corresponded to a week.

We analyzed these data using a multilevel model for dyadic diary data that treats the three levels of distinguishable dyadic diary data (days nested within persons nested within couples) as two levels of random variation. The lower level represents variability due to within-person repeated measures for male partners and female partners, and the upper level represents between-couples variability across male partners and across female partners (see Laurenceau & Bolger, 2005, and Raudenbush et al., 1995, for more details).

In this model, we specified a within-couple process of reactivity in end-of-the-day relationship dissatisfaction to daily work stressors that was hypothesized to be significant, on average, for both male and female partners. Figure 1 shows thin fitted regression lines for male partners and female partners together with thick fitted lines for the average male and female partner. Visual inspection of the thick lines suggests that our prediction was borne out: The slope of the lines representing the link between number of work stressors and end-of-the-day relationship dissatisfaction are positive for both male and female partners.

For a statistical test of the hypothesis, we refer to the upper panel of

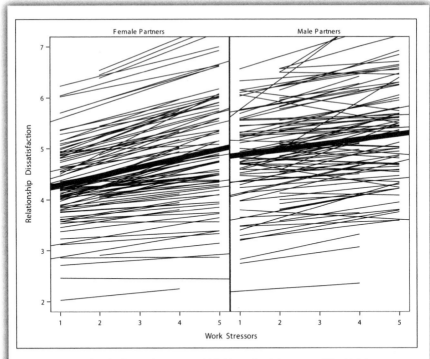

Figure 1. Spaghetti plots of average (thick) and subject-specific (thin) regression lines for evening relationship dissatisfaction as a function of work stressors for female (left) and male (right) partners.

Table 1, which shows the fixed or average effects for the model. On days with a typical number of work stressors, on average, male and female partners reported relationship dissatisfaction levels of approximately 5.1 and 4.6 units, respectively; that is, at the middle of the 0–10 scale. For every one additional work stressor experienced, female partners were, on average, 0.11 units higher in relationship dissatisfaction (CI_{95} = 0.06, 0.16; all subsequent CIs are 95%); male partners were, on average, 0.16 units higher on relationship dissatisfaction (CI = 0.11, 0.21).

The lower panel of Table 1 presents random effects, that is, estimates of between-couples variability around the average or fixed effects. Random effects are reported as within- and between-couples

Table 1. Parameter Estimates for Dyadic Multilevel Model of Evening Relationship Dissatisfaction as a Function of Number of Work Stressors for Male and Female Dyad Partners

Fixed effects (intercepts, slopes)	Estimate	(SE)	t^a	p^b	CI_{95} Lower	Upper
M_Intercept	5.09	(0.10)	48.98	<.001	4.88	5.29
F_Intercept	4.65	(0.10)	46.98	<.001	4.45	4.84
M_Work stressor Slope	0.11	(0.03)	4.27	<.001	0.06	0.16
F_Work stressor Slope	0.16	(0.03)	6.37	<.001	0.11	0.21
M_Time Slope	0.01	(0.02)	0.51	.61	−0.03	0.06
F_Time Slope	−0.02	(0.03)	−0.97	.33	−0.08	0.03
Mean M_Work Stressor Slope	−0.14	(0.44)	−0.33	.75	−1.01	0.73
Mean F_Work Stressor Slope	0.62	(0.43)	1.45	.15	−0.23	1.47

Random effects ([co-]variances)	Estimate	(SE)	z	p^b	CI_{95}^c Lower	Upper
Level-2 (between-couples)^d						
M_Intercept	1.03	(0.15)	6.76	<.001	0.79	1.41
F_Intercept	0.92	(0.14)	6.66	<.001	0.70	1.27
M_Work Stressor Slope	0.028	(0.009)	3.10	.001	0.02	0.06
F_Work Stressor Slope	0.016	(0.009)	1.79	.04	0.01	0.07
M-F Intercept covariance	0.26	(0.11)	2.39	.02	0.05	0.47
M-F Slope covariance	0.011	(0.007)	1.57	.12	-0.003	0.024
Level-1 (within-couples)						
M_Residual	0.761	(0.025)	30.81	<.001	0.72	0.81
F_Residual	1.00	(0.03)	30.81	<.001	0.94	1.06
M–F Residual covariance	0.064	(0.020)	3.21	.001	0.02	0.10
Autocorrelation	0.010	(0.017)	0.60	.55	-0.02	0.04

Note: N = 100 couples, 21 days. M, male partner; F, female partner.

[a]Degrees of freedom are 98 for tests of intercepts and mean work stressors and 99 for work stressors and time slopes.

[b]All p-values are two-tailed except in the case of variances, where one-tailed p-values are used (because variances are constrained to be non-negative).

[c]Confidence intervals for variances were computed using the Satterthwaite method (see Littell, Milliken, Stroup, Wolfinger, & Schabenberger, 2006).

[d]Covariances among male and female partner intercepts and slopes were estimated but, for the sake of brevity, are not shown.

variances and covariances. The intercept and work stressor slope coefficients show substantial and statistically significant variability across both male and female partners. Expressed in standard deviation units, the variation for work stressor reactivity is $\sqrt{.028} = 0.17$ units and $\sqrt{0.016} = 0.13$, for male and female partners, respectively. To get a better sense of these differences in work stressor reactivity, it is useful to examine $\pm SD$ around the average reactivity coefficients for males and females. In the present sample, approximately 95% of male partners' reactivity coefficients fall between -0.23 and 0.45 (0.11 ± 0.34). For female partners, approximately 95% of their reactivity coefficients fall between -0.10 and 0.42 (0.16 ± 0.26) units.

Also in the lower panel of Table 1 are covariances showing the dyad-level interdependence of male and female partners. These are (i) the covariance between male partner and female partner intercepts and (ii) the covariance between male partner and female partner slopes. Figure 2 represents these as 95% confidence ellipses for their respective bivariate normal distributions. Both covariances are positive, indicating that male partners with above-average relationship dissatisfaction tended to be paired with similarly above-average female partners;

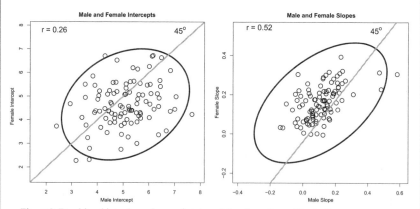

Figure 2. Dyad-level interdependence of male and female partners: Ninety-five percent confidence ellipses for bivariate normal distribution of male and female intercepts (left) and slopes (right). Small circles are empirical Bayes predictions from the dyadic longitudinal model.

and male partners with above-average tendencies to show increases in relationship dissatisfaction following stressful work days tended to be paired with similarly above-average female partners. The parameter labeled M–F residual covariance in Table 1 reflects the within-day association between male and female relationship dissatisfaction residuals on a given day. This association can come about through experiences during the day that both partners may share and lead to unusually high- or low-relationship dissatisfaction in both partners. Finally, we note that there is no evidence of autocorrelation in the level-1 (within-person) residuals.

8.5 CHAPTER SUMMARY

Dyadic relationships play a central role in daily life. In this chapter, we discussed intensive longitudinal studies of dyads, highlighting the opportunities and challenges of modeling dyadic interdependence at multiple levels and focusing on distinguishable dyads (e.g., wife-husband). The data example in this chapter was one where the within-subject processes for each partner within a couple (i.e., linking changes in daily work stressors to changes in dissatisfaction) were analyzed in parallel, allowing for correlated residuals between partners at the within-couple level and correlations between partner random effects at the between-couple level. Although not demonstrated, the model we proposed can also be extended to contain within-couple partner effects (Kenny et al., 2006) by including, for example, the male partner's daily work stressors as an additional cause of the female partner's relationship dissatisfaction.

8.6 RECOMMENDED READINGS

Gable, S. L., Reis, H. T., & Downey, G. (2003). He said, she said: A quasi-signal detection analysis of daily interactions between close relationship partners. *Psychological Science, 14,* 100–105.

The authors use a dyadic longitudinal design to identify partners' congruent and incongruent perceptions of relationship events.

Gonzalez, R., & Griffin, D. (2000). The statistics of interdependence: Treating dyadic data with respect. In W. Ickes & S. W. Duck (Eds.), *The social psychology of personal relationships* (pp. 181–213). Chichester, UK: Wiley.

This chapter presents an excellent discussion of the challenges and opportunities presented when working with dyadic data.

Kenny, D. A., Kashy, D. A., & Cook, W. L. (2006). *Dyadic data analysis.* New York: Guilford Press.

This book is the current bible on dyadic data analysis.

Laurenceau, J.-P., & Bolger, N. (2012). Analyzing diary and intensive longitudinal data from dyads. In M. R. Mehl & T. S. Conner (Eds.), *Handbook of research methods for studying daily life* (pp. 407–422). New York: Guilford Press.

Focusing specifically on Mplus, this chapter provides another data analysis example of the type covered in this chapter.

Appendix to Chapter 8

IBM SPSS

```
MIXED reldis WITH male female time7c wrkstrscw
    wrkstrscb

/FIXED=female male male*time7c female*time7c
    male*wrkstrscw female*wrkstrscw male*wrkstrscb

female*wrkstrscb | NOINT SSTYPE(3)

/METHOD=reml

/PRINT= G  TESTCOV SOLUTION

/RANDOM=female male male*wrkstrscw female*wrkstrscw
    | SUBJECT(coupleid) COVTYPE(UN)

/REPEATED=time | SUBJECT(coupleid*gender)
    COVTYPE(ar1).
```

SAS

```
PROC MIXED DATA=ild.dyads COVTEST METHOD=reml CL;

CLASS coupleid gender time;

MODEL reldis=male female male*time7c female*time7c
    male*wrkstrscw female*wrkstrscw
```

```
    male*wrkstrscb female*wrkstrscb/noint S CL
        DDF=98,98,99,99,99,99,98,98;

    RANDOM male female male*wrkstrscw female*wrkstrscw /
        SUBJECT=coupleid TYPE=un S G GCORR;

    REPEATED gender time /SUBJECT=coupleid TYPE=un@ar(1);
```

Mplus

```
    TITLE:      Dyadic Process Model in Mplus ;

    DATA:       FILE IS dyadsmplus.dat;

    VARIABLE: NAMES ARE coupleid personid time time7c
                freldis fwrkstrs fwrkstrsc fwrkstrscb
                fwrkstrscw mreldis mwrkstrs mwrkstrsc
                mwrkstrscb mwrkstrscw;

                USEVAR = time7c freldis mreldis fwrkstrscw
                mwrkstrscw mwrkstrscb fwrkstrscb;

                BETWEEN = mwrkstrscb fwrkstrscb;

                WITHIN =  time7c mwrkstrscw fwrkstrscw;

                CLUSTER = coupleid;

    ANALYSIS: TYPE = TWOLEVEL RANDOM; ESTIMATOR=ml;

    MODEL:      %WITHIN%

                cf | freldis ON fwrkstrscw;

                cm | mreldis ON mwrkstrscw;

                freldis mreldis ON time7c;

                freldis WITH mreldis;

                %BETWEEN%

                freldis ON fwrkstrscb;
```

```
          mreldis ON mwrkstrscb;

          freldis WITH cf cm;

          mreldis WITH cf cm;

          freldis WITH mreldis (covint);

          cf WITH cm (covslp);

          freldis (freldis);

          mreldis (mreldis);

          cf (cf);

          cm (cm);

       MODEL CONSTRAINT:

          NEW rint; rint = covint/sqrt(freldis *
          mreldis);

          NEW rslp; rslp = covslp/sqrt(cf * cm);

OUTPUT:   cinterval;
```

9

Within-Subject Mediation Analysis

Statistical mediation analysis has been used extensively in the social sciences over the past 30 years because it allows researchers to find evidence of a causal chain linking an initial variable X to an intervening or mediating variable M and thereby to an outcome variable Y. Between-subjects mediation analyses form the vast majority of examples in the literature (Cole & Maxwell, 2003; MacKinnon, 2008). In this chapter, we consider a type of mediation—mediation at the within-subject level—that is uncommon but one for which intensive longitudinal data are especially suited. Because in intensive longitudinal studies each subject can provide many assessments of putative causes, mediators, and outcomes, one can allow each subject to have his or her own specific mediation process. By summarizing these processes one can describe mediation for the average subject as well as between-subjects heterogeneity around that average. In this chapter we illustrate these ideas by further analyses of the example dataset on work–home stress spillover from Chapter 8.

9.1 SINGLE-LEVEL MEDIATION TO MULTILEVEL MEDIATION

A more general introduction to statistical mediation is necessary before we proceed. It is common in behavioral and social science research to posit both the existence of a causal relationship and a mediating process that explains the relationship. Let us assume that we have a theoretical model specifying that an X-to-Y relationship can be explained by a mediating variable, M, as represented in Figure 9.1. As shown, mediation is a two-step process: X is a cause of Y because X causes M, and M, in turn, causes Y.

There is a variety of research strategies that can be used to assess mediation (e.g., see Cook & Groom, 2004), but for simplicity we describe two major ones. The first involves investigating the two-step theoretical model in two separate experiments. In one experiment, X is manipulated and its effect on M is assessed; in the second, M is manipulated and its effect on Y is assessed. If both effects are confirmed, they can be combined to infer an indirect effect through M (Spencer, Zanna, & Fong, 2005). This approach has much in its favor, especially the fact that both X and M are manipulated variables. The principal drawback is that it cannot be used if either X or M cannot be manipulated experimentally.

The second research strategy investigates mediation in a single

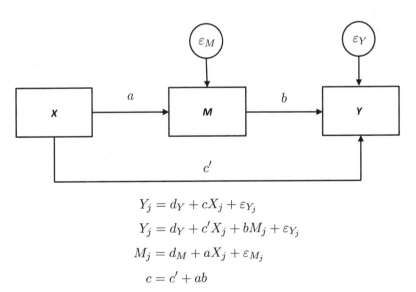

$$Y_j = d_Y + cX_j + \varepsilon_{Y_j}$$

$$Y_j = d_Y + c'X_j + bM_j + \varepsilon_{Y_j}$$

$$M_j = d_M + aX_j + \varepsilon_{M_j}$$

$$c = c' + ab$$

FIGURE 9.1. Between-subjects mediation: Diagram and structural equations. Subscripts j indicate that the measures vary between subjects only. The final equation shows the key identity underlying statistical mediation, that the total effect c from the X-to-Y equation is equal to an X-to-M effect, a, multiplied by an M-to-Y effect, b, plus a residual effect, c'.

study. X can be either a manipulated or a measured variable, but M and Y are always measured (nonmanipulated) variables. Mediation is assessed through a form of structural equation modeling. By far the most highly cited source for this approach is Baron and Kenny (1986), who specified a sequence of steps for assessing the presence of mediation, and they popularized the Sobel test, a statistical test for this purpose (Sobel, 1982, 1986). In recent years, more statistically powerful alternatives to the Sobel test have been proposed and are beginning to be adopted (MacKinnon, Lockwood, Hoffman, West, & Sheets, 2002; Shrout & Bolger, 2002). It should be noted that the majority of work and examples of mediation in this literature has focused on the designs where X, M, and Y come from cross-sectional data.

Several types of mediation scenarios can exist with multilevel data that come from intensive longitudinal designs. This is because X, M, and Y can vary either within-subjects (level-1), between-subjects (level-2), or both. Krull and MacKinnon (2001) outline three specific multilevel mediation scenarios: $2 \rightarrow 2 \rightarrow 1$, $2 \rightarrow 1 \rightarrow 1$, and $1 \rightarrow 1 \rightarrow 1$. A level-2, between-subjects variable can act as a mediator of the link between another level-2, between-subjects variable and a level-1 outcome (i.e., $2 \rightarrow 2 \rightarrow 1$). A level-1 variable can act as a mediator of the link between a level-2, between-subjects variable and a level-1 outcome (i.e., $2 \rightarrow 1 \rightarrow 1$). Finally, a level-1 variable can act as a mediator of the link between a level-1 variable and another level-1 outcome (i.e., $1 \rightarrow 1 \rightarrow 1$). The first two multilevel mediation scenarios, $2 \rightarrow 2 \rightarrow 1$ and $2 \rightarrow 1 \rightarrow 1$, are more straightforward to estimate and interpret than the third, and the corresponding formulae for doing this are detailed in Krull and MacKinnon (2001).

With intensive longitudinal data, we describe a more complex version of mediation, where the X to M to Y pathway is assessed within-subjects (i.e., $1 \rightarrow 1 \rightarrow 1$). As we know from earlier chapters, intensive longitudinal data allow us to examine within-subject psychological and interpersonal processes and between-subjects heterogeneity in these processes. Thus, the paths from X to M and from M to Y in Figure 9.1 can vary across subjects; this would be indicated by subscripts j on the a, b, and c' coefficients. Because the within-subject level is the lower level in a multilevel model, within-subject mediation is sometimes also called lower-level mediation or $1 \rightarrow 1 \rightarrow 1$ mediation (Bauer, Preacher, & Gil, 2006; Kenny,

Korchmaros, & Bolger, 2003; Krull & MacKinnon, 2001). Within-subject mediation, by allowing between-subjects heterogeneity in mediated paths, affords a realistic conceptualization of psychological and interpersonal processes, but as we will see, it also involves some conceptual and analytic complexities.

9.2 EMPIRICAL EXAMPLE

In the dyads chapter (Chapter 8), we examined the extent to which work stressors on a given day (assessed at the end of the workday) predicted increased relationship dissatisfaction later that day. In this chapter, we examine the extent to which work dissatisfaction (again assessed at the end of the workday) can explain this relationship. For the sake of simplicity, we use data from female partners only.

We already saw in Chapter 8 that for female partners, work stressors on a given day robustly predicted greater relationship tension at the end of the day. Figures 8.4 and 8.5 showed raw data and individual fitted regression lines, and Table 8.1 showed the fixed and random effects that underlie the fitted lines. The fixed effect coefficient for the average female partner was 0.16 relationship distress units for each additional work stressor. The associated random effect was 0.016 variance units, which was 0.13 standard deviation units.

We now turn to the question of whether this relationship can be explained by the female partner's work dissatisfaction measured at the end of the workday, which we presume persists to some degree after the workday is over and can affect the relationship with the partner at home. A full account of this would involve showing individual scatterplots of the X-to-M and the M-to-Y relationship for each couple, but for brevity's sake we omit these. Interested readers are encouraged to create their own scatterplots of the data using the commands shown in previous chapters.

Figure 9.2 depicts a version of a within-subjects path diagram corresponding to our empirical example. Beneath the path diagram are multilevel equations for the mediation model. The equations use the same general notation used in Figure 9.1, such that work stressors are labeled X, work dissatisfaction is labeled M, and relationship dissatisfaction is labeled Y.

These equations need special attention, as they differ in important

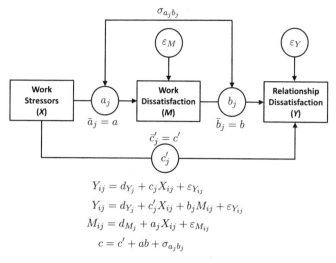

$$Y_{ij} = d_{Y_j} + c_j X_{ij} + \varepsilon_{Y_{ij}}$$
$$Y_{ij} = d_{Y_j} + c'_j X_{ij} + b_j M_{ij} + \varepsilon_{Y_{ij}}$$
$$M_{ij} = d_{M_j} + a_j X_{ij} + \varepsilon_{M_{ij}}$$
$$c = c' + ab + \sigma_{a_j b_j}$$

FIGURE 9.2. Within-subjects mediation: Diagram and structural equations. To reduce clutter, we have omitted time as a predictor and we treat X, M, and Y as varying within-subjects only. These are the essential features of an actual within-subjects mediation analysis (see section 9.3).

ways from conventional meditation equations of the sort discussed in standard sources (e.g., Baron & Kenny, 1986; Kenny et al., 1998; MacKinnon, 2008). One obvious difference is that the regression coefficients in the first two equations have subscripts j, such that each subject in the population has a potentially distinct mediation model linking X to M to Y. It is the final equation, however, that is the most unusual. Here we see that c, the relationship between X and Y for the typical subject, is equal to the sum of (1) ab, the product of the X-to-M and the M-to-Y coefficients for the typical subject; (2) c', the coefficient representing the unmediated portion of the X-to-Y relationship for the typical subject; and (3) $\sigma_{a_j b_j}$, the covariance of between-subjects differences in the X-to-M and M-to-Y relationships.

The need to include this final covariance term was shown in a paper by Kenny et al. (2003), and it can have important implications for estimates of mediated effects. To the extent that those female partners whose work dissatisfaction is most affected by work stressors are the same women whose relationship dissatisfaction is most affected by their work dissatisfaction, then the overall mediated effect will be greater than one would expect from the ab product alone. More will be said about this important point later in the chapter.

9.3 IMPLEMENTING WITHIN-SUBJECT MEDIATION IN STATISTICAL SOFTWARE

Currently there were two main ways to implement a multilevel mediation analysis using commercial statistical software. The first involves using conventional multilevel software in a clever but somewhat convoluted way, as detailed in Bauer et al. (2006). The complexity is because an appropriate test of within-subject mediation involves estimating two multilevel regression equations simultaneously: an X-to-M equation and an M-to-Y equation. A data restructuring trick is needed to get conventional multilevel software to do this, which we briefly detail below. The Bauer paper uses SAS software, but the same approach has been implemented in HLM (see Bauer's website: *www.unc.edu/~dbauer/manuscripts/HLMinstructions.pdf*) as well as SPSS MIXED (*www.unc.edu/~dbauer/manuscripts/SPSSinstructions.pdf*).

The second approach is based on a conceptual and technical innovation whereby multilevel random effects are conceptualized as latent variables, and as such, can be treated as part of a more general latent variable modeling framework (Muthén & Asparouhov, 2011). This is how the software package Mplus, that is at its core a structural equation modeling (SEM) program, can be used to conduct multilevel modeling, including assessment of multilevel mediation. We realize that many readers may not be familiar with Mplus for multilevel modeling and that the Mplus syntax we provide later in the chapter may be intimidating and require some practice. Nevertheless, we believe the gain in ease and flexibility can be worth it, particularly for multilevel mediation. It should be noted that both approaches provide the same parameter estimates (within rounding error) for equivalent models.

As we have been doing in the example analyses in earlier chapters of this book, we will continue to isolate and focus on the within-subject links among the variables that have been intensively assessed, but in this case they will be part of a trivariate mediation system. Thus far, we have been doing this by splitting the predictor into two independent pieces: the within-subject deviations and the between-subjects means. When both pieces of the predictor are entered into the model, the coefficient for the subject-mean deviated piece (which reflects within-subject variability only) represents a pure within-subject effect, and the coefficient for the subject-means piece (which reflects between-subjects variability only) represents the corresponding between-subjects effect. However, one of the complexities that comes with examining within-subject mediation is that M is both an outcome and a predictor in the same $X \rightarrow M \rightarrow Y$ model (a situation we have not yet encountered in this book). As a result, when we demonstrate how to do the analyses below, we will be using subject-mean deviated versions of X, M, and Y. Although we will obtain the correct estimate of the within-subject mediated effect, a necessary consequence of using subject-mean deviated variables is that the intercepts for the M and Y equations will equal zero, and the intercept random effect will equal zero (because the variables have been purged of between-subjects variance).

We now describe how to implement a within-subject mediation analysis using a conventional multilevel program, namely SAS PROC MIXED. Following this, we will show the corresponding analysis in Mplus.

Implementation Using SAS

To understand the first approach to within-subject mediation analysis, bear in mind that a mediation analysis involves two multilevel regression equations, one predicting M and the other predicting Y. A correct analysis requires that we estimate both regressions simultaneously, an approach that for single-level models is routine in SEM (e.g., Kline, 2011). However, multilevel models consider only one equation in isolation, and, in standard multilevel software at least, there is no easy way to jointly estimate a two-equation system.

As described in Bauer et al. (2006), the key to doing so is to create a special type of stacked dataset. In Chapter 8 we saw that the analysis of distinguishable dyads required us to stack male partner and female partner data lines and to include dummy variables in our statistical model that identified which data lines pertained to which dyad partner. We then ran what, in effect, were two analyses in parallel, one for the male partner and one for the female partner. In the Bauer et al. approach to multilevel mediation, a similar strategy is required, except in this case we stack the data according to whether the regression equation has M or Y as the dependent variable, and we estimate the two regressions in the same analysis.

Concretely, this involves data restructuring of the kind shown in Figure 9.3. Notice first the simplified dataset on the left representing X, M, and Y for two subjects and 4 time points. This is restructured into the larger dataset such that each subject on each day has two data lines, one for M and one for Y. The SAS code to accomplish this restructuring was originally published in Bauer et al. (2006). As with all analyses in each chapter, the complete SAS code, datasets, and sample output are available on the website for this book. The restructured dataset also contains dummy variables (DY, DM) to identify the data lines for M and Y, and there is another column, labeled $DVCODE$, that contains the same information in text form, using the text m when the data line pertains to M and y when the data line pertains to Y.

Once the data have been restructured (i.e., stacked) in this way, the PROC MIXED code for the analysis is as follows:

id	timec	X fwkstrcw	M fwkdiscw	Y freldiscw
101	-10	0.333333	0.982878	-1.44207
101	-9	0.333333	0.927983	0.144134
101	-8	0.333333	-0.71886	-1.62598
101	-7	1.333333	0.745001	1.921912
102	-10	1.714286	-1.51483	0.249225
102	-9	-0.28571	1.760554	-0.59369
102	-8	0.714286	2.519932	-0.90786
102	-7	0.714286	0.12286	-0.11093

id	timec	X fwkstrcw	M fwkdiscw	M & Y z	DM	DY	DVCODE
101	-10	0.333333	0.982878	0.982878	1	0	m
101	-10	0.333333	0.982878	-1.44207	0	1	y
101	-9	0.333333	0.927983	0.927983	1	0	m
101	-9	0.333333	0.927983	0.144134	0	1	y
101	-8	0.333333	-0.71886	-0.71886	1	0	m
101	-8	0.333333	-0.71886	-1.62598	0	1	y
101	-7	1.333333	0.745001	0.745001	1	0	m
101	-7	1.333333	0.745001	1.921912	0	1	y
102	-10	1.714286	-1.51483	-1.51483	1	0	m
102	-10	1.714286	-1.51483	0.249225	0	1	y
102	-9	-0.28571	1.760554	1.760554	1	0	m
102	-9	-0.28571	1.760554	-0.59369	0	1	y
102	-8	0.714286	2.519932	2.519932	1	0	m
102	-8	0.714286	2.519932	-0.90786	0	1	y
102	-7	0.714286	0.12286	0.12286	1	0	m
102	-7	0.714286	0.12286	-0.11093	0	1	y

FIGURE 9.3. Data restructuring necessary for a within-subjects mediation analysis using multilevel software. On the left is a conventional longitudinal data structure for X, M, and Y for $N = 2$ females and $T = 4$ time points (from the dyads dataset). On the right is a restructured version with stacked data lines for M and Y. Note that X (fwkstrcw), M (fwkdiscw), and Y (freldiscw) have between-subjects means removed.

```
PROC MIXED COVTEST NOCLPRINT CL METHOD=ml;
CLASS DVCODE TIME ID;
MODEL Z = DM*FWKSTRCW DM*TIMEC
          DY*FWKDISCW DY*FWKSTRCW DY*TIMEC /noint
          solution covb cl
ddf= 97 , 97 , 97 , 97 , 97 , 97 , 97 , 97 , 97 , 97;
RANDOM DM*FWKSTRCW DY*FWKDISCW DY*FWKSTRCW/g gcorr
     TYPE=un SUBJECT=id;
REPEATED TIME/TYPE=vc GROUP=DVCODE SUBJECT=ID;
RUN;
```

The syntax will look somewhat familiar to readers who have studied the previous chapter on analysis models for distinguishable dyads. In the MODEL statement, the dummy variables DM and DY serve the same function as the dummy variables MALE and FEMALE did in a dyadic context. Note that we have not estimated the DM and DY intercept effects because they will necessarily be equal to zero due to M and Y being subject-mean deviations. The RANDOM statement estimates between-subjects random effects for the a (DM*FWKSTRCW), b (DY*FWKDISCW), and c' (DY*FWKSTRCW) within-subjects fixed effects. Also analogous to the dyadic analysis is the use of a REPEATED statement, which allows the error variance to differ according to whether the dependent variable is M or Y. The text variable DV is used for this purpose. The output for this analysis is in Table 9.1.

Implementation Using Mplus

The first point to note when using Mplus to do within-subject mediation is that no data restructuring involving stacking is necessary, so long as the data are in the standard univariate setup for multilevel modeling of intensive longitudinal data. The structure of the data is displayed in Figure 9.4. *id* is an identification variable unique to each subject in the dataset; *time* is an index of each of the days 1 to 21; *timec* is an index of the 21 days of assessment centered on the middle time point (11); *freldis* (Y) is the daily relationship dissatisfaction

TABLE 9.1. SAS Within-Subject Mediation Output

Covariance Parameter Estimates

Cov Parm	Subject	Group	Estimate	Standard Error	Z Value	Pr Z	Alpha	Lower	Upper
UN(1,1)	id		0.06645	0.01787	3.72	0.0001	0.05	0.04174	0.1221
UN(2,1)	id		0.03074	0.01040	2.96	0.0031	0.05	0.01036	0.05111
UN(2,2)	id		0.04400	0.01106	3.98	<.0001	0.05	0.02839	0.07723
UN(3,1)	id		0.007773	0.008028	0.97	0.3329	0.05	-0.00796	0.02351
UN(3,2)	id		0.02068	0.006424	3.22	0.0013	0.05	0.008087	0.03327
UN(3,3)	id		0.002049	0.006292	0.33	0.3723	0.05	0.000214	4.519E11
time	id	dv m	1.1866	0.03754	31.61	<.0001	0.05	1.1163	1.2637
time	id	dv y	0.8623	0.02785	30.96	<.0001	0.05	0.8102	0.9196

Fit Statistics

-2 Log Likelihood	12117.6
AIC (smaller is better)	12147.6
AICC (smalleris better)	12147.7
BIC (smaller is better)	12186.7

Solution for Fixed Effects

Effect	Estimate	Standard Error	DF	t Value	Pr > |t|	Alpha	Lower	Upper
dm	2.474E-6	0.02377	97	0.00	0.9999	0.05	-0.04718	0.04718
dm*FWKSTRCW	0.1904	0.03534	97	5.39	<.0001	0.05	0.1202	0.2605
dm*timec	-0.00584	0.003975	97	-1.47	0.1452	0.05	-0.01373	0.002052
dy	-0.00008	0.02026	97	-0.00	0.9970	0.05	-0.04029	0.04014
dy*FWKDISCW	0.1498	0.02799	97	5.35	<.0001	0.05	0.09421	0.2053
FWKSTRCW*dy	0.1053	0.02122	97	4.96	<.0001	0.05	0.06313	0.1474
timec*dy	-0.00239	0.003382	97	-0.71	0.4812	0.05	-0.00910	0.004321

id	time	timec	fwkstrs	fwkdis	freldis	...	fwkstrcw	fwkdiscw	freldiscw
							X_{ij}	M_{ij}	Y_{ij}
101	1	-10	3	5.5901	3.0345		0.333333	0.982878	-1.44207
101	2	-9	3	5.5352	4.6207		0.333333	0.927983	0.144134
101	3	-8	3	3.8884	2.8506		0.333333	-0.71886	-1.62598
101	4	-7	4	5.3522	6.3985		1.333333	0.745001	1.921912
101	5	-6	1	4.4831	2.5441		-1.66667	-0.12417	-1.93249
101	6	-5	2	3.3394	5.1648		-0.66667	-1.26781	0.688196
101	7	-4	3	4.1354	2.705		0.333333	-0.47183	-1.77157
101	8	-3	4	5.8005	5.0038		1.333333	1.193308	0.527276
101	9	-2	3	5.4346	4.0996		0.333333	0.827343	-0.37694
101	10	-1	2	4.8307	5.4713		-0.66667	0.2235	0.994709
101	11	0	2	3.3669	5.7011		-0.66667	-1.24036	1.224594
101	12	1	1	5.0046	5.8851		-1.66667	0.397334	1.408502
101	13	2	3	4.6203	4.8966		0.333333	0.01307	0.419996
101	14	3	4	3.312	4.8582		1.333333	-1.29526	0.381682
101	15	4	0	5.0229	3.9923		-2.66667	0.415632	-0.48422
101	16	5	1	4.8216	3.2414		-1.66667	0.214351	-1.23518
101	17	6	1	4.721	4.2146		-1.66667	0.113711	-0.262
101	18	7	3	4.5929	4.3985		0.333333	-0.01438	-0.07809
101	19	8	4	4.0073	4.7203		1.333333	-0.59992	0.243751
101	20	9	4	4.9222	4.751		1.333333	0.314992	0.274402
101	21	10	5	3.9707	5.4559		2.333333	-0.63652	0.979383
102	1	-10	5	4.3458	4.567		1.714286	-1.51483	0.249225
102	2	-9	3	7.6212	3.7241		-0.28571	1.760554	-0.59369
102	3	-8	4	8.3806	3.41		0.714286	2.519932	-0.90786
102	4	-7	4	5.9835	4.2069		0.714286	0.12286	-0.11093

FIGURE 9.4. Data structure for within-subjects mediation analysis using Mplus. Note X, M, and Y are subject-mean deviated.

score for females; *fwkdis* (M) is the daily work dissatisfaction score for females; and *fwkstrs* (X) is a count of the number of daily stressors that took place at work for females. For ease of focusing on the structure and function of the Mplus syntax, we use X, M, and Y as corresponding variable names.

Below is the Mplus syntax that we use to estimate the within-subject multilevel mediation model for the example data, where capitalized terms refer to Mplus-specific commands and options, and lower-case terms are user-defined variables or options.

```
TITLE: Ch. 9 Within-subject mediation(all between-
    subject deviated variables); (X, M, and Y are
    subject-mean deviated.)

DATA: FILE IS mediate.dat;

VARIABLE: NAMES ARE id time timec fwkstr fwkdis
                    freldis fwkstrc fwkdisc freldisc
                    fwkstrcb fwkdiscb freldiscb
                    fwkstrcw fwkdiscw freldiscw x m y;
        USEVAR = id timec x m y;
        WITHIN = timec x m y;
        CLUSTER = id;

ANALYSIS: TYPE = twolevel random; ESTIMATOR=ml;

MODEL: %WITHIN%
        cp | y ON x;
        a | m ON x;
        b | y ON m;
        y m ON timec;
         [m@0 y@0];
      %BETWEEN%
        cp WITH a b;
        [a] (ma); a (vara); [b] (mb); b (varb);
        [cp] (mcp);
        a WITH b (covab);

MODEL CONSTRAINT:
        NEW med te pme corr;
        med=ma*mb+covab;
        te=ma*mb+covab+mcp;
        pme=(ma*mb+covab)/(ma*mb+covab+mcp);
        corr=covab/sqrt(vara*varb);

OUTPUT: sampstat cinterval;
```

After the TITLE and DATA specifications, the VARIABLE command lists the names of the variables in the dataset that are read in by Mplus. The USEVAR statement lists the variables that are actually used in the analysis. Note that we have taken the variables freldis fwkdis fwkstr and have constructed subject-mean devi-ated versions that are called y, m, and x, respectively, in the data-set. This is the equivalent of doing so-called *group-mean centering* (Raudenbush & Bryk, 2002). The %WITHIN% statement specifies the variables in the analysis that vary only within subject. The group-ing or clustering variable (id) is specified in the CLUSTER state-ment.

The TYPE = twolevel random option on the ANALYSIS com-mand tells Mplus that this is a two-level multilevel model with ran-dom intercepts and slopes. ESTIMATOR=ml allows us to specify full maximum likelihood as the estimation method, just as we did for the SAS analyses. Restricted maximum likelihood (REML) is not available as an estimator in Mplus.

The first three lines of syntax in the MODEL command under the %WITHIN% specification make use of the "|" symbol, which tells Mplus to create random intercepts and slopes for the within-subject regression relationship that follows it. In the first of these lines, cp is a label that is given to the random slope of the regression of y ON x, which is the within-subject c' coefficient. Using the Mplus syntax logic, the random slope effect will be called cp and the ran-dom intercept will be called y. The two lines that follow create the a and b random slope effects. The line y m ON timec is used to control for any possible linear time trends in the y and m outcomes over days. (Although we do not do this in the example, we can also remove variability in x due to a linear time trend by regressing x ON timec.) The final line under the %WITHIN% part of the model, [m@0 y@0], tells Mplus to fix the intercept of the m and y equations to be zero. Fixing these intercepts to zero is a necessary by-product of the fact that m and y were subject-mean centered.

The lines under the %BETWEEN% statement specify the between-subjects part of the multilevel mediation model. The next line, cp WITH a b, requests the covariances of the cp random effect with the a and b random effects. We then ask Mplus to label sev-eral parameters that will be used as part of the calculation of the mediated (indirect) effect, direct effect, and total effect. The syn-tax [a] (ma) and a (vara) label the mean, or fixed effect, of the a slope and the variance of the a slope random effect as "ma" and "vara," respectively. The next two lines provide corresponding labeling for the mean b effect, the b random effect, and the mean of the cp effect. The final model line labels the covariance of the a and b random effects as "covab."

The set of lines under MODEL CONSTRAINT creates new parameters for the mediated effect (med), total effect (te), percent mediated effect (pme), and the covariance of the a and b random effects in a correlation metric (corr). Finally, the OUTPUT statement requests confidence intervals for all effects in the output.

9.4 INTERPRETATION OF RESULTS

Inspection of Tables 9.1 and 9.2 reveals that SAS and Mplus (as expected) give the same results to two significant digits. We continue with a description of the Mplus version of the results, which are summarized in Figure 9.5. For the typical female partner, there is clear evidence that work stressors (X) predict greater work dissatisfaction (M). For each additional work stressor on a given day, a female partner's work dissatisfaction is predicted to be 0.19 units higher at the end of that work day ($SE = 0.04$, $z = 5.38$, $p < .001$). The standard deviation of 0.26 (based on taking the square root of the .067 random effect) associated with this average effect indicates that the spread of values is large. The model predicts that approximately 95% of the population of female partners has slopes in the range 0.19 ± 1.96 * 0.26, that is, −0.32 to 0.70.

The work dissatisfaction (M) to relationship dissatisfaction (Y) slope for the average female partner is 0.15, $SE = 0.03$, $z = 5.10$, $p < .001$, indicating that, for days equated on work stressors, each additional unit of work dissatisfaction at the end of the workday predicts that relationship dissatisfaction is 0.15 units higher at the end of the waking day. Once again, this average within-subject effect must be viewed in the context of striking between-subjects heterogeneity. The model predicts that approximately 95% of the population of female partners has slopes in the range 0.15 ± 1.96 * 0.21, that is, −0.26 to 0.56.

There is also evidence of a direct effect of negative work events (X) on relationship dissatisfaction for the average female partner, such that after adjusting for work dissatisfaction (M), each additional

TABLE 9.2. Mplus Within-Subject Multilevel Mediation Results

MODEL RESULTS

	Estimate	S.E.	Est./S.E.	Two-Tailed P-Value
Within Level				
Y ON				
TIMEC	-0.002	0.003	-0.724	0.469
M ON				
TIMEC	-0.006	0.004	-1.464	0.143
Intercepts				
M	0.000	0.000	999.000	999.000
Y	0.000	0.000	999.000	999.000
Residual Variances				
M	1.187	0.038	31.610	0.000
Y	0.855	0.027	31.171	0.000
Between Level				
CP WITH				
A	0.009	0.009	0.929	0.353
B	0.018	0.008	2.353	0.019
A WITH				
B	0.031	0.011	2.883	0.004
Means				
CP	0.105	0.024	4.432	0.000
A	0.190	0.035	5.379	0.000
B	0.149	0.029	5.097	0.000
Variances				
CP	0.008	0.009	0.972	0.331
A	0.067	0.018	3.716	0.000
B	0.046	0.012	3.937	0.000
New/Additional Parameters				
MED	0.059	0.014	4.245	0.000
TE	0.164	0.027	6.096	0.000
PME	0.361	0.077	4.692	0.000
CORR	0.555	0.165	3.374	0.001

work stressor on a given day predicts an increase in relationship dissatisfaction of 0.11 units later that day, $SE = 0.02$, $z = 4.43$, $p < .001$. Between-subjects heterogeneity is not as large in this case, with 95% of the population of female partners predicted to have slopes between $0.11 \pm 1.96 * 0.07$, that is, -0.02 to 0.25.

The next step in evaluating these results is to assemble the components that comprise the within-subject multilevel mediation

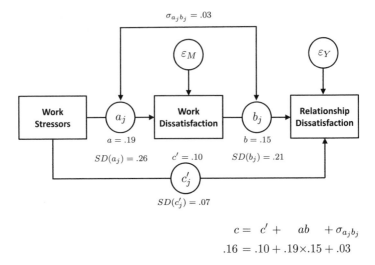

$$c = c' + ab + \sigma_{a_j b_j}$$
$$.16 = .10 + .19 \times .15 + .03$$

FIGURE 9.5. Results for within-subject mediation example.

model. We repeat below the Kenny et al. (2003) formula for the average total effect:

$$c = c' + ab + \sigma_{a_j b_j}$$

The average total effect c (across all women) is composed of three quantities: (1) the average direct effect, c'; (2) the product of the average X-to-M and M-to-Y effects, ab; and (3) the covariance of between-female partners differences in those effects, $\sigma_{a_j b_j}$. This final component, $\sigma_{a_j b_j}$, does not reflect traditional mediation but, rather, a form of moderation. Moreover, it does not reflect simple moderation but what we term *co-moderation*, that is, the extent to which moderation in the X-to-M link covaries with moderation of the M-to-Y link. For the current dataset $\sigma_{a_j b_j}$ is non-zero, positive, and statistically significant, 0.03, $SE = 0.01$, $p < .01$. Thus, the total effect for the average female partner (using the more precise estimates from the computer output) is .1053 + (0.1904 * 0.1498) + .03074 = 0.1646. Note that the total effect is the same, to two decimal places, as the work stressors slope for women found in the previous chapter (0.16).

Given these results, we can calculate that 36% (0.06/0.16) of the overall average relationship between work stressors and relationship dissatisfaction is explained by work dissatisfaction. A useful feature of Mplus is its ability to calculate standard errors and tests of significance for this proportion. These can be found under the heading New/Additional Parameters in the Mplus output on Table 9.2, and it can be seen there that this effect has a standard error of 0.077, is statistically significant ($z = 4.69$, $p < .001$), and has a CI_{95} that ranges from 21 to 51% (using the CI_{95} formula of $0.36 \pm 1.96 * 0.077$).

The size of the *ab* covariance, $\sigma_{a_j b_j}$, accounts for approximately half of the explained effect ($0.031/0.59 = 0.52$); it is statistically significant ($z = 2.99$, $p = .004$) and has a CI_{95} that ranges approximately from 0.01 to 0.05. A substantive interpretation of the covariance is that women who demonstrate stronger reactivity to work stressors in terms of work dissatisfaction tend to be the same women for whom work dissatisfaction spills over to feelings of relationship dissatisfaction later that evening. The magnitude of this link association in correlation metric is .56.

Further empirical research is needed to see the typical size and sign of co-moderation effects. For example, in datasets where the co-moderation effect is of the opposite sign to the mediation effect but of similar size, then we would observe a type of suppression (e.g., see Kline, 2011), where there would be no overall *X*-to-*Y* relationship, but there would be an average mediated component, were a mediation analysis to be conducted.

We have illustrated two methods for implementing the appropriate within-subject mediation analysis. Each has strengths and weaknesses. The strengths of the SAS approach is that multilevel modeling in SAS may be more readily available to readers, and PROC MIXED has been used already in this book. Its weakness is that it involves creating an unfamiliar data structure that is paired with an equally unfamiliar type of PROC MIXED model.

Mplus is stand-alone SEM software that is well supported and is constantly gaining new features. We suspect, however, that many readers will be unfamiliar with it. As an SEM program, its traditional strength is that it can estimate indirect effects in multi-equation systems. In recent years, it has added special syntax for implementing multilevel modeling. Moreover, Mplus can calculate the standard errors of the estimated indirect and total effects, which allows for inferential tests of these statistics. The combination of multi-equation SEM and multilevel modeling capabilities is precisely what is required for within-subject multilevel mediation, and in the near future we see Mplus emerging as the preferred method of conducting such within-subject mediation analyses.

9.5   CHAPTER SUMMARY

Researchers in the behavioral and social sciences are very interested in statistical mediation analysis because it is one of the main ways they can identify a chain of causal links between two variables. Although within-subject multilevel mediation is a new and relatively complex form of data analysis, analysts of intensive longitudinal data should be aware of it because it showcases the strengths of this type of data: A mediation process can be demonstrated within each subject over time, and between-subjects differences in the process can be evaluated, quantified, and modeled.

9.6   RECOMMENDED READINGS

Atlas, L. Y., Bolger, N., Lindquist, M. A., & Wager, T. D. (2010). Brain mediators of predictive cue effects on perceived pain. *The Journal of Neuroscience, 30,* 12964–12977.

> This is an application of within-subject mediation to intensive longitudinal (fMRI) data where *X* is an experimentally manipulated variable, expectation, *M* is brain activation, and *Y* is pain rating.

Baron, R. M., & Kenny, D. A. (1986). The moderator–mediator variable distinction in social psychological research: Conceptual, strategic, and statistical considerations. *Journal of Personality and Social Psychology, 51,* 1173–1182.

> This is the classic reference on mediation analysis in the behavioral and social sciences.

Bauer, D. J., Preacher, K. J., & Gil, K. M. (2006). Conceptualizing and testing random indirect effects and moderated mediation in multilevel models: New procedures and recommendations. *Psychological Methods, 11,* 142–163.

> This is the article that showed how multilevel modeling software could be used to conduct lower-level (e.g., within-subject) mediation analyses.

Kenny, D. A., Korchmaros, J. D., & Bolger, N. (2003). Lower level mediation in multilevel models. *Psychological Methods, 8,* 115–128.

This article discusses mediation in multilevel data where all the lower-level causal links have random effects. It derives the formula for decomposing a total effect into its explanatory components.

MacKinnon, D. P. (2008). *Introduction to statistical mediation analysis.* Mahwah, NJ: Erlbaum.

This book provides a comprehensive and accessible review of statistical mediation and shows how mediation analyses can be conducted using commonly available software.

Kristopher J. Preacher (Vanderbilt University) maintains an excellent website containing resources for implementing mediation analyses: *www.quantpsy.org/medn.htm*

10

Statistical Power for Intensive Longitudinal Designs

In this final chapter we tackle statistical power calculation, which for intensive longitudinal designs means determining the number of subjects and time points needed for adequate tests of one's key hypotheses. It is unfortunate that a relatively advanced skill is necesssary at the very first step in an intensive longitudinal study. Furthermore, it is fair to say that our simulation-based approach requires considerable effort. For doctoral students planning their dissertation research or for aspiring National Institutes of Health grant recipients, however, this will be effort well spent.

10.1 APPROACHES TO POWER

Power, the probability of detecting a hypothesized effect if one actually exists, is the most important statistical concept in planning an empirical study. Although the concept was first introduced nearly 80 years ago (Neyman & Pearson, 1933), the practice of calculating power remains foreign to many researchers, and it is rarely used outside of the context of grant writing. Yet, conducting a power analysis before beginning a study is a wise policy and can save researchers much wasted time, resources, and effort: Why embark on a research project that has little chance of success?

Unfortunately, conducting a power analysis for an intensive longitudinal study is a complex task. As we have seen in the earlier chapters of this book, because data from intensive longitudinal designs involve multiple sources of randomness, assumptions about each source, together with the traditional assumptions about effect sizes, must be made. Nonetheless, as we demonstrate in this chapter, it is possible with moderate effort to carry out a useful power analysis for an intensive longitudinal study, particularly if there are some prior data available on which to base the necessary assumptions.

Considered from a more positive angle, if you are able to conduct a power analysis for a particular intensive longitudinal study, this means that you already have gained considerable knowledge about the phenomenon of interest and how it can be modeled statistically. We illustrate how this specific knowledge comes into play by providing five examples of power analyses, one for each of the major types of research questions and datasets presented in earlier chapters. The research questions concern (1) the time course of continuous outcomes (Chapter 4), (2) the within-subject causal process for continuous outcomes (Chapter 5), (3) the within-subject causal process for categorical outcomes (Chapter 6), (4) the within-subject causal process for continuous outcomes in dyads (Chapter 8), and (5) within-subject causal mediation for continuous mediators and outcomes (Chapter 9). For readers who are interested in a more compact introduction to power analysis that focuses on process modeling for continuous outcomes only, see Bolger, Stadler, and Laurenceau (2012).

Researchers wishing to conduct a power analysis for an intensive longitudinal study have a variety of options, from (1) applying formulae that are available in books covering multilevel modeling, repeated-measures designs, and longitudinal designs (Fitzmaurice et al., 2011; Gelman & Hill, 2007; Hox, 2010; Snijders & Bosker, 2012); (2) using specialized software designed for power analyses for multilevel models such as PinT (Bosker, Snijders, & Guldemond, 2007) and Optimal Design (Raudenbush, Spybrook, Liu, & Congdon, 2006); to (3) using simulation methods in general purpose programming environments such as SAS (Littell, Milliken, Stroup,

Wolfinger, & Schabenberger, 2006; SAS Institute Inc., 2011), R (Gelman & Hill, 2007; R Development Core Team, 2011), or MATLAB (MathWorks Inc., 2011). All have advantages and drawbacks. The most flexible and comprehensive approach that we are aware of involves using the Monte Carlo simulation capabilities that are part of the Mplus statistical software. This is the approach we recommend and use in this chapter.

10.2 POWER IN MULTILEVEL MODELS

A power analysis fundamentally involves an assessment of whether the effect or signal one wishes to detect is large enough to be detected against the background noise likely to be encountered in the study design. *Noise*, in the language of statistics, is how much the value of a statistic is likely to vary from sample to sample. If it varies a lot, then one cannot put a lot of trust in the value obtained; if it varies very little, then the results obtained from a study can be taken as trustworthy. This statistical noise is typically assessed by the standard error of the effect in question. A ratio of the effect size to its standard error is a signal-to-noise ratio, one that we see most often as t- or z-ratio statistics.

The issue of power, then, can be reduced to assessing the standard error one can expect from a given research design. A design that yields a smaller standard error will be more powerful, more capable of allowing us to detect a given signal in the midst of background noise. Note that because different hypotheses are usually reflected in different parameters having different standard errors associated with them, when one speaks of a study being sufficiently powered, one is referring to a particular hypothesis or group of hypotheses to be tested.

So what leads to smaller standard errors? We have all learned in introduction to statistics classes that increasing the sample size increases the power of a hypothesis test, and this is true in intensive longitudinal designs as much as in more conventional designs. Similarly, reducing the error variance in Y (e.g., through blocking or using covariates) is another approach that decreases standard errors and increases power. Increasing the variance in X is a third way to increase power, and can be accomplished by using stronger manipulations or long study durations wherein X can be expected to change more.

A new element in multilevel designs, however, is the influence of random effects of intercepts and slopes. Let us consider random slopes, for as we have seen, slopes tend to be the focus of most intensive longitudinal studies. Other things being equal, an average, fixed slope will be easier to detect the smaller its corresponding random effect is. In other words, if, for example, we are interested in the typical slope for the effect of marital conflicts on marital intimacy, the less people vary from one another in that effect, the less the typical slope will vary from sample to sample, and the more power one has in any given study. Random slopes, therefore, lead to reduced power to detect an average slope. As we will see, the key pieces of information that we use to compute power are the four just mentioned: sample size, residual variance in Y, variance in X (or X's), and the random effects associated with the fixed effect of X (or X's) of interest.

Taken from Snijders and Bosker (1993) but re-expressed in the Raudenbush and Byrk (2002) notation introduced in Chapter 4, the following equation shows the interrelationships of the standard error of an average within-person slope and other key parameters of a multilevel model. To keep the formula simple and increase its heuristic value, we assume a model with a binary (0,1) X with equal numbers of time points of "0" and "1" across all subjects. Additionally, we assume that X varies within subjects only. Finally, we assume a random intercept, a random slope for X, no between-subjects predictors, and a common nonautocorrelated level-1 error variance for Y. In this case, the sampling variance of the average slope for X (the square root of which is the standard error of the slope) is

$$\sigma^2_{\hat{\gamma}_{10}} = \frac{\sigma^2}{NT\sigma^2_X} + \frac{\tau_{11}}{N} \tag{10.1}$$

Here, N refers to the number of subjects (e.g., persons) in the sample, T refers to the number of time points (e.g., diary days) per subject, σ^2 is the level-1 error variance for Y, σ^2_X is the within-subject variance in X, and τ_{11} is the variance of the random slope for X (see also Moerbeek, Van Breukelen, & Berger, 2008).

We can see that the sampling variance of the slope is composed of two parts, what we call a *within-subjects* part and a *between-subjects* part. How can the size of this variance be reduced? If we focus only on changing the sample sizes of subjects and time points, it can be seen that the within-subject part can be reduced in size equally well by increasing the number of subjects or the number of time points. The between-subjects part can be reduced in size only by increasing the number of subjects. This means that no matter how many repeated measurements are taken, there will be no decrease in the second component. Increasing the number of subjects, however, can decrease both.

10.3 POWER FOR THE TIME COURSE EXAMPLE

For the case of change over time, we return to the dataset on changes in women's intimacy over 16 weeks in a treatment study of couples with marital difficulties. As we saw in Chapter 4, the intimacy data represent a treatment study involving only the female partners from 50 couples, 25 in the treatment group and 25 controls. The dependent measure is the weekly report of intimacy by the woman, and the key hypothesis under question is whether the treatment altered the time slope for intimacy such that women in the treatment group showed increases in intimacy compared to those in the control group. Time is scaled such that 0 is the value for week 1 and 1 is the value for week 16, with the intervening 14 weeks spaced equally across the 0–1 interval. This somewhat unorthodox scaling of time has the virtue that the slope for time estimates the total change in intimacy over the complete therapeutic period.

The results from Chapter 4 revealed a treatment effect corresponding to a 0.92 unit increase in the time slope for the treatment group relative to that of the control group. However, it had a confidence interval that ranged from −0.07 to 1.91. Thus, although the best estimate of the effectiveness of the treatment was that it was twice that of the control condition, we could not rule out the possibility that it was no better than the control condition.

To begin our discussion of power, it is useful to calculate what the *post-hoc power* was for this analysis. If we use the observed effect size and assume it to be the true (population) effect size, we can calculate, post hoc, how much power we had. For this and all the power analyses we conduct in this chapter, we use Mplus (Muthén & Muthén, 1998–2010; Muthén & Muthén, 2002). Mplus is a general-purpose SEM program that in the past decade has expanded its range to include multilevel models. It is noteworthy for its ability to conduct Monte Carlo power simulations for any model in its broad repertoire (Muthén & Muthén, 2002). This capacity allows one to run, for example, an analysis on actual data and to use the estimates from that model as inputs for a power analysis. This is the approach we take to evaluate the power characteristics of the time course dataset.

The first step in the process is to replicate in Mplus the analysis already conducted in Chapter 4 using the SPSS MIXED or SAS PROC MIXED programs. As noted in the earlier chapter, for readers familiar only with the mixed model approach to estimating multilevel models, the SEM approach used in Mplus will take some getting used to. The syntax below reads in the same data file used by SPSS/ SAS earlier, specifies the same model, and produces nearly identical results.

```
TITLE:      Chapter 4 Intimacy Intervention Example;

DATA:       FILE IS intimacy.dat;

VARIABLE: NAMES ARE id time time01 intimacy treatment;

            USEVAR ARE intimacy treatment time01;

            WITHIN =  time01;

            BETWEEN = treatment;

            CLUSTER = id;

ANALYSIS: TYPE = twolevel random;

            ESTIMATOR=ml;

MODEL:      %WITHIN%

            slope | intimacy on time01;
```

```
%BETWEEN%

intimacy slope on treatment;

intimacy with slope;
```

OUTPUT: cinterval;

The following is an excerpted portion of the resulting Mplus output:

MODEL RESULTS

				Two-Tailed
	Estimate	S.E.	Est./S.E.	P-Value
Within Level				
Residual Variances				
INTIMACY	1.693	0.091	18.701	0.000
Between Level				
SLOPE ON				
TREATMENT	0.921	0.479	1.921	0.055
INTIMACY ON				
TREATMENT	-0.056	0.286	-0.196	0.844
INTIMACY WITH				
SLOPE	-0.462	0.282	-1.639	0.101
Intercepts				
INTIMACY	2.899	0.202	14.335	0.000
SLOPE	0.735	0.339	2.168	0.030
Residual Variances				
INTIMACY	0.637	0.204	3.115	0.002
SLOPE	1.752	0.573	3.055	0.002

We hope the reader will notice that the key coefficient in the table above is the estimate of 0.921 for the regression of *intimacy* on *treatment by time* (SLOPE ON TREATMENT), a value identical to the SPSS MIXED or SAS PROC MIXED estimate in Chapter 4. The next step in producing the power analysis in Mplus is to conduct power simulations using the parameter estimates from the results of an actual analysis. The Mplus code for this analysis is also included as a part of the simulation code. The basic rationale of simulation-based power analysis is that we (1) assume that the estimated parameter values from an analysis of sample data are the true population values for these parameters, (2) draw samples from this population model using the original N and T, and (3) determine the number of samples for which a particular parameter of interest is found to be statistically significant. By this reckoning, statistical power for a particular effect is the percentage of samples for which a parameter estimate was statistically significant (Muthén & Muthén, 2002). Although the Mplus parameter estimates are virtually identical to those of SPSS/SAS, they differ slightly in some places because Mplus does not use REML estimation and cannot incorporate an autocorrelated error structure (as explained in more detail in Chapter 4). Thus, we use the parameter estimates from the SPSS MIXED/SAS PROC MIXED runs as well as sample values for the means and variances of predictor values in the Mplus simulation code. The code used is presented below.

```
MONTECARLO:
        NAMES ARE time intimacy treatment;
        NOBSERVATIONS = 800;
        NCSIZES = 1;
        CSIZES = 50 (16);
        SEED = 5859;
        NREPS = 1000;
        WITHIN = time;
        BETWEEN = treatment;
ANALYSIS:
        TYPE = twolevel random;
        MODEL POPULATION:
        %WITHIN%
```

```
      slope | intimacy ON time;
      [time*0.500];
      intimacy*1.693;
      time*0.094;
      %BETWEEN%
      slope ON treatment*0.921;
      intimacy ON treatment*-0.056;
      intimacy WITH slope*-0.516;
      [treatment*0.500];
      [intimacy*2.899];
      [slope*0.735];
      treatment*0.250;
      intimacy*0.687;
      slope*1.894;
MODEL:
      %WITHIN%
      slope | intimacy ON time;
      [time*0.500];
      intimacy*1.693;
      time*0.094;
      %BETWEEN%
      slope ON treatment*0.921;
      intimacy ON treatment*-0.056;
      intimacy WITH slope*-0.516;
      [treatment*0.500];
      [intimacy*2.899];
      [slope*0.735];
      treatment*0.250;
      intimacy*0.687;
      slope*1.894;
OUTPUT:
```

The code starts with telling Mplus the names of the variables in the analysis (NAMES ARE time intimacy treatment). We then specify the total number of observations in the samples we would like to draw (NOBSERVATIONS = 800) which is determined as the product of $N = 50$ subjects and $T = 16$ time points (CSIZES = 50 (16)). NREPS = 1000 tells Mplus to simulate or draw 1,000 samples for this simulation run. We recommend that this number be at least 1,000 and ideally 5,000 or 10,000 for the sake of stability; however, the time for running the simulation may be considerable for increasingly complex models, so we recommend starting with a smaller number initially. We then tell Mplus that time is a predictor that varies only within subjects and that treatment is a predictor that varies only between subjects using WITHIN = time and BETWEEN = treatment. Specifying TYPE = twolevel random has Mplus run a multilevel model with random intercepts and random slopes.

The lines of code under the section starting with MODEL POPULATION specifies the Mplus model we ran originally but uses an asterisk (*) to indicate the fixing of values of the population model's parameters. For example, slope ON treatment*0.921 specifies the parameter for the treatment by time slope effect to be equal to 0.921 in the population from which Mplus will be drawing samples. Note that the code in brackets (e.g., [intimacy*2.899]) refers to means (e.g., fixed effects) or intercepts and code without brackets refers to variances, slopes, or covariances. Once the population model has been specified, then an analysis model used to analyze each sample drawn from the population must also be specified. When the analysis and population models (along with specified starting values) are the same, Mplus provides post hoc power estimates for all parameters in the resulting output. Partial output is shown below.

```
MODEL RESULTS
                    ESTIMATES              S. E.     M. S. E.   95%   % Sig
           Population  Average  Std. Dev.  Average            Cover  Coeff
Within Level
  Means
    TIME       0.500   0.4999    0.0111    0.0107    0.0001  0.927  1.000
  Variances
    TIME       0.094   0.0938    0.0046    0.0046    0.0000  0.937  1.000
```

Residual Variances							
INTIMACY	1.693	1.6952	0.0898	0.0888	0.0081	0.934	1.000
Between Level							
SLOPE ON							
TREATMENT	0.921	0.9111	0.5198	0.4959	0.2701	0.933	0.466
INTIMACY ON							
TREATMENT	-0.056	-0.0560	0.3098	0.2906	0.0959	0.914	0.088
INTIMACY WITH							
SLOPE	-0.516	-0.4724	0.2984	0.2888	0.0909	0.896	0.316
Means							
TREATMENT	0.500	0.5020	0.0722	0.0693	0.0052	0.938	1.000
Intercepts							
INTIMACY	2.899	2.8938	0.2239	0.2062	0.0501	0.920	1.000
SLOPE	0.735	0.7510	0.3659	0.3514	0.1340	0.937	0.558
Variances							
TREATMENT	0.250	0.2423	0.0491	0.0467	0.0025	0.911	1.000
Residual Variances							
INTIMACY	0.687	0.6358	0.2071	0.2055	0.0455	0.882	0.955
SLOPE	1.894	1.7977	0.5944	0.5882	0.3623	0.899	0.962

The output summarizes the results for each parameter averaged across the 1,000 simulations. For the treatment-by-time slope (boxed above), we can see that the average value found across the simulations is equal to the value used to simulate the data. The statistical power estimate for this parameter, reported under the final column headed "% Sig Coeff," is the proportion of the 1,000 replications in which the treatment-by-time slope coefficient was significant at $p < .05$. Its value, .466, suggests that the original study design was not adequately powered for the test of this hypothesis, according to the widely held convention of .80 power or greater. The fact that the p-value for the treatment-by-time coefficient in SPSS/SAS run of the original sample was marginally significant (i.e., $p = .067$) is consistent with a post hoc power estimate of slightly under 50%. In sum, the Monte Carlo simulation results show that the study had low power to detect (i.e., find a significant coefficient at alpha = .05) an effect of the size found in the sample, were it to be the true effect size in the population.

If we now regard the time course study as a pilot for a larger, more definitive study, a power analysis would be of great help in the rational planning of such a future study. Figure 10.1 shows power estimates for the treatment-by-time coefficient for various combinations of sample sizes and numbers of time points. The highlighted data point is the .466 power estimate for the results of the simulation we just discussed, that is, for the originally observed dataset sample size (N = 50 women) and number of weeks (T = 16). Each of the remaining data points are for equivalent simulations (with 1,000 replications each) for other combinations of sample size (32, 63, 94, 125, 157, 188) keeping the number of time points constant, and number of time points (10, 20, 30, 40, 50, 60) keeping the number of subjects constant. As far as the treatment-by-time slope is concerned, the simulations predict that a study with 125 women and 16 time points would slightly exceed the usual power requirement of 80% for grant submissions.

For readers unfamiliar with power analyses, the more than two-fold increase in sample size may be shocking. Unfortunately, it is typical of what one can expect to find when planning replications of studies with marginally significant results.

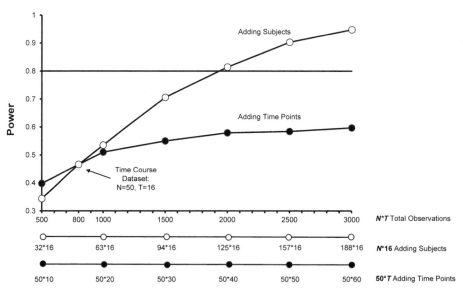

FIGURE 10.1. Power curves for the key hypothesis in the Chapter 4 time course dataset. This figure shows the relative benefits of adding subjects or time points for testing the treatment by time hypothesis.

The effect of increasing the number of repeated measurements also may be shocking to some readers, for it turns out to be impossible to reach 80% power using this approach (while holding the sample size at its original value of 50 people). More than doubling the number of measurements to 40 increases power to .58. Increasing it again to 60 increases power further by only a trivial amount, to .60. In fact, no matter how many repeated measurements are taken, the power will not rise above approximately .65. Figure 10.1 also contains a graphical representation of each of these potential design changes, respectively. The clear implication—one made often in the past regarding multilevel datasets (e.g., Snijders & Bosker, 2012)—is that increasing level-2 units (in our case, persons) is typically more effective than increasing level-1 units (in our case, time points). The inspection of Equation 10.1 earlier in the chapter underlies this state of affairs.

10.4 POWER FOR THE CAUSAL PROCESS EXAMPLE

In the first example, the within-subject independent variable was time itself. In the second example, we turn to a more general problem of investigating within-subject variables and their consequences. Our example involves a causal analysis of a within-subject process focusing on the consequences of interpersonal conflicts in intimate adult relationships. We again begin by reminding the reader of the results already presented in Chapter 5. There we saw that on days when an interpersonal conflict with the partner occurred, female subjects showed a marked decrease in end-of-day ratings of intimacy, an effect that was moderated by relationship quality such that those in high-quality relationships showed less intimacy reactivity to daily conflict. This moderation effect was statistically significant. but it had a large confidence interval, ranging from just above zero to approximately twice its estimated value of 1.0 units. As before, we begin by calculating the post-hoc power associated with this result by using the following Mplus code.

```
TITLE:     Ch. 5 Daily conflict and intimacy example;

DATA:      FILE IS process.dat;
```

```
VARIABLE: NAMES ARE id time time7c intimacy conflict confc
          confcb confcw relqual;

          USEVAR ARE time7c intimacy confcw confcb relqual
                 confcbrq;

          WITHIN = confcw time7c;

          BETWEEN = relqual confcb confcbrq;

          CLUSTER = id;

DEFINE:   confcbrq=confcb*relqual;

ANALYSIS: TYPE = twolevel random;

          ESTIMATOR=ml;

MODEL:    %WITHIN%

          confslp | intimacy ON confcw;

          intimacy ON time7c;

          %BETWEEN%

          intimacy WITH confslp;

          intimacy ON confcb confcbrq;

          intimacy confslp ON relqual;

Output:   sampstat cinterval;
```

The following is an excerpted portion of the resulting Mplus output:

```
MODEL RESULTS
```

	Estimate	S.E.	Est./S.E.	Two-Tailed P-Value
Within Level				
INTIMACY ON				
TIME7C	-0.028	0.039	-0.737	0.461
Residual Variances				
INTIMACY	3.589	0.122	29.329	0.000

Between Level

CONFSLP ON				
RELQUAL	1.032	0.483	2.138	0.033

INTIMACY ON				
CONFCB	-0.840	1.071	-0.784	0.433
CONFCBRQ	2.524	1.630	1.549	0.121
RELQUAL	0.647	0.274	2.367	0.018
INTIMACY WITH				
CONFSLP	0.385	0.226	1.702	0.089
Intercepts				
INTIMACY	4.532	0.215	21.116	0.000
CONFSLP	-2.022	0.363	-5.566	0.000
Residual Variances				
INTIMACY	0.746	0.152	4.899	0.000
CONFSLP	2.564	0.625	4.102	0.000

The key coefficient in the table above is the estimate of 1.032 for the regression of *intimacy* on *relqual by conflict* (CONFSLP ON REL-QUAL), a value almost identical to the SPSS MIXED or SAS PROC MIXED estimate in Chapter 5. Again, the reason the estimates are not identical is because Mplus does not use REML estimation and cannot model residual autocorrelation. As in the previous example, the next step is to conduct power simulations in Mplus using the parameter estimates from the results of the SPSS MIXED/SAS PROC MIXED actual analysis as well as sample means and variances for predictors. The simulation code is presented below.

```
MONTECARLO:
    NAMES ARE day7c intimacy confcw confcb relqual
             rqconfcb;

        NOBSERVATIONS = 1848;

        NCSIZES = 1;
```

```
            CSIZES = 66 (28);

            SEED = 5859;

            NREPS = 1000;

            WITHIN = day7c confcw;

            BETWEEN = confcb relqual rqconfcb;

ANALYSIS:

            TYPE = TWOLEVEL RANDOM;

                  MODEL POPULATION:

            %WITHIN%

            slope | intimacy ON confcw;

            intimacy ON day7c*-0.028;

            intimacy*3.579;

            [confcw*0]; confcw*0.146;

            %BETWEEN%

            slope ON relqual*1.016;

            intimacy ON confcb*-0.841;

            intimacy ON relqual*0.647;

            intimacy ON rqconfcb*2.527;

            intimacy WITH slope*0.401;

            [relqual*0.610];

            [confcb*0];

            [rqconfcb*-0.041];

            [intimacy*4.532];

            [slope*-2.011];

            relqual*0.239;

            confcb*0.027;

            rqconfcb*0.009;

            intimacy*0.812;

            slope*2.711;

    MODEL:
```

```
%WITHIN%

slope | intimacy ON confcw;

intimacy ON day7c*-0.028;

intimacy*3.579;

%BETWEEN%

slope ON relqual*1.016;

intimacy ON confcb*-0.841;

intimacy ON relqual*0.647;

intimacy ON rqconfcb*2.527;

intimacy WITH slope*0.401;

[intimacy*4.532];

[slope*-2.011];

intimacy*0.812;

slope*2.711;
```

OUTPUT:

Note that we use sample size specifications from the original study, as this is a post-hoc power analysis (i.e., NOBSERVATIONS = 1848 and (CSIZES = 66   (28)). Partial output from this run is presented below.

```
MODEL RESULTS
                          ESTIMATES          S. E.      M. S. E.   95%  % Sig
             Population   Average   Std. Dev.  Average     Cover Coeff
Within Level
  INTIMACY    ON
    DAY7C      -0.028    0.1121   4.5261   4.4316   20.4850 0.936 0.064
  Residual Variances
    INTIMACY   3.579    3.5765   0.1215   0.1204    0.0148 0.947 1.000
Between Level
  SLOPE       ON
    RELQUAL    1.016    1.0088   0.5273   0.4697    0.2778 0.915 0.573
  INTIMACY    ON
    CONFCB     -0.841   -0.8366   0.7536   0.6978    0.5673 0.917 0.265
    RELQUAL    0.647    0.6537   0.2506   0.2399    0.0628 0.939 0.768
```

RQCONFCB	2.527	2.5575	1.3218	1.2100	1.7464	0.927	0.572
INTIMACY WITH							
SLOPE	0.401	0.3993	0.2385	0.2225	0.0568	0.927	0.432
Intercepts							
INTIMACY	4.532	4.5269	0.1981	0.1931	0.0392	0.939	1.000
SLOPE	-2.011	-1.9919	0.3996	0.3677	0.1599	0.926	0.999
Residual Variances							
INTIMACY	0.812	0.7612	0.1647	0.1510	0.0297	0.883	1.000
SLOPE	2.711	2.6127	0.6236	0.6014	0.3981	0.900	1.000

For the relationship quality-by-conflict slope (boxed above), we can see that the post-hoc statistical power estimate for this parameter, reported under the final column headed "% Sig Coeff," is .573, an uncomfortably low value. Working from this base of $N = 66$ persons and $T = 28$ time points, Figure 10.2 displays two power curves: One shows the predicted power for studies that increase the number of level-2 units (subjects), and the second shows the equivalent predictions for increases in level-1 units (time points). The 80% power value is indicated by a horizontal line. The reader can easily see that 80% power is nearly reached at $N = 118$, for $T = 28$, but it

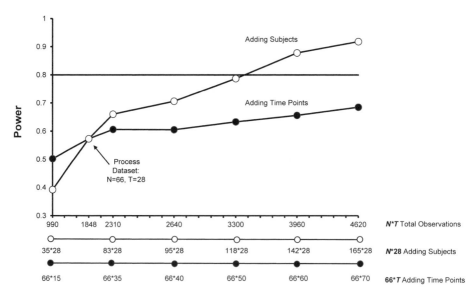

FIGURE 10.2. Power curves for the key hypothesis in the Chapter 5 causal process dataset. This figure shows the relative benefits of adding subjects or time points for testing the relationship quality by daily conflict hypothesis.

is never reached when N is held at 66 and T is increased to 70 and beyond. Again, the power analysis demonstrates the relatively limited value of increasing time points relative to persons for intensive longitudinal designs.

10.5 POWER FOR THE CATEGORICAL OUTCOMES EXAMPLE

We now turn to evaluating the power characteristics of the diary dataset we analyzed in the categorical outcomes chapter (Chapter 6). The first step in the process is to replicate in Mplus the analysis already conducted in Chapter 6 using the GLIMMIX program in SAS and the GENLINMIXED program in SPSS. The key hypothesis is that levels of morning anger/irritability of female partners on a given day increase the risk of conflicts reported by the male relationship partner later that evening. The syntax below reads in the same file as was used by SAS/SPSS earlier, specifies the same model, and produces nearly identical results.

```
TITLE:     Morning anger and conflict model;
DATA:      FILE IS gcsmall.dat;
VARIABLE: NAMES ARE couple sex day pconf
           camang mcamang clpconf cday7;
           USEVAR ARE pconf camang mcamang clpconf
                  cday7;
           CATEGORICAL = pconf;
           WITHIN = camang clpconf cday7;
           BETWEEN = mcamang;
           CLUSTER = couple;
ANALYSIS: TYPE = twolevel random;
           ESTIMATOR=ml;
           ALGORITHM = INTEGRATION
MODEL:     %WITHIN%
           pconf ON camang clpconf cday7;
           %BETWEEN%
           pconf ON mcamang;
```

```
OUTPUT:    sampstat CINTERVAL;
```

As can be seen by the CATEGORICAL = pconf statement, the analysis treats partner reports of conflict as categorical, which results in a logistic rather than linear form for the model for *pconf*. There are also statements that specify which variables have within-subjects versus between-subjects variability. The key output of the analysis is given below.

```
MODEL RESULTS
```

	Estimate	S.E.	Est./S.E.	Two-Tailed P-Value
Within Level				
PCONF ON				
CAMANG	0.216	0.068	3.191	0.001
CDAY7	-0.193	0.071	-2.703	0.007
CLPCONF	0.314	0.211	1.492	0.136
Between Level				
PCONF ON				
MCAMANG	-0.441	0.243	-1.813	0.070
Thresholds				
PCONF$1	1.902	0.110	17.256	0.000
Residual Variances				
PCONF	0.255	0.124	2.051	0.040

The reader will notice that the key coefficient in the table above is the estimate of 0.216 for the regression of *pconf* on *camang*, a value almost identical to the SAS/SPSS estimates in Chapter 6. The next step in producing the power analysis in Mplus is to conduct power simulations using the parameter estimates above. The original study ran for 28 days, but the average person in the sample provided 22 days, or just over 3 weeks. With this finding in mind, we conducted simulations for a 3-week study with no missing data. A 3-week study would produce 21 − 1 = 20 usable data points, given that we include the lagged value of *pconf* in the analysis. The code used is presented below.

```
MONTECARLO: NAMES ARE pconf camang mcamang clpconf
                  day7;
```

```
        NOBSERVATIONS = 1220;

        NCSIZES = 1;

        CSIZES = 61 (20);

        SEED = 5859;

        NREPS = 1000;

        WITHIN = cday7 camang clpconf;

        BETWEEN = mcamang;

        CATEGORICAL = pconf;

        GENERATE = pconf (1);
ANALYSIS:  TYPE = TWOLEVEL RANDOM;
MODEL POPULATION:

        %WITHIN%

        camang*1.241; clpconf*0.132; cday7*1.321;

        [camang*0 clpconf*0 cday7*0];

        pconf ON camang*0.216;

        pconf ON cday7*-0.193 clpconf*0.314;

        %BETWEEN%

        mcamang*0.244;[mcamang*0];

        pconf ON mcamang*-0.441;

        [conf$1*-1.902];

        pconf*0.255;
MODEL:    %WITHIN%

        pconf ON camang*0.216;

        pconf ON cday7*-0.193 clpconf*0.314;

        %BETWEEN%

        pconf ON mcamang*-0.441;

         [pconf$1*-1.902];

        pconf*0.255;
OUTPUT:    SAMPSTAT;
```

Partial output from this run is shown below.

```
MODEL RESULTS
```

		ESTIMATES		S. E.	M. S. E.	95%	% Sig
		Population	Average	Std. Dev.	Average	Cover	Coeff
Within Level							
PCONF	ON						
CAMANG		0.216	0.2134	0.0775	0.0747	0.0060 0.936	0.784
CDAY7		-0.193	-0.1982	0.0748	0.0727	0.0056 0.933	0.765
CLPCONF		0.314	0.3133	0.2326	0.2271	0.0541 0.937	0.281
Between Level							
PCONF	ON						
MCAMANG		-0.441	-0.4464	0.2245	0.2107	0.0504 0.920	0.565
Thresholds							
PCONF$1		-1.902	-1.9068	0.1117	0.1147	0.0125 0.950	1.000
Residual Variances							
PCONF		0.255	0.2327	0.1269	0.1490	0.0166 0.889	0.437

The output summarizes the results for each parameter averaged across the 1,000 simulations. For the slope for *camang* (in the first boxed line highlighted above) we can see that the average value found across the simulations was very close to the value used to simulate the data. The power estimate, reported in the column headed "% Sig Coeff," is the proportion of the 1,000 replications in which the *camang* coefficient was significant at $p < .05$. Its value, .78, suggests that the original study design was adequately powered for this coefficient. This contrasts with the *pconf* variance estimate (the second boxed line), for which the equivalent power estimate was .44. This coefficient had a p-value of approximately .04 in the analysis of the original dataset. Note that there is no necessary contradiction between a design being underpowered and an effect being significant. The post-hoc power of a just-significant effect is approximately .5, and the simulated value of .44 is consistent with this.

Readers can use the simulation code above to try out various combinations of samples sizes for persons and time points to obtain corresponding predictions of power. For example, a design with 120 persons and 27 days of data would meet the usual requirements of 80% power for both the *amang* slope (94% power) and the random intercept variance coefficient (80% power).

10.6 POWER FOR THE DYADIC PROCESS EXAMPLE

The key hypothesis for the dyadic process example in Chapter 8 was that the number of daily stressors at work predicts degree of end-of-the-day relationship dissatisfaction for both male and female partners. The dataset was simulated to represent 100 dual-career heterosexual couples who completed two online daily diaries (i.e., end of workday and end of evening) for each of 21 consecutive days. We used the Mplus analysis code as well as the parameter estimates from the SPSS/SAS results that we presented in Chapter 8 to create the necessary Mplus simulation code shown below.

```
MONTECARLO:
      NAMES ARE time7c freldis mreldis fwrkstrscw
      mwrkstrscw mwrkstrscb fwrkstrscb;
      NOBSERVATIONS = 2100;
        NCSIZES = 1;
        CSIZES = 100 (21);
        SEED = 5859;
        NREPS = 1000;
        WITHIN = time7c fwrkstrscw mwrkstrscw;
        BETWEEN = mwrkstrscb fwrkstrscb;
ANALYSIS:
      TYPE = twolevel random;
      MODEL POPULATION:
      %WITHIN%
      slopef | freldis ON fwrkstrscw;
      slopem | mreldis ON mwrkstrscw;
      freldis ON time7c*-0.025;
```

```
mreldis ON time7c*0.012;

freldis WITH mreldis*0.064;

freldis*0.997; mreldis*0.761;

[fwrkstrscw*0 mwrkstrscw*0 time7c*-0.071];

fwrkstrscw*1.007 mwrkstrscw*1.015 time7c*749;

%BETWEEN%

freldis ON fwrkstrscb*0.621;

mreldis ON mwrkstrscb*-0.143;

freldis WITH mreldis*0.257;

freldis WITH slopef*0.058;

freldis WITH slopem*-0.003;

mreldis WITH slopef*0.001;

mreldis WITH slopem*0.031;

slopef WITH slopem*0.011;

[ freldis*4.648 ];

[ mreldis*5.086 ];

[ slopef*0.160 ];

[ slopem*0.109 ];

freldis*0.921;

mreldis*1.031;

slopef*0.016;

slopem*0.028;

[fwrkstrscb*-0.022 mwrkstrscb*0.022];

fwrkstrscb*0.047 mwrkstrscb*0.051;

MODEL:

%WITHIN%

slopef | freldis ON fwrkstrscw;

slopem | mreldis ON mwrkstrscw;

freldis ON time7c*-0.025;

mreldis ON time7c*0.012;
```

```
freldis WITH mreldis*0.064;
freldis*0.997; mreldis*0.761;
%BETWEEN%
freldis ON fwrkstrscb*0.621;
mreldis ON mwrkstrscb*-0.143;
freldis WITH mreldis*0.257;
freldis WITH slopef*0.058;
freldis WITH slopem*-0.003;
mreldis WITH slopef*0.001;
mreldis WITH slopem*0.031;
slopef WITH slopem*0.011;
[ freldis*4.648 ];
[ mreldis*5.086 ];
[ slopef*0.160 ];
[ slopem*0.109 ];
freldis*0.921;
mreldis*1.031;
slopef*0.016;
slopem*0.028;
```

OUTPUT:

Partial output from this run is shown below.

```
MODEL RESULTS
```

	ESTIMATES			S. E.	M. S. E.	95%	% Sig
	Population	Average	Std. Dev.	Average		Cover	Coeff
Between Level							
Means							
SLOPEF	0.160	0.1602	0.0252	0.0256	0.0006	0.949	1.000
SLOPEM	0.109	0.1086	0.0272	0.0257	0.0007	0.940	0.987
Intercepts							
FRELDIS	4.648	4.6509	0.1008	0.0982	0.0102	0.946	1.000
MRELDIS	5.086	5.0850	0.1051	0.1029	0.0110	0.945	1.000

```
Variances
  SLOPEF       0.016   0.0174   0.0078   0.0097   0.0001 0.987 0.404
  SLOPEM       0.028   0.0277   0.0090   0.0092   0.0001 0.933 0.929
Residual Variances
  FRELDIS      0.921   0.9029   0.1398   0.1319   0.0198 0.929 1.000
  MRELDIS      1.031   1.0085   0.1529   0.1452   0.0239 0.910 1.000
```

The key work stress–relationship dissatisfaction spillover hypothesis is represented by the female partner and male partner fixed effect coefficients boxed in the above output under the heading "Means." Summarized across 1,000 replications, the post-hoc power estimates of 1.00 and .99 for female and male partner spillover coefficients, respectively, indicate that this design was well powered for testing this hypothesis and suggest that a replication, assuming these are the true effects in the population, is highly likely to detect these effects as statistically significant at .05 alpha level. In fact, one could drop down to 2 weeks instead of 3 weeks of daily diary data and still be very well powered.

10.7 POWER FOR THE WITHIN-SUBJECT MEDIATION EXAMPLE

In Chapter 9 we used Mplus to conduct a within-subject multilevel mediation analysis; we use its results here as a basis for power simulation. We assume that readers of this section will have already familiarized themselves with those earlier Mplus results. As recommended in Chapter 9, we focus on mediation using person-mean deviated scores on X, M, and Y. Below is the key Mplus code to simulate power for the actual dataset used in Chapter 9.

```
MONTECARLO:
                names are timec x m y;
                nobservations = 2100;
                ncsizes = 1;
                csizes = 100 (21);
```

```
                   seed = 5859;
                   nreps = 500;
                   within = x m y timec;
ANALYSIS:   TYPE = TWOLEVEL RANDOM;
MODEL POPULATION:
              %WITHIN%
              [timec*0 x*0 m*0 y *0];
              timec*36.7 x*1.0 m*1.29 y *0.99;
              cp | y  ON x;
               a | m ON x;
               b | y  ON m;
              y  on timec*0; m on timec*0;
              y *.855; m*1.86;
              %BETWEEN%
              cp WITH a*.008 b*.018;
              [a*.189] (ma); a*.067 (vara);
              [b*.149] (mb); b*.046 (varb);
              [cp*.106] (mcp); cp*.009;
              a WITH b*.031 (covab);
MODEL:
              %WITHIN%
              [timec*0 x*0 m*0 y *0];
              timec*36.7 x*1.0 m*1.29 y *0.99;
              cp | y  ON x;
               a | m ON x;
               b | y  ON m;
              y  on timec*0; m on timec*0;
              y *.855; m*1.86;
              %BETWEEN%
              cp WITH a*.008 b*.018;
```

```
          [a*.189] (ma); a*.067 (vara);

          [b*.149] (mb); b*.046 (varb);

          [cp*.106] (mcp); cp*.009;

          a WITH b*.031 (covab);

MODEL CONSTRAINT:

          NEW CORAB*.531 MED*.056 VMED*.00892
            TE*.162 PME*.347;

          CORAB=covab/sqrt(vara*varb);

          MED=ma*mb+covab;

          VMED=(mb^2)*vara+(ma^2)*varb+vara*varb+2*m
            *mb*covab+covab^2;

          TE=ma*mb+covab+mcp;

          PME=(ma*mb+covab)/(ma*mb+covab+mcp);
```

The code above is identical to that shown in Chapter 9, except now we treat the values already obtained from the sample as the population values; these population values are used to generate simulated samples. As we did for the earlier examples, for the assessment of post hoc power we generated 1,000 samples and analyzed each of the samples as if it contained real data. We then summarized the power results, which was the proportion of samples in which a given effect of interest was found to be statistically significant. As before, we treat 80% as the desirable level of power.

In addition to the sections of code introduced earlier, we now include a new section, called MODEL CONSTRAINT. Here we use the parameter estimates and equations from Kenny et al. (2003) to construct estimates of the average mediated effect (MED), the variance of the mediated effect (VMED), the total effect (TE), and the proportion of the total effect that is mediated. Below is the table of results for the 1,000 samples simulated, based on 100 female partners and 21 days (100 female partners and 21 days were used in the design of the original dataset). The reader will notice (as explained in Chapter 9) that because of the removal of between-persons variability in the predictors and outcomes, certain means and intercepts are fixed at zero.

MODEL RESULTS

		ESTIMATES			S. E.	M. S. E.	95%	% Sig
		Population	Average	Std. Dev.	Average		Cover	Coeff
Within Level								
Y	ON							
TIMEC		0.000	0.0000	0.0034	0.0034	0.0000	0.954	0.046
M	ON							
TIMEC		0.000	0.0000	0.0046	0.0049	0.0000	0.954	0.046
Means								
TIMEC		0.000	0.0083	0.1391	0.1312	0.0194	0.922	0.078
X		0.000	-0.0005	0.0224	0.0215	0.0005	0.944	0.056
Intercepts								
Y		0.000	0.0000	0.0214	0.0205	0.0005	0.934	0.066
M		0.000	0.0011	0.0306	0.0297	0.0009	0.940	0.060
Variances								
TIMEC		36.700	36.6227	1.1497	1.1149	1.3253	0.932	1.000
X		1.000	0.9989	0.0317	0.0306	0.0010	0.938	1.000
Residual Variances								
Y		0.855	0.8526	0.0266	0.0274	0.0007	0.950	1.000
M		1.860	1.8568	0.0613	0.0582	0.0038	0.916	1.000
Between Level								
CP	WITH							
A		0.008	0.0081	0.0082	0.0101	0.0001	0.980	0.076
B		0.018	0.0169	0.0057	0.0063	0.0000	0.968	0.826
A	WITH							
B		0.031	0.0309	0.0109	0.0107	0.0001	0.940	0.864
Means								
CP		0.106	0.1072	0.0234	0.0233	0.0005	0.956	0.994
A		0.189	0.1872	0.0405	0.0397	0.0016	0.940	0.998

B	0.149	0.1505	0.0269	0.0263	0.0007	0.950	1.000
Variances							
CP	0.009	0.0110	0.0053	0.0083	0.0000	0.994	0.154
A	0.067	0.0678	0.0234	0.0220	0.0005	0.928	0.916
B	0.046	0.0451	0.0093	0.0094	0.0001	0.924	1.000
New/Additional Parameters							
CORAB	0.531	0.5699	0.1652	0.1756	0.0287	0.930	0.864
MED	0.056	0.0593	0.0139	0.0139	0.0002	0.946	0.998
VMED	0.009	0.0092	0.0034	0.0032	0.0000	0.902	0.986
TE	0.162	0.1665	0.0275	0.0272	0.0008	0.946	1.000
PME	0.347	0.3587	0.0753	0.0754	0.0058	0.958	0.998

Consistent with the significant findings using the actual data, the power simulation confirms that the design was more than adequately powered, particularly for the within-subject mediated effect and the *ab* covariance. Given this (perhaps unusual) circumstance, we reran the simulations for other combinations of subjects and time points. For the mediated effect, 80% power can be obtained in a variety of ways. Instead of 100 couples and 21 days, the simulations indicated that 50 couples and 21 days would have sufficed, or 75 couples and 14 days. Even 100 couples and 7 days was close, with almost 70% power.

We also examined the *ab* covariance because of its crucial role in the mediated effect. For the actual data, it constituted over half of the mediated effect, 0.031 out of 0.056. Expressed as a correlation, it is $r = .53$. The power curve for the *ab* covariance also crossed the 80% line for 100 women and 21 days. Seventy-five couples and 21 days resulted in a power of 74%, which, depending on future research resources, is a risk some might consider acceptable.

10.8 CHAPTER SUMMARY

We have shown in this chapter how to conduct a power analysis for five important analysis types presented in earlier chapters: (1) modeling time for continuous outcomes, (2) modeling process for continuous outcomes, (3) modeling process for categorical outcomes, (4) modeling process for continuous outcomes in dyads, and (5) modeling within-subject mediation for continuous outcomes. Although it was not presented in this chapter, one could use the same approach and adapt code provided earlier to conduct a power analysis for assessing the reliability of within-subject change using multi-item scales (as covered in Chapter 7). A take-home message from this chapter might be that, all other things being equal, one generally gets more power by adding subjects than by adding time points to one's design. Although power analysis for intensive longitudinal studies is clearly an advanced topic and one that requires considerable effort, we hope that it will prove useful, especially for readers who are planning dissertation studies or are writing grant applications.

10.9 RECOMMENDED READINGS

Bolger, N., Stadler, G., & Laurenceau, J.-P. (2012). Power analysis for intensive longitudinal studies. In M. R. Mehl & T. S. Conner (Eds.), *Handbook of research methods for studying daily life* (pp. 285–301). New York: Guilford Press.

This chapter is a stand-alone introduction to power analysis in intensive longitudinal designs. It presents a worked example on calculating power for a study of how within-subject changes in daily physical activity influence depressed mood.

Fitzmaurice, G. M., Laird, N. M., & Ware, J. H. (2011). *Applied longitudinal analysis* (2nd ed.). Hoboken, NJ: Wiley.

In Chapter 20 of their book, the authors provide a lucid account of factors that affect statistical power in models of the time course of continuous and categorical outcomes.

Muthén, L. K., & Muthén, B. O. (2002). How to use a Monte Carlo study to decide on sample size and determine power. *Structural Equation Modeling, 9,* 599–620.

This article provides an excellent introduction to using simulation in Mplus to calculate statistical power.

Snijders, T. A. B., & Bosker, R. J. (1993). Standard errors and sample sizes for two-level research. *Journal of Educational Statistics, 18,* 237–259.

This article explains the link between standard errors, lower- and upper-level sample sizes, and power for multilevel models.

References

Ackerman, R. A., Donnellan, M. B., & Kashy, D. A. (2011). Working with dyadic data in studies of emerging adulthood: Specific recommendations, general advice, and practical tips. In F. Fincham & M. Cui (Eds.), *Romantic relationships in emerging adulthood* (pp. 67–98). New York: Cambridge University Press.

Affleck, G., Zautra, A., Tennen, H., & Armeli, S. (1999). Multilevel daily process designs for consulting and clinical psychology: A preface for the perplexed. *Journal of Consulting and Clinical Psychology, 67*, 746–754.

Agresti, A. (2007). *An introduction to categorical data analysis* (2nd ed.). Hoboken, NJ: Wiley.

Aharony, N., Pan, W., Ip, C., Khayal, I., & Pentland, A. (2011). Social fMRI: Investigating and shaping social mechanisms in the real world. *Pervasive and Mobile Computing, 7*, 643–659.

Aiken, L. S., & West, S. G. (1991). *Multiple regression: Testing and interpreting interactions.* Newbury Park, CA: Sage.

Allison, P. D. (2005). *Fixed effects regression methods for longitudinal data using SAS.* Cary, NC: SAS Institute.

Allison, P. D. (2009). *Fixed effects regression models.* Thousand Oaks, CA: Sage.

Alloy, L. B., Just, N., & Panzarella, C. (1997). Attributional style, daily life events, and hopelessness depression: Subtype validation by prospective variability and specificity of symptoms. *Cognitive Therapy and Research, 21*, 321–344.

Allport, G. W. (1942). *The use of personal documents in psychological science.* New York: Social Science Research Council.

Almeida, D. M., & Kessler, R. C. (1998). Everyday stressors and gender differences in daily distress. *Journal of Personality and Social Psychology, 75*, 670–680.

American Psychological Association. (2009). *Publication manual of the American Psychological Association* (6th ed.). Washington, DC: Author.

Atlas, L. Y., Bolger, N., Lindquist, M. A., & Wager, T. D. (2010). Brain mediators of predictive cue effects on perceived pain. *The Journal of Neuroscience, 30*, 12964–12977.

Baltes, P. B., Reese, H. W., & Nesselroade, J. R. (1988). *Life-span developmental psychology: Introduction to research methods.* Hillsdale, NJ: Erlbaum.

Barnett, R. C., Marshall, N. L., Raudenbush, S. W., & Brennan, R. T. (1993). Gender and the relationship between job experiences and psychological distress: A study of dual-earner couples. *Journal of Personality and Social Psychology, 64*, 794–806.

Baron, R. M., & Kenny, D. A. (1986). The moderator–mediator variable distinction in social psychological research: Conceptual, strategic, and statistical considerations. *Journal of Personality and Social Psychology, 51*, 1173–1182.

Barrett, L. F. (2004). Feelings or words?: Understanding the content in self-report ratings of emotional experience. *Journal of Personality and Social Psychology, 87*, 266–281.

Barta, W., Tennen, H., & Litt, M. D. (2012). Measurement reactivity in diary research. In M. R. Mehl & T. S. Conner (Eds.), *Handbook of research methods for studying daily life* (pp. 108–123). New York: Guilford Press.

Bauer, D. J., Preacher, K. J., & Gil, K. M. (2006). Conceptualizing and testing random indirect effects and moderated mediation in multilevel models: New procedures and recommendations. *Psychological Methods, 11*, 142–163.

Baumeister, R. F., Vohs, K. D., & Funder, D. C. (2007). Psychology as the science of self-reports and finger movements: Whatever happened to actual behavior? *Perspectives on Psychological Science, 2*, 396–403.

Belcher, A. J., Laurenceau, J.-P., Graber, E. C., Cohen, L. H., Dasch-Yee, K. B., & Siegel, S. D. (2011). Daily support in couples coping with early stage breast cancer: Maintaining intimacy during adversity. *Health Psychology, 30*, 665–673.

Berscheid, E. (1999). The greening of relationship science. *American Psychologist, 54*, 260–266.

Bevans, G. E. (1913). *How working men spend their spare time.* New York: Columbia University Press.

Black, A. C., Harel, O., & Matthews, G. (2012). Techniques for analyzing intensive longitudinal data with missing values. In M. R. Mehl & T. S. Conner (Eds.), *Handbook of research methods for studying daily life* (pp. 339–356). New York: Guilford Press.

Boker, S. M., & Laurenceau, J.-P. (2006). Dynamical systems modeling: An application to the regulation of intimacy and disclosure in marriage.

In T. A. Walls & J. L. Schafer (Eds.), *Models for intensive longitudinal data* (pp. 195–218). New York: Oxford University Press.

Bolger, N. (1990). Coping as a personality process: A prospective study. *Journal of Personality and Social Psychology, 59,* 525–537.

Bolger, N., Davis, A., & Rafaeli, E. (2003). Diary methods: Capturing life as it is lived. *Annual Review of Psychology, 54,* 579–616.

Bolger, N., DeLongis, A., Kessler, R. C., & Schilling, E. A. (1989). Effects of daily stress on negative mood. *Journal of Personality and Social Psychology, 57,* 808–818.

Bolger, N., DeLongis, A., Kessler, R. C., & Wethington, E. (1989). The contagion of stress across multiple roles. *Journal of Marriage and the Family, 51,* 175–183.

Bolger, N., DeLongis, A., Kessler, R. C., & Wethington, E. (1990). The microstructure of daily role-related stress in married couples. In J. Eckenrode & S. Gore (Eds.), *Stress between work and family* (pp. 95–115). New York: Plenum Press.

Bolger, N., & Schilling, E. A. (1991). Personality and the problems of everyday life: The role of neuroticism in exposure and reactivity to daily stressors. *Journal of Personality, 59,* 355–386.

Bolger, N., & Shrout, P. E. (2007). Accounting for statistical dependency in longitudinal data on dyads. In T. D. Little, J. A. Bovaird, & N. A. Card (Eds.), *Modeling contextual effects in longitudinal studies* (pp. 285–298). Mahwah, NJ: Erlbaum.

Bolger, N., Stadler, G., & Laurenceau, J.-P. (2012). Power analysis for intensive longitudinal studies. In M. R. Mehl & T. S. Conner (Eds.), *Handbook of research methods for studying daily life* (pp. 285–301). New York: Guilford Press.

Bolger, N., Stadler, G., Paprocki, C., & DeLongis, A. (2009). Grounding social psychology in behavior in daily life: The case of conflict and distress in couples. In C. Agnew, D. E. Carlston, W. G. Graziano, & J. E. Kelly (Eds.), *Then a miracle occurs: Focusing on behavior in social psychological theory and research* (pp. 368–390). New York: Oxford University Press.

Bolger, N., & Zuckerman, A. (1995). A framework for studying personality in the stress process. *Journal of Personality and Social Psychology, 69,* 890–902.

Bolger, N., Zuckerman, A., & Kessler, R. C. (2000). Invisible support and adjustment to stress. *Journal of Personality and Social Psychology, 79,* 953–961.

Bollen, K. A., & Curran, P. J. (2006). *Latent curve models: A structural equation perspective.* Hoboken, NJ: Wiley.

Borsboom, D., Mellenbergh, G. J., & van Heerden, J. (2003). The theoretical status of latent variables. *Psychological Review, 110,* 203–219.

Bosker, R. J., Snijders, T. A. B., & Guldemond, H. (2007). *PinT: (Power in two-level designs) Estimating standard errors of regression coefficients in hierarchical linear models for power calculations (Version 2.12)*. Groningen, The Netherlands: Authors.

Brennan, R. L. (2001). *Generalizability theory*. New York: Springer.

Byerly, M. J., Fisher, R., Carmody, T. J., Rush, A. J. (2005). A trial of compliance therapy in outpatients with schizophrenia or schizoaffective disorder. *Journal of Clinical Psychiatry, 66,* 997–1001.

Cohen, J. (1988). *Statistical power analysis for the behavioral sciences* (2nd ed.). Hillsdale, NJ: Erlbaum.

Cohen, L. H., Gunthert, K., Butler, A., Parrish, B., Wenze, S., & Beck, J. (2008). Negative affective spillover from daily events predicts early response to cognitive therapy for depression. *Journal of Consulting and Clinical Psychology, 76,* 955–965.

Cole, D. A., & Maxwell, S. E. (2003). Testing mediational models with longitudinal data: Questions and tips in the use of structural equation modeling. *Journal of Abnormal Psychology, 112,* 558–577.

Collins, L. M. (2006). Analysis of longitudinal data: The integration of theoretical model, temporal design, and statistical model. *Annual Review of Psychology, 57,* 505–528.

Collins, L. M., & Graham, J. W. (2002). The effect of the timing and temporal spacing of observations in longitudinal studies of tobacco and other drug use: Temporal design considerations. *Drug and Alcohol Dependence, 68,* S85–S96.

Conner, T. S., & Lehman, B. J. (2012). Getting started: Launching a study in daily life. In M. R. Mehl & S. T. Conner (Eds.), *Handbook of research methods for studying daily life* (pp. 89–107). New York: Guilford Press.

Cook, T. D., & Groom, C. (2004). The methodological assumptions of social psychology: The mutual dependence of substantive theory and method choice. In C. Sansone, C. C. Morf, & A. T. Panter (Eds.), *The Sage handbook of methods in social psychology* (pp. 19–44). Thousand Oaks, CA: Sage.

Cranford, J. A., Shrout, P. E., Iida, M., Rafaeli, E., Yip, T., & Bolger, N. (2006). A procedure for evaluating sensitivity to within-person change: Can mood measures in diary studies detect change reliably? *Personality and Social Psychology Bulletin, 32,* 917–929.

Crocker, L., & Algina, J. (1986). *Introduction to classical and modern test theory*. Belmont, CA: Wadsworth.

Cronbach, L. J. (1951). Coefficient alpha and the internal structure of tests. *Psychometrika, 16,* 297–334.

Cronbach, L. J., & Furby, L. (1970). How should we measure "change"—or should we? *Psychological Bulletin, 74,* 68–80.

Cronbach, L. J., Gleser, G. C., Nanda, H., & Rajaratnam, N. (1972). *The dependability of behavioral measurements: Theory of generalizability for scores and profiles*. New York: Wiley.

Csikszentmihalyi, M., & Larson, R. (1984). *Being adolescent: Conflict and growth in the teenage years.* New York: Basic Books.

Csikszentmihalyi, M., Larson, R., & Prescott, S. (1977). The ecology of adolescent activity and experience. *Journal of Youth and Adolescence, 6,* 281–294.

Cummings, E. M., Goeke-Morey, M. C., Papp, L. M., & Dukewich, T. L. (2002). Children's responses to mothers' and fathers' emotionality and tactics in marital conflict in the home. *Journal of Family Psychology, 16,* 478–492.

Delespaul, P. A. E. G. (1995). *Assessing schizophrenia in daily life.* Maastricht: Universitaire Pers Maastricht.

deVries, M. W. (Ed.). (1992). *The experience of psychopathology: Investigating mental disorders in their natural settings.* New York: Cambridge University Press.

Diener, E., & Emmons, R. A. (1985). The independence of positive and negative affect. *Journal of Personality and Social Psychology, 47,* 1105–1117.

Diener, E., & Larsen, R. J. (1984). Temporal stability and cross-situational consistency of affective, cognitive, and behavioral responses. *Journal of Personality and Social Psychology, 47,* 871–883.

Diggle, P., Heagerty, P., Liang, K.-Y., & Zeger, S. L. (2002). *Analysis of longitudinal data* (2nd ed.). New York: Oxford University Press.

Duck, S. W. (1991). Diaries and logs. In B. M. Montgomery & S. W. Duck (Eds.), *Studying social interaction* (pp. 141–161). New York: Guilford Press.

Eckenrode, J., & Bolger, N. (1995). Daily and within-day event measurement. In S. Cohen, R. C. Kessler, & L. U. Gordon (Eds.), *Measuring stress: A guide for health and social scientists* (pp. 80–101). New York: Oxford University Press.

Enders, C. K. (2010). *Applied missing data analysis.* New York: Guilford Press.

Fabes, R. A., & Eisenberg, N. (1997). Regulatory control and adults' stress-related responses to daily life events. *Journal of Personality and Social Psychology, 73,* 1107–1117.

Fahrenberg, J., & Myrtek, M. (Eds.). (2001). *Progress in ambulatory assessment.* Seattle: Hogrefe & Huber.

Fahrenberg, J., Myrtek, M., Pawlik, K., & Perrez, M. (2007). Ambulatory assessment-monitoring in daily life settings: A behavioral-scientific challenge for psychology. *European Journal of Psychological Assessment, 23,* 206–213.

Feldman, L. A. (1995). Valence focus and arousal focus: Individual differences in the structure of affective experience. *Journal of Personality and Social Psychology, 69,* 153–166.

Ferguson, G. A., & Takane, Y. (1989). *Statistical analysis in psychology and education* (6th ed.). New York: McGraw-Hill.

Fitzmaurice, G. M., Davidian, M., Verbeke, G., & Molenberghs, G. (Eds.). (2009). *Longitudinal data analysis*. Boca Raton, FL: CRC Press.

Fitzmaurice, G. M., Laird, N. M., & Ware, J. H. (2011). *Applied longitudinal analysis* (2nd ed.). Hoboken, NJ: Wiley.

Froehlich, J., Chen, M., Smith, I., & Potter, F. (2006, September 17–21). *Voting with your feet: An investigative study of the relationship between place visit behavior and preference*. Paper presented at UbiComp 2006, Orange County, CA.

Gable, S. L., Reis, H. T., & Downey, G. (2003). He said, she said: A quasi-signal detection analysis of daily interactions between close relationship partners. *Psychological Science, 14*, 100–105.

Gelman, A., & Hill, J. (2007). *Data analysis using regression and multilevel/hierarchical models*. New York: Cambridge University Press.

Gleason, M. E. J., Iida, M., Bolger, N., & Shrout, P. E. (2003). Daily supportive equity in close relationships. *Personality and Social Psychology Bulletin, 29*, 1036–1045.

Gleason, M. E. J., Iida, M., Shrout, P. E., & Bolger, N. (2008). Receiving support as a mixed blessing: Evidence for dual effects of support on psychological outcomes. *Journal of Personality and Social Psychology, 94*, 824–838.

Gonzalez, R., & Griffin, D. (1999). The correlational analysis of dyad-level data in the distinguishable case. *Personal Relationships, 6*, 449–469.

Gonzalez, R. & Griffin, D. (2000). The statistics of interdependence: Treating dyadic data with respect. In W. Ickes & S. W. Duck (Eds.), *The social psychology of personal relationships* (pp. 181–213). Chichester, UK: Wiley.

Graham, J. W. (2009). Missing data analysis: Making it work in the real world. *Annual Review of Psychology, 60*, 549–576.

Greene, W. H. (2008). *Econometric analysis* (6th ed.). Upper Saddle River, NJ: Pearson/Prentice Hall.

Grimm, K. J., & Ram, N. (2009). Nonlinear growth models in Mplus and SAS. *Structural Equation Modeling, 16*, 676–701.

Hamaker, E. L. (2012). Why researchers should think "within-person": A paradigmatic rationale. In M. R. Mehl & T. S. Conner (Eds.), *Handbook of research methods for studying daily life* (pp. 43–61). New York: Guilford Press.

Hedeker, D. (2003). A mixed-effects multinomial logistic regression model. *Statistics in Medicine, 22*, 1433–1446.

Hedeker, D. (2008). Multilevel models for ordinal and nominal variables. In J. de Leeuw & E. Meijer (Eds.), *Handbook of multilevel analysis* (pp. 237–274). New York: Springer.

Hedeker, D., & Mermelstein, R. J. (2011). Multilevel analysis of ordinal outcomes related to survival data. In J. J. Hox & J. K. Roberts (Eds.),

Handbook of advanced multilevel analysis (pp. 115–136). New York: Routledge.

Hektner, J. M., Schmidt, J. A., & Csikszentmihalyi, M. (2007). *Experience sampling method: Measuring the quality of everyday life.* Thousand Oaks, CA: Sage.

Holland, P. (1986). Statistics and causal inference (with comments). *Journal of the American Statistical Association, 81,* 945–970.

Hormuth, S. E. (1986). The sampling of experiences in situ. *Journal of Personality, 54,* 262–293.

Hox, J. J. (2010). *Multilevel analysis: Techniques and applications* (2nd ed.). New York: Routledge.

Hurlburt, R. T., & Sipprelle, C. N. (1978). Random sampling of cognitions in alleviating anxiety attacks. *Cognitive Therapy and Research, 2*(2), 165–169.

IBM Inc. (2010). *IBM SPSS Statistics (Version 19).* Armonk, NY: Author.

Iida, M., Shrout, P. E., Laurenceau, J.-P., & Bolger, N. (2012). Using diary methods in psychological research. In H. Cooper, P. M. Camic, D. L. Long, A. T. Panter, D. Rindskopf, & K. J. Sher (Eds.), *APA handbook of research methods in psychology: Vol. 1. Foundations, planning, measures and psychometrics* (pp. 277–305). Washington, DC: American Psychological Association.

Intille, S. S. (2005). Technological innovations enabling automatic, context-sensitive ecological momentary assessment. In A. A. Stone, S. Shiffman, A. A. Atienza, & L. Nebeling (Eds.), *The science of real-time data capture: Self-reports in health research* (pp. 308–337). New York: Oxford University Press.

Intille, S. S. (2012). Emerging technology for studying daily life. In M. R. Mehl & T. S. Conner (Eds.), *Handbook of research methods for studying daily life* (pp. 267–284). New York: Guilford Press.

Intille, S. S., Rondoni, J., Kukla, C., Anacona, I., & Bao, L. (2003). A context-aware experience sampling tool. In *Proceedings of CHI '03 extended abstracts on human factors in computing systems* (pp. 972–973). New York: ACM Press.

Judge, C. G., Griffiths, W. E., Hill, R. C., & Lee, T. C. (1980). *The theory and practice of econometrics.* New York: Wiley.

Kennedy, J. K., Bolger, N., & Shrout, P. E. (2002). Witnessing interpersonal psychological aggression in childhood: Implications for daily conflict in adult intimate relationships. *Journal of Personality, 70,* 1051–1077.

Kenny, D. A., & Kashy, D. A. (2011). Dyadic data analysis using multilevel modeling. In J. Hox & J. K. Roberts (Eds.), *Handbook of advanced multilevel analysis* (pp. 335–370). New York: Taylor & Francis.

Kenny, D. A., Kashy, D. A., & Bolger, N. (1998). Data analysis in social psychology. In D. T. Gilbert, S. T. Fiske, & G. Lindzey (Eds.), *The handbook of social psychology* (4th ed., Vol. 1, pp. 233–265). New York: McGraw-Hill.

Kenny, D. A., Kashy, D. A., & Cook, W. L. (2006). *Dyadic data analysis.* New York: Guilford Press.

Kenny, D. A., Korchmaros, J. D., & Bolger, N. (2003). Lower level mediation in multilevel models. *Psychological Methods, 8,* 115–128.

Kenny, D. A., Mannetti, L., Pierro, A., Livi, S., & Kashy, D. A. (2002). The statistical analysis of data from small groups. *Journal of Personality and Social Psychology, 83,* 126–137.

Kenny, D. A., & Zautra, A. (1995). The trait–state–error model for multiwave data. *Journal of Consulting and Clinical Psychology, 63,* 52–59.

Kline, R. B. (2011). *Principles and practice of structural equation modeling* (3rd ed.). New York: Guilford Press.

Kreft, I. G. G., de Leeuw, J., & Aiken, L. S. (1995). Effects of different forms of centering in hierarchical linear models. *Multivariate Behavioral Research, 30*(1), 1–22.

Krull, J. L., & MacKinnon, D. P. (2001). Multilevel modeling of individual and group level mediated effects. *Multivariate Behavioral Research, 36,* 249–277.

Kuppens, P., Oravecz, Z., & Tuerlinckx, F. (2010). Feelings change: Accounting for individual differences in the temporal dynamics of affect. *Journal of Personality and Social Psychology, 99,* 1042–1060.

Kurdek, L. A. (1994). Conflict resolution styles in gay, lesbian, heterosexual nonparent, and heterosexual parent couples. *Journal of Marriage and the Family, 56,* 705–722.

Larson, R. W., & Almeida, D. M. (1999). Emotional transmission in the daily lives of families: A new paradigm for studying family process. *Journal of Marriage and the Family, 61,* 5–20.

Larson, R., & Csikszentmihalyi, M. (1983). The experience sampling method. *New Directions for Methodology of Social and Behavioral Science, 15,* 41–56.

Laurenceau, J.-P., & Bolger, N. (2005). Using diary methods to study marital and family processes. *Journal of Family Psychology, 19,* 86–97.

Laurenceau, J.-P., & Bolger, N. (2012). Analyzing diary and intensive longitudinal data from dyads. In R. M. Mehl & T. S. Conner (Eds.), *Handbook of research methods for studying daily life* (pp. 407–422). New York: Guilford Press.

Laurenceau, J.-P., Feldman Barrett, L., & Rovine, M. J. (2005). The interpersonal process model of intimacy in marriage: A daily-diary and multilevel modeling approach. *Journal of Family Psychology, 19,* 314–323.

Litt, M. D., Cooney, N. L., & Morse, P. (1998). Ecological momentary assessment (EMA) with treated alcoholics: Methodological problems and potential solutions. *Health Psychology, 17,* 48–52.

Littell, R. C., Milliken, G. A., Stroup, W. W., Wolfinger, R. D., &

Schabenberger, O. (2006). *SAS for mixed models* (2nd ed.). Cary, NC: SAS Institute.

Little, R. J. A., & Rubin, D. B. (2002) *Statistical analysis with missing data* (2nd ed.). New York: Wiley.

Lord, F. M. (1963). Elementary models for measuring change. In C. W. Harris (Ed.), *Problems in measuring change* (pp. 21–38). Madison: University of Wisconsin Press.

Lord, F. M., & Novick, M. R. (1968). *Statistical theories of mental test scores.* Reading, MA: Addison-Wesley.

MacCallum, R. C., Kim, C., Malarkey, W. B., & Kiecolt-Glaser, J. K. (1997). Studying multivariate change using multilevel models and latent curve models. *Multivariate Behavioral Research, 32,* 215–253.

MacKinnon, D. P. (2008). *Introduction to statistical mediation analysis.* Mahwah, NJ: Erlbaum.

MacKinnon, D. P., Lockwood, C. M., Hoffman, J. M., West, S. G., & Sheets, V. (2002). A comparison of methods to test mediation and other intervening variable effects. *Psychological Methods, 7,* 83–104.

MathWorks Inc. (2011). *Matlab (Version 7.12).* Sherborn, MA: Author.

McAdams, D. P., & Constantian, C. A. (1983). Intimacy and affiliation motives in daily living: An experience sampling analysis. *Journal of Personality and Social Psychology, 45,* 851–861.

McCulloch, C. E., Searle, S. R., & Neuhaus, J. M. (2008). *Generalized, linear, and mixed models* (2nd ed.). New York: Wiley.

McDonald, R. P. (1999). *Test theory: A unified treatment.* Mahwah, NJ: Erlbaum.

Mehl, M. R., & Conner, T. S. (Eds.). (2012). *Handbook of research methods for studying daily life.* New York: Guilford Press.

Mehl, M., Pennebaker, J. W., Crow, D. M., Dabbs, J., & Price, J. (2001). The Electronically Activated Recorder (EAR): A device for sampling naturalistic daily activities and conversations. *Behavior Research Methods, Instruments, and Computers, 33,* 517–523.

Mehl, M. R., Vazire, S., Ramirez-Esparza, N., Slatcher, R. B., & Pennebaker, J. W. (2007). Are women really more talkative than men? *Science, 317,* 82.

Moerbeek, M., Van Breukelen, G. J. P., & Berger, M. P. F. (2008). Optimal designs for multilevel studies. In J. de Leeuw & E. Meijer (Eds.), *Handbook of multilevel analysis* (pp. 177–205). New York: Springer.

Molenaar, P. C. M. (2004). A manifesto on psychology as idiographic science: Bringing the person back into scientific psychology, this time forever. *Measurement, 2*(4), 201–218.

Molenaar, P. C. M., & Campbell, C. G. (2009). The new person-specific paradigm in psychology. *Current Directions in Psychology, 18,* 112–117.

Multivariate Software Inc. (2011). *EQS 6.1.* Encino, CA: Author.

Muthén, B. O. (1994). Multilevel covariance structure analysis. *Sociological Methods and Research, 22,* 376–398.

Muthén, B. O., & Asparouhov, T. (2011). Beyond multilevel regression modeling: Multilevel analysis in a general latent variable framework. In J. Hox & J. K. Roberts (Eds.), *Handbook of advanced multilevel analysis* (pp. 15–40). New York: Taylor & Francis.

Muthén, L. K., & Muthén, B. O. (1998–2010). *Mplus user's guide* (6th ed.). Los Angeles, CA: Authors.

Muthén, L. K., & Muthén, B. O. (2002). How to use a Monte Carlo study to decide on sample size and determine power. *Structural Equation Modeling, 9*, 599–620.

Neyman, J. (1990). On the application of probability theory to agricultural experiments: Essay on statistical principles, Section 9 (D. M. Dabrowska & T. P. Speed, Trans.). *Statistical Science, 5*, 465–480. (Original work published 1923)

Neyman, J., & Pearson, E. S. (1933). The testing of statistical hypotheses in relation to probabilities a priori. *Proceedings of the Cambridge Philosophical Society, 29*, 492–510.

Nilsen, W. J., Haverkos, L., Nebeling, L., & Taylor, M. V. (2010). Maintenance of long-term behavior change. *American Journal of Health Behavior, 34*, 643–646.

Nusser, S. M., Intille, S. S., & Maitra, R. (2006). Emerging technologies and next-generation intensive longitudinal data collection. In T. A. Walls & J. L. Schafer (Eds.), *Models for intensive longitudinal data* (pp. 254–278). New York: Oxford University Press.

Pawlik, K., & Buse, L. (1982). *Rechnergestutzte verhaltensregistrierung im field: Beschreibung und erste psychometrische Uberprufung einer neuen erhebungsmethode* [Computer-aided behavior recording in the field: Description and first psychometric test of a new investigative method]. *Zeitschrift für Differentielle and Diagnostische Psychologie, 3*, 101–118.

Pember-Reeves, M. (1913). *Round about a pound a week*. London: Bell.

Perrez, M., Schoebi, D., & Wilhelm, P. (2000). How to assess social regulation of stress and emotions in daily family life?: A computer-assisted family self-monitoring system (FASEM-C). *Clinical Psychology and Psychotherapy, 7*, 326–339.

R Development Core Team. (2011). *R: A language and environment for statistical computing (Version 2.8)*. Vienna, Austria: R Foundation for Statistical Computing.

Rabe-Hesketh, S., & Skrondal, A. (2009). Generalized linear mixed-effects models. In G. M. Fitzmaurice, M. Davidian, G. Verbeke, & G. Molenberghs (Eds.), *Longitudinal data analysis* (pp. 79–106). Boca Raton: CRC Press.

Rao, C. R. (1971). Estimation of variance and covariance components: MINQUE theory. *Journal of Multivariate Analysis, 1*, 257–275.

Rasbash, J., Charlton, C., Browne, W. J., Healy, M., & Cameron, B. (2011).

MLwiN Version 2.23. Bristol, UK: Centre for Multilevel Modelling, University of Bristol.

Raudenbush, S. W., Brennan, R. T., & Barnett, R. C. (1995). A multivariate hierarchical model for studying psychological change within married couples. *Journal of Family Psychology, 9*, 161–174.

Raudenbush, S. W., & Bryk, A. S. (2002). *Hierarchical linear models: Applications and data analysis methods* (2nd ed.). Thousand Oaks, CA: Sage.

Raudenbush, S. W., Bryk, A. S., Cheong, Y. F., Congdon, R. T., Jr., & du Toit, M. (2011). *HLM 7: Hierarchical linear and nonlinear modeling.* Lincolnwood, IL: Scientific Software International.

Raudenbush, S. W., Spybrook, J., Liu, X.-F., & Congdon, R., Jr. (2006). *Optimal design (Version 1.77).* Ann Arbor, MI: HLM Software.

Raykov, T., & Marcoulides, G. A. (2011). *Introduction to psychometric theory.* New York: Taylor & Francis.

Reis, H. T. (1994). Domains of experience: Investigating relationship processes from three perspectives. In R. Erber & R. Gilmour (Eds.), *Theoretical frameworks for personal relationships* (pp. 87–110). Hillsdale, NJ: Erlbaum.

Reis, H. T., Collins, W. A., & Berscheid, E. (2000). The relationship context of human behavior and development. *Psychological Bulletin, 126*, 844–872.

Reis, H. T., & Gable, S. L. (2000). Event sampling and other methods for studying daily experience. In H. T. Reis & C. M. Judd (Eds.), *Handbook of research methods in social and personality psychology* (pp. 190—222). New York: Cambridge University Press.

Reis, H. T., & Gosling, S. D. (2010). Social psychological methods outside the laboratory. In S. Fiske, D. Gilbert, & G. Lindzey (Eds.), *Handbook of social psychology* (5th ed., Vol. 1, pp. 82–114). New York: Wiley.

Reis, H. T., Nezlek, J. B., & Wheeler, L. (1980). Physical attractiveness in social interaction. *Journal of Personality and Social Psychology, 48*, 1204–1217.

Reis, H. T., & Shaver, P. R. (1988). Intimacy as an interpersonal process. In S. Duck (Ed.), *Handbook of relationships* (pp. 367–389). Chichester, UK: Wiley.

Reis, H. T., & Wheeler, L. (1991). Studying social interaction with the Rochester Interaction Record. In M. P. Zanna (Ed.), *Advances in experimental social psychology* (Vol. 24, pp. 270–318). San Diego, CA: Academic Press.

Repetti, R. L. (1989). Effects of daily workload on subsequent behavior during marital interaction: The roles of social withdrawal and spouse support. *Journal of Personality and Social Psychology, 57*, 651–659.

Repetti, R. L., & Wood, J. (1997). Effects of daily stress at work on mothers' interactions with preschoolers. *Journal of Family Psychology, 11*, 90–108.

Robinson, M. D., & Clore, G. L. (2002). Belief and feeling: Evidence for an accessibility model of emotional self-report. *Psychological Bulletin, 128,* 934–960.

Robinson, W. S. (1950). Ecological correlations and the behavior of individuals. *American Sociological Review, 15,* 351–357.

Rubin, D. B. (1974). Estimating causal effects of treatments in randomized and nonrandomized studies. *Journal of Educational Psychology, 66,* 688–701.

SAS Institute Inc. (2011). *SAS 9.2.* Cary, NC: Author.

Schafer, J. L., & Graham, J. W. (2002). Missing data: Our view of the state of the art. *Psychological Methods, 7,* 147–177.

Schneiders, J., Nicolson, N. A., Berkhof, J., Feron, F. J., deVries, M. W., van Os, J. (2007). Mood in daily contexts: Relationships with risk in early adolescence. *Journal of Research on Adolescence, 17,* 697–722.

Schwartz, J. E., & Stone, A. A. (2007). The analysis of real-time momentary data: A practical guide. In A. A. Stone, S. Shiffman, A. A. Atienza, & L. Nebeling (Eds.), *The science of real-time data capture: Self-reports in health research* (pp. 76–114). New York: Oxford University Press.

Schwarz, N. (2007). Retrospective and concurrent self-reports: The rationale for real-time data capture. In A. A. Stone, S. Shiffman, A. Atienza, & L. Nebeling (Eds.), *The science of real-time data capture: Self-reports in health research* (pp. 11–26). New York: Oxford University Press.

Shavelson, R. J., & Webb, N. M. (1991). *Generalizability theory: A primer.* Thousand Oaks, CA: Sage.

Shiffman, S., Stone, A. A., & Hufford, M. R. (2008). Ecological momentary assessment. *Annual Review of Clinical Psychology, 4,* 1–32.

Shrout, P. E., & Bolger, N. (2002). Mediation in experimental and nonexperimental studies: New procedures and recommendations. *Psychological Methods, 7,* 422–445.

Shrout, P. E., & Lane, S. P. (2012a). Psychometrics. In M. R. Mehl & T. S. Conner (Eds.), *Handbook of research methods for studying daily life* (pp. 302–320). New York: Guilford Press.

Shrout, P. E., & Lane, S. P. (2012b). Reliability. In H. Cooper, P. M. Camic, D. L. Long, A. T. Panter, D. Rindskopf, & K. J. Sher (Eds.), *APA handbook of research methods in psychology: Vol. 1. Foundations, planning, measures, and psychometrics* (pp. 643–660). Washington, DC: American Psychological Association.

Singer, J. D., & Willett, J. B. (2003). *Applied longitudinal data analysis: Modeling change and event occurrence.* New York: Oxford University Press.

Smith, A. (2011, July). Pew Internet Project and American Life Project. Retrieved August 18, 2011, from *pewinternet.org/Reports/2011/Smartphones.aspx.*

Snijders, T. A. B., & Bosker, R. J. (1993). Standard errors and sample sizes for two-level research. *Journal of Educational Statistics, 18,* 237–259.

Snijders, T. A. B., & Bosker, R. J. (2012). *Multilevel analysis: An introduction to basic and advanced multilevel modeling* (2nd ed.). Thousand Oaks, CA: Sage.

Sobel, M. E. (1982). Asymptotic confidence intervals for indirect effects in structural equation models. In S. Leinhardt (Ed.), *Sociological methodology 1982* (pp. 290–312). San Francisco: Jossey-Bass.

Sobel, M. E. (1986). Some new results on indirect effects and their standard errors in covariance structure models. In N. Tuma (Ed.), *Sociological methodology* (Vol. 16, pp. 159–186). Washington, DC: American Sociological Association.

Sorokin, P. A., & Berger, C. Q. (1939). *Time budgets of human behaviour.* Cambridge, MA: Harvard University Press.

Spencer, S. J., Zanna, M. P., & Fong, G. T. (2005). Establishing a causal chain: Why experiments are often more effective than mediational analyses in examining psychological processes. *Journal of Personality and Social Psychology, 89,* 845–851.

SSI Inc. (2010). *LISREL 8.8.* Chicago: Author.

StataCorp LP. (2011). *Stata 12.* College Station, TX: Author.

Stigler, S. M. (1986). *The history of statistics: The measurement of uncertainty before 1900.* Cambridge, MA: Harvard University Press.

Stone, A. A., & Shiffman, S. (1992). Recollections on the intensive measurement of stress, coping and mood. *Psychology and Health, 7,* 115–129.

Stone, A. A., & Shiffman, S. (1994). Ecological momentary assessment (EMA) in behavioral medicine. *Annals of Behavioral Medicine, 16,* 199–202.

Stone, A. A., & Shiffman, S. (2002). Capturing momentary, self-report data: A proposal for reporting guidelines. *Annals of Behavioral Medicine, 24,* 236–243.

Stone, A. A., Shiffman, S., Atienza, A., & Nebeling, L. (2007). *The science of real-time data capture: Self-reports in health research.* New York: Oxford University Press.

Stone, A. A., Shiffman, S., & DeVries, M. (1999). Rethinking our self-report assessment methodologies: An argument for collecting ecologically valid, momentary measurements. In D. Kahneman, E. Diener, & N. Schwarz (Eds.), *Well-being: The foundations of hedonic psychology* (pp. 26–39). New York: Sage.

Swim, J. K., Hyers, L. L., Cohen, L. L., & Ferguson, M. J. (2001). Everyday sexism: Evidence for its incidence, nature, and psychological impact from three daily diary studies. *Journal of Social Issues, 57,* 31–54.

Swim, J. K., Hyers, L. L., Cohen, L. L., Fitzgerald, D. F., & Bylsma, W. B. (2003). African American college students' experiences with everyday anti-black racism: Characteristics of and responses to these incidents. *Journal of Black Psychology, 29,* 38–67.

Tennen, H., Affleck, G., & Armeli, S. (2003). Daily processes at the interface of social and health psychology. In J. Suls & K. Wallston (Eds.), *The social foundations of health and illness* (pp. 495–529). Oxford, UK: Blackwell.

Thompson, A., & Bolger, N. (1999). Emotional transmission in couples under stress. *Journal of Marriage and the Family, 61*, 38–48.

Tidwell, M., Reis, H. T., & Shaver, P. R. (1996). Attachment styles, attractiveness, and emotions in social interactions: A diary study. *Journal of Personality and Social Psychology, 71*, 729–745.

Tversky, A., & Kahneman, D. (1982). Evidential impact of base rates. In D. Kahneman, P. Slovic, & A. Tversky (Eds.), *Judgment under uncertainty: Heuristics and biases* (pp. 153–160). New York: Cambridge University Press.

U.S. Food and Drug Administration. (2009, December). Guidance for industry. Patient reported outcome measures: Use in medical product development to support labelling claims. Retrieved December 17, 2009, from *www.fda.gov/downloads/Drugs/GuidanceComplianceRegulatoryInformation/Guidances/UCM193282.pdf*.

Walls, T. A., & Schafer, J. L. (Eds.). (2006). *Models for intensive longitudinal data.* New York: Oxford University Press.

Wheeler, L., & Nezlek, J. B. (1977). Sex differences in social participation. *Journal of Personality and Social Psychology, 35*, 742–754.

Wheeler, L., & Reis, H. T. (1991). Self-recording of everyday events: Origins, types, and uses. *Journal of Personality, 59*, 339–354.

Wills, T. A., Weiss, R. L., & Patterson, G. R. (1974). A behavioral analysis of the determinants of marital satisfaction. *Journal of Consulting and Clinical Psychology, 42*, 802–811.

Winer, B. J. (1971). *Statistical principles in experimental design* (2nd ed.). New York: McGraw-Hill.

Wold, H. (1938). *A study in the analysis of stationary time series.* Uppsala, Sweden: Almqvist & Wiksells.

Yule, G. U. (1926). Why do we sometimes get nonsense correlations between time-series?: A study in sampling and the nature of time-series. *Journal of the Royal Statistical Society, 89*, 2–9, 30–41.

Author Index

Subject Index

f indicates a figure; *t* indicates a table.

About the Authors

Niall Bolger, PhD, is Professor of Psychology and Chairperson of the Department of Psychology at Columbia University, where he teaches courses on social relationships, linear statistical models, and longitudinal data analysis. His main research interests include adjustment processes in close relationships using intensive longitudinal methods and laboratory-based studies of dyadic behavior, emotion and physiology, and personality processes as they are revealed in patterns of behavior, emotion, and physiology in daily life. He is also interested in statistical methods for analyzing longitudinal and multilevel data. Dr. Bolger is a Charter Member and Fellow of the Association for Psychological Science, a Fellow of the Society of Experimental Social Psychology and of the Society for Personality and Social Psychology, and a member of the Society for Multivariate Experimental Psychology. He has served on National Institutes of Health and National Science Foundation grant review panels, and as Associate Editor of the *Journal of Personality and Social Psychology: Interpersonal Relations and Group Processes*.

Jean-Philippe Laurenceau, PhD, is Professor of Psychology at the University of Delaware. His research interests focus on understanding the processes by which partners in marital and romantic relationships develop and maintain intimacy within the context of everyday life. His methodological interests include intensive longitudinal methods for studying close relationship processes and applications of modern methods for the analysis of change in individuals and dyads. Dr. Laurenceau is an appointed member of the Social, Personality, and Interpersonal Processes grant review panel of the National Institutes of Health, and has served on the editorial boards of the *Journal of Consulting and Clinical Psychology* and the *Journal of Family Psychology*. He has been principal investigator or co-investigator on research projects funded by the National Institute of Mental Health, the National Institute of Child Health and Human Development, and the National Cancer Institute.